RECORDED VERSIONS GUITAR®

AUTHENTIC TRANSCRIPTIONS WITH NOTES AND TABLATURE

Music transcriptions by Pete Billman, Colin Higgins, and Hemme Luttjeboer.

ISBN 0-7935-8740-9

HAL•LEONARD® CORPORATION

7777 W. Bluemound Rd. P.O. Box 13819 Milwaukee, WI 53213

SEE REVERSE SIDE FOR OPENING INSTRUCTIONS

adam gaynor

brian yale

rob thomas

paul doucette

kyle cook

20

20

matchbo

matchbox 20

Art Direction and Design by Ria Lewerke / Digital Gypsies.

Photography by Andrew Macpherson,
Neal Preston, Rankin, and Patrice Bilawka.

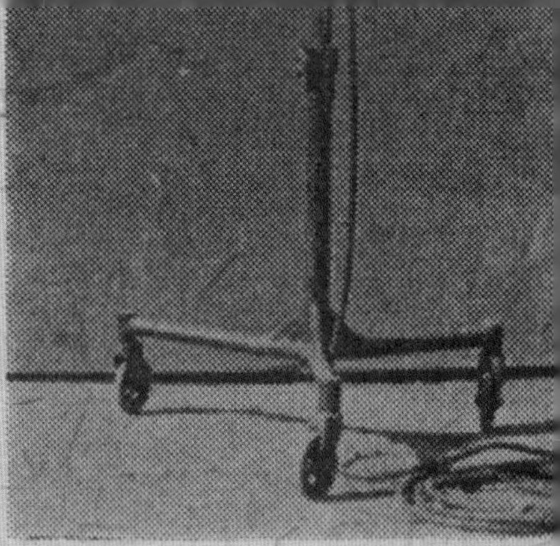

Produced by Matt Serletic
for Melisma Productions, Inc.

Engineered by Jeff Tomei.

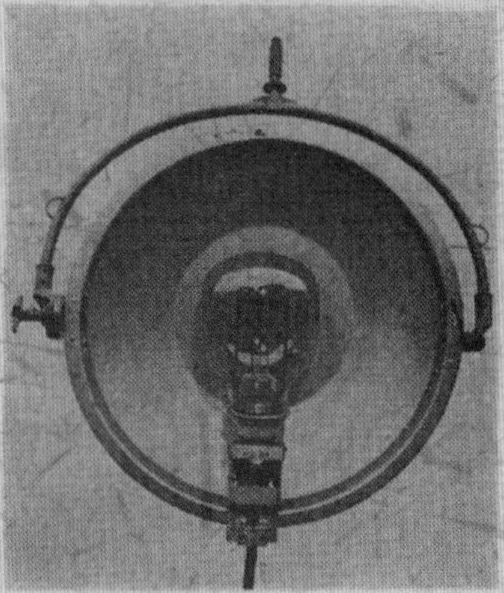

Mixed by Greg Archilla
and Matt Serletic.

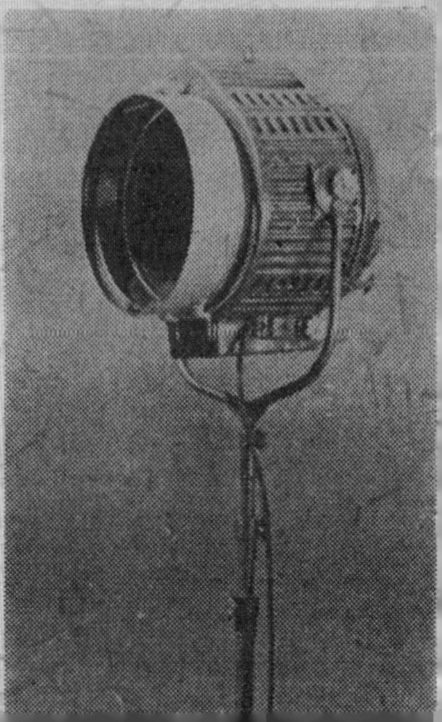

www.matchbox20.com

Real World

Written by Rob Thomas

*Symbols in parentheses represent chord names respective to capoed guitar and do not reflect actual sounding chord.

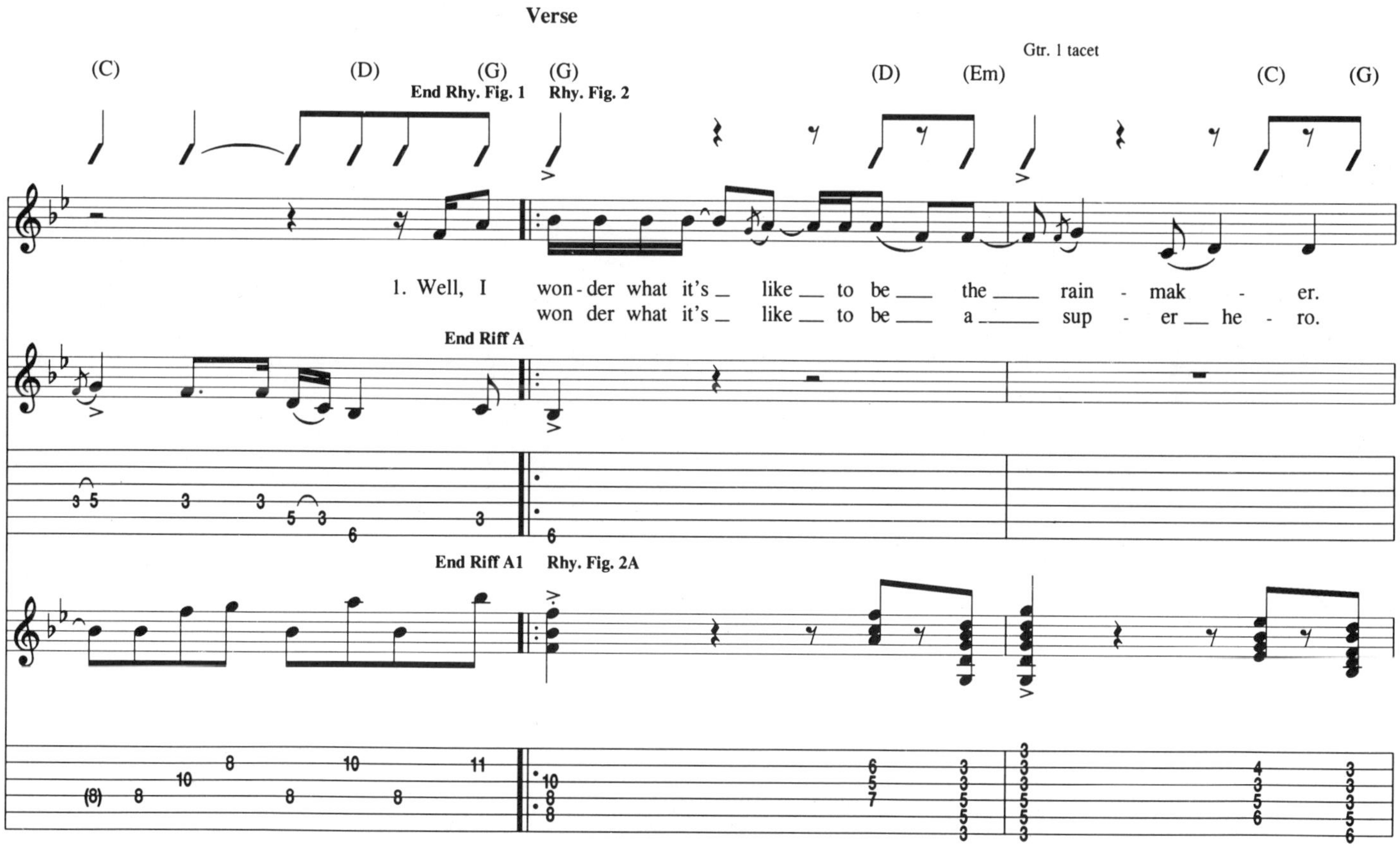

*Symbols in parentheses represent chord names respective to capoed guitar.
Symbols above reflect actual sounding chord.

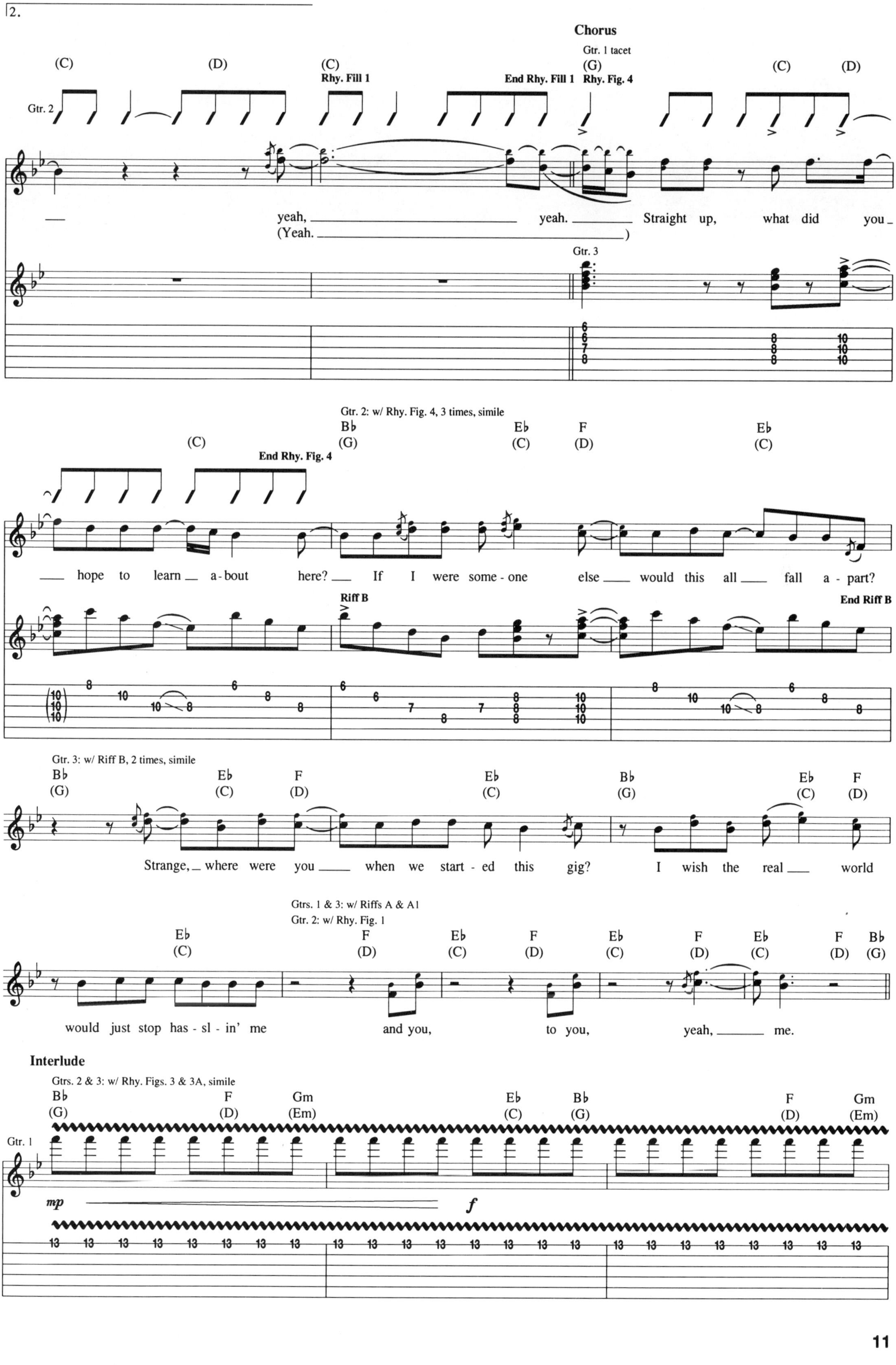
2.
Chorus
Gtr. 1 tacet
(C) (D) (C) (G) (C) (D)
Rhy. Fill 1
End Rhy. Fill 1
Rhy. Fig. 4
Gtr. 2
yeah, yeah. Straight up, what did you
(Yeah.)
Gtr. 3
Gtr. 2: w/ Rhy. Fig. 4, 3 times, simile
(C) Bb (G) Eb (C) F (D) Eb (C)
End Rhy. Fig. 4
hope to learn about here? If I were some-one else would this all fall a-part?
Riff B
End Riff B
Gtr. 3: w/ Riff B, 2 times, simile
Bb (G) Eb (C) F (D) Eb (C) Bb (G) Eb (C) F (D)
Strange, where were you when we start-ed this gig? I wish the real world
Gtrs. 1 & 3: w/ Riffs A & A1
Gtr. 2: w/ Rhy. Fig. 1
Eb (C) F (D) Eb (C) F (D) Eb (C) F (D) Eb (C) F (D) Bb (G)
would just stop has-sl-in' me and you, to you, yeah, me.
Interlude
Gtrs. 2 & 3: w/ Rhy. Figs. 3 & 3A, simile
Bb (G) F (D) Gm (Em) Eb (C) Bb (G) F (D) Gm (Em)
Gtr. 1
mp
f

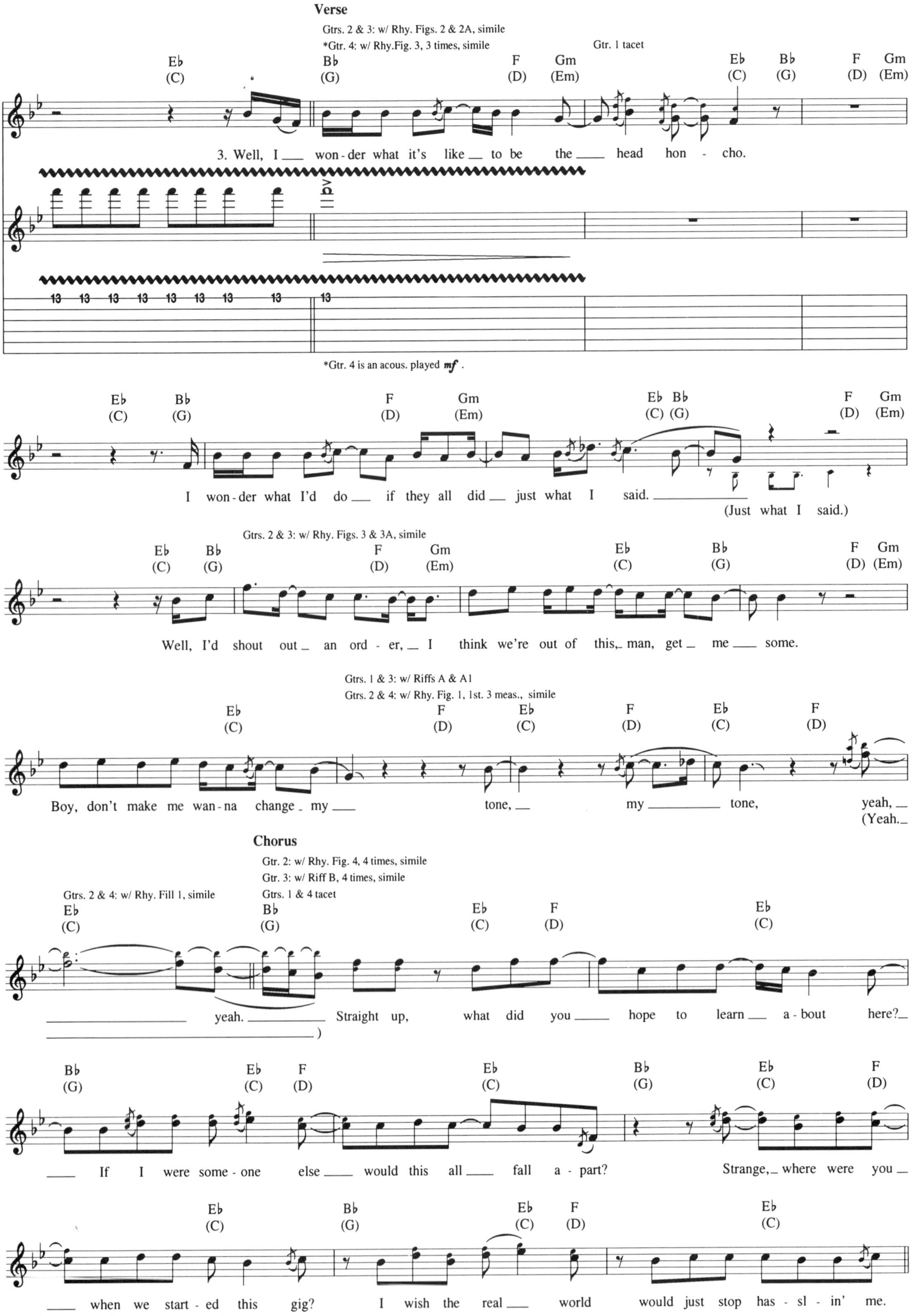
Verse
Gtrs. 2 & 3: w/ Rhy. Figs. 2 & 2A, simile
*Gtr. 4: w/ Rhy.Fig. 3, 3 times, simile
Gtr. 1 tacet
Eb (C) Bb (G) F (D) Gm (Em) Eb (C) Bb (G) F (D) Gm (Em)
3. Well, I wonder what it's like to be the head honcho.
*Gtr. 4 is an acous. played mf.
Eb (C) Bb (G) F (D) Gm (Em) Eb (C) Bb (G) F (D) Gm (Em)
I wonder what I'd do if they all did just what I said.
(Just what I said.)
Gtrs. 2 & 3: w/ Rhy. Figs. 3 & 3A, simile
Eb (C) Bb (G) F (D) Gm (Em) Eb (C) Bb (G) F (D) Gm (Em)
Well, I'd shout out an order, I think we're out of this, man, get me some.
Gtrs. 1 & 3: w/ Riffs A & A1
Gtrs. 2 & 4: w/ Rhy. Fig. 1, 1st. 3 meas., simile
Eb (C) F (D) Eb (C) F (D) Eb (C) F (D)
Boy, don't make me wanna change my tone, my tone, yeah,
(Yeah.
Chorus
Gtr. 2: w/ Rhy. Fig. 4, 4 times, simile
Gtr. 3: w/ Riff B, 4 times, simile
Gtrs. 1 & 4 tacet
Gtrs. 2 & 4: w/ Rhy. Fill 1, simile
Eb (C) Bb (G) Eb (C) F (D) Eb (C)
yeah. Straight up, what did you hope to learn about here?
)
Bb (G) Eb (C) F (D) Eb (C) Bb (G) Eb (C) F (D)
If I were someone else would this all fall apart? Strange, where were you
Eb (C) Bb (G) Eb (C) F (D) Eb (C)
when we started this gig? I wish the real world would just stop hasslin' me.

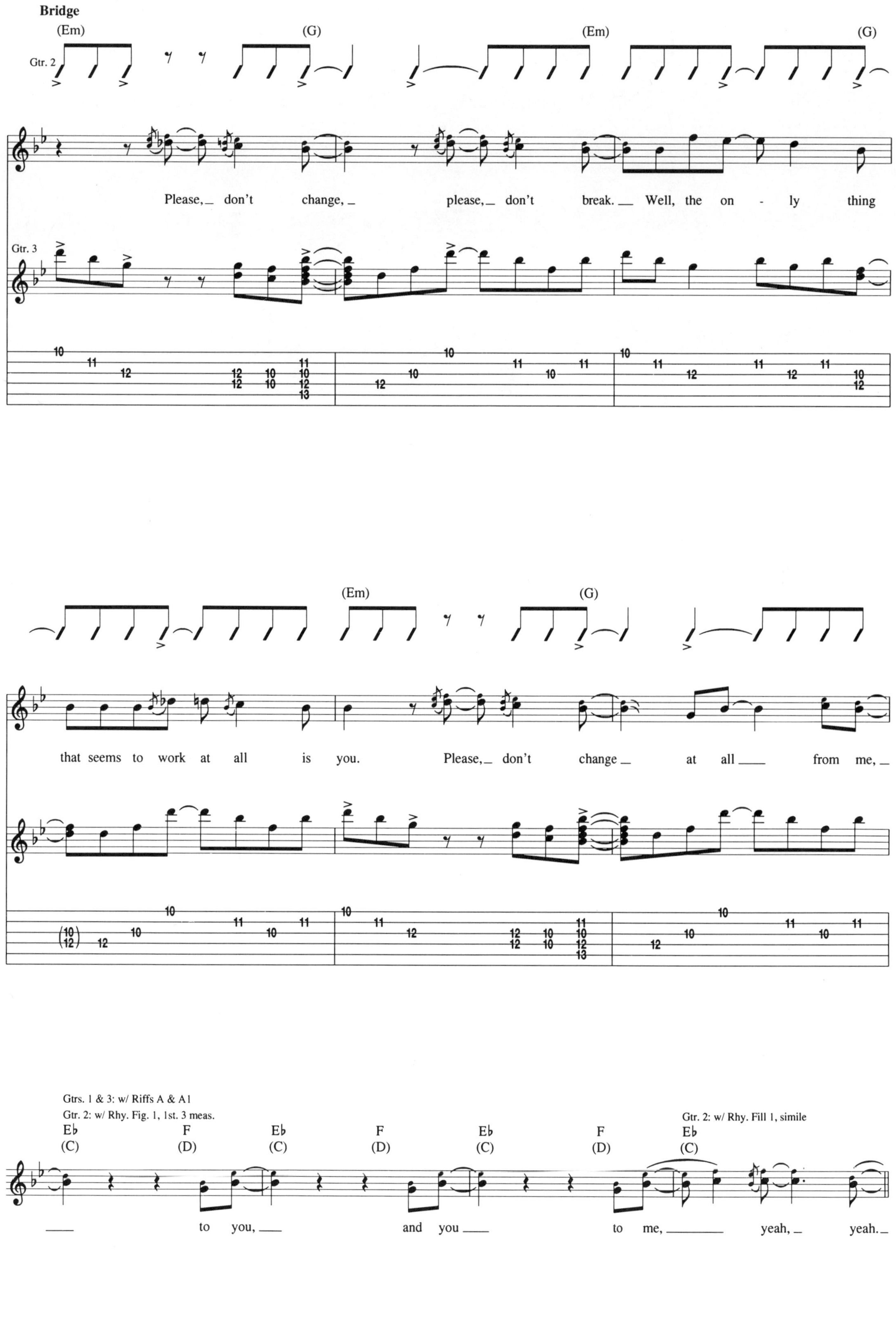
Bridge
(Em)
(G)
Gtr. 2
Please, don't change, please, don't break. Well, the on - ly thing
Gtr. 3
that seems to work at all is you. Please, don't change at all from me,
Gtrs. 1 & 3: w/ Riffs A & A1
Gtr. 2: w/ Rhy. Fig. 1, 1st. 3 meas.
Gtr. 2: w/ Rhy. Fill 1, simile
E♭ (C) F (D) E♭ (C) F (D) E♭ (C) F (D) E♭ (C)
to you, and you to me, yeah, yeah.

Guitar Solo

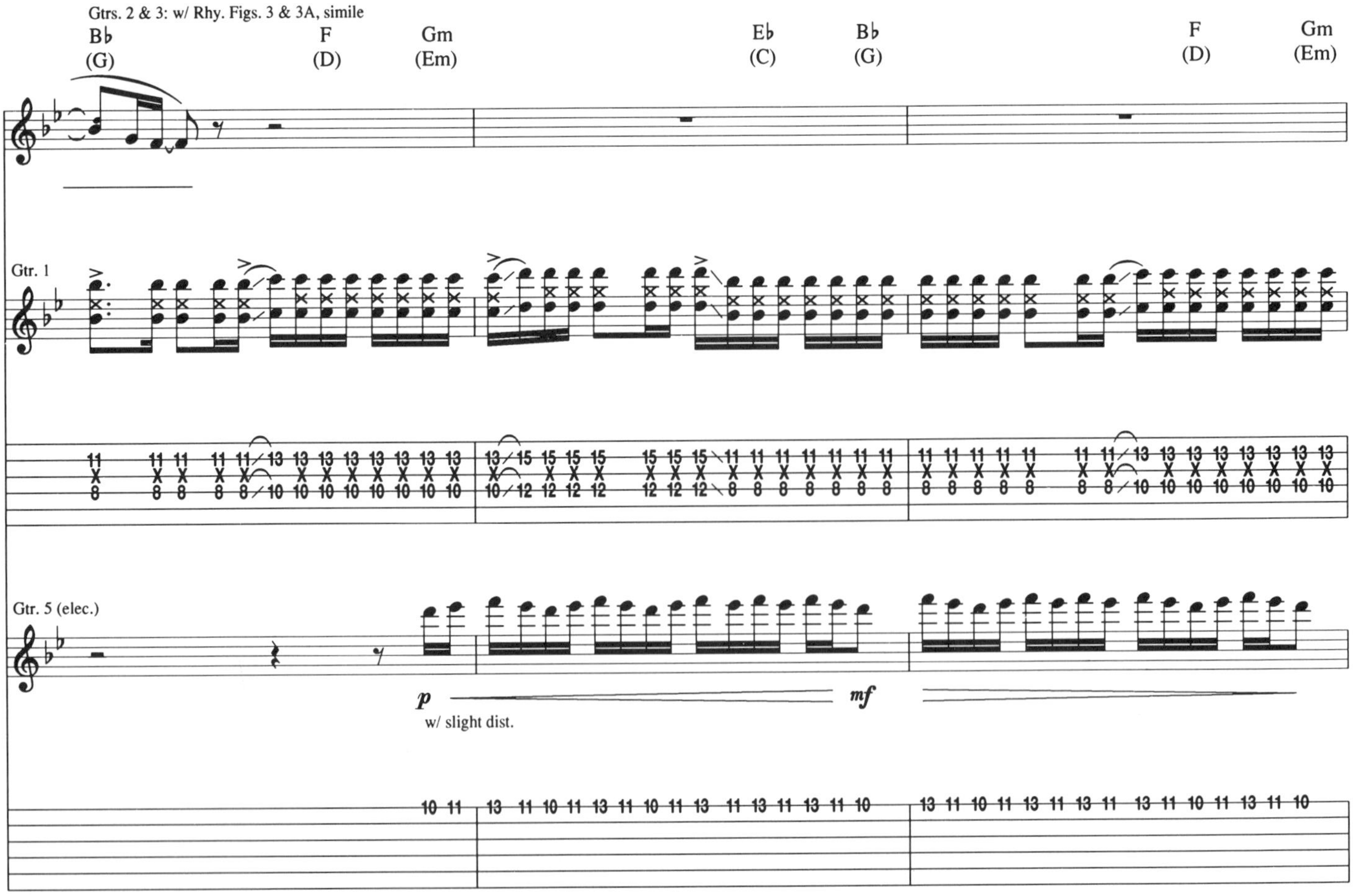
Gtrs. 2 & 3: w/ Rhy. Figs. 3 & 3A, simile
B♭ (G)
F (D)
Gm (Em)
E♭ (C)
B♭ (G)
F (D)
Gm (Em)
Gtr. 1
Gtr. 5 (elec.)
p
mf
w/ slight dist.

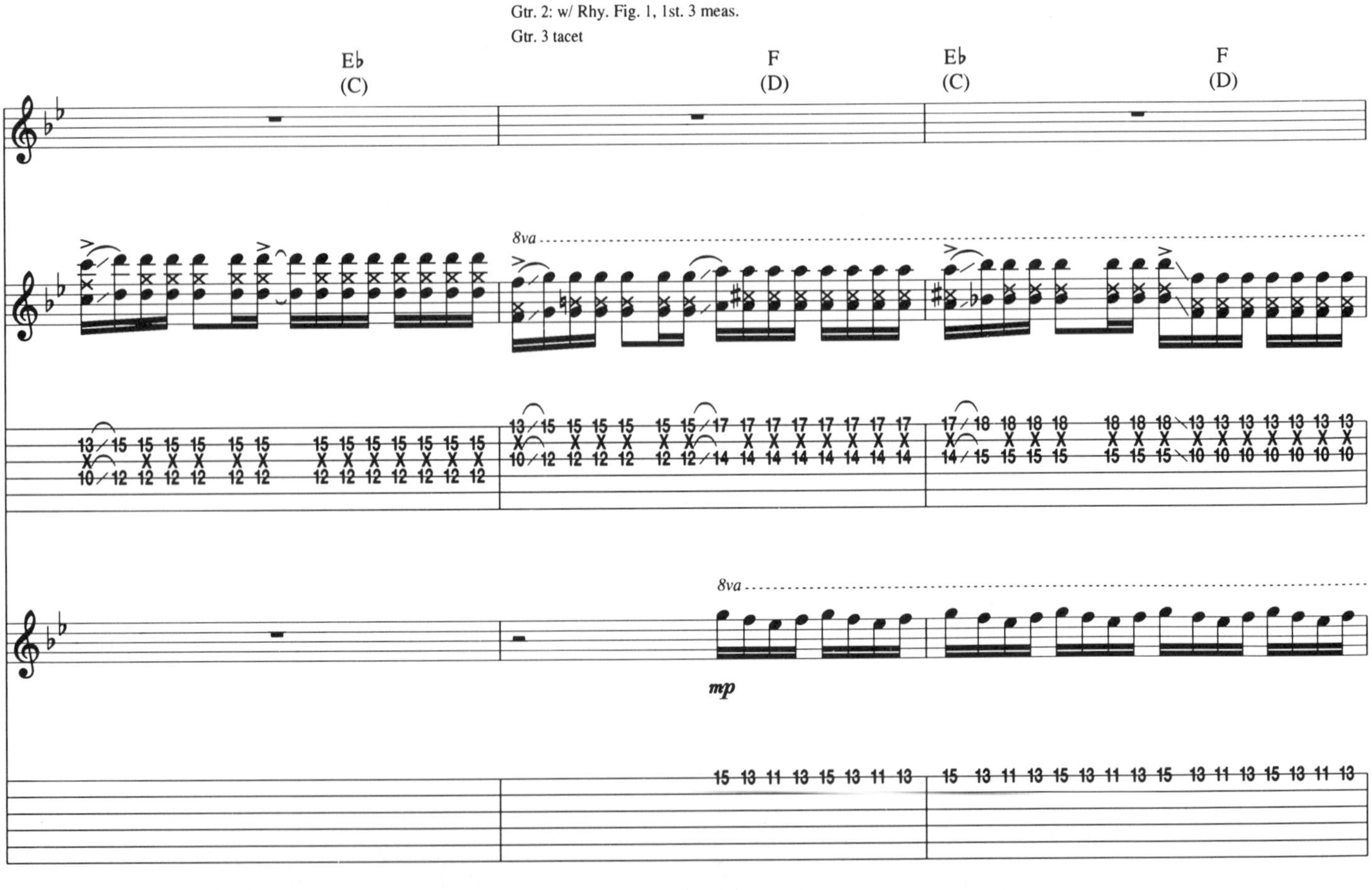
Gtr. 2: w/ Rhy. Fig. 1, 1st. 3 meas.
Gtr. 3 tacet
E♭ (C)
F (D)
E♭ (C)
F (D)
8va
8va
mp

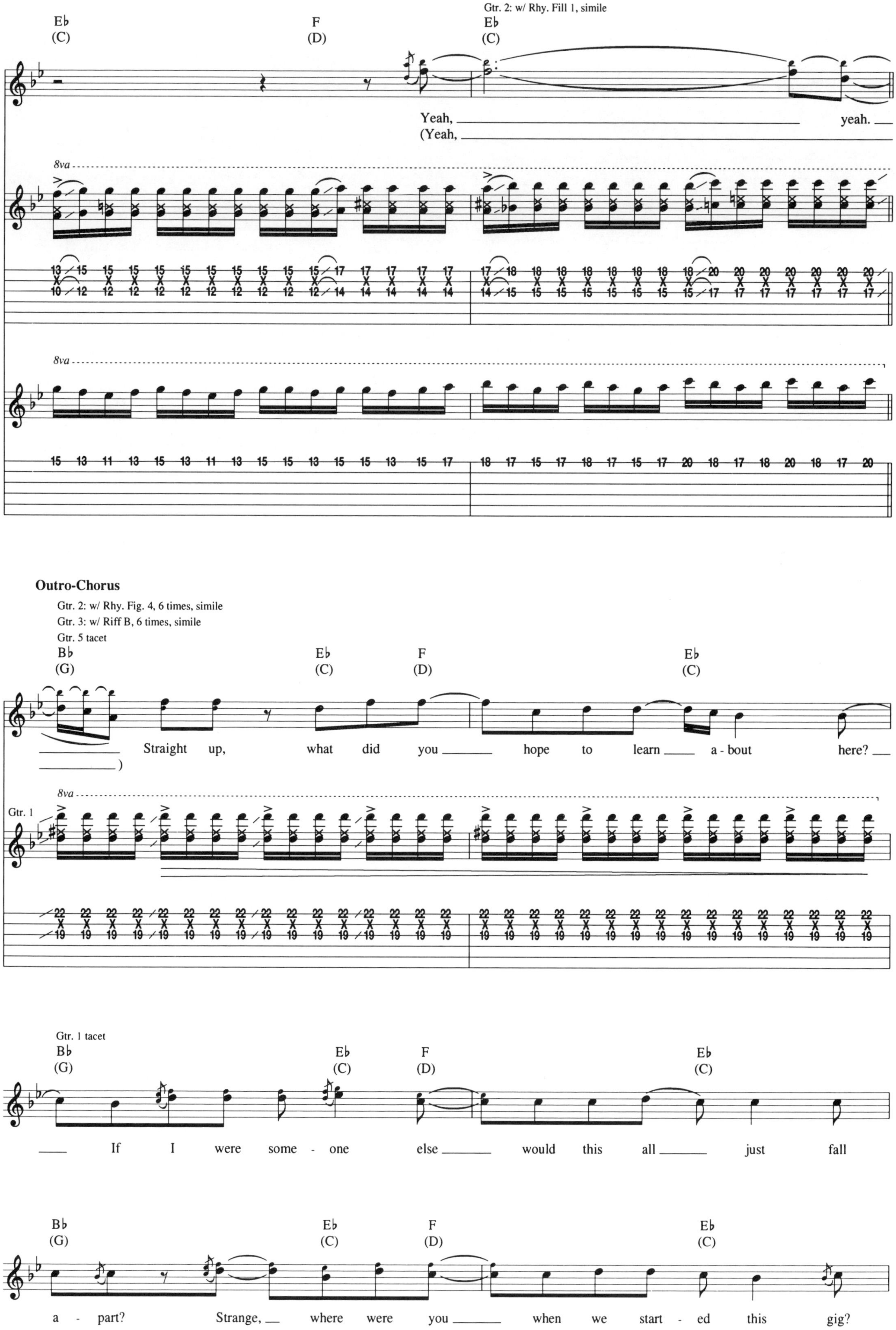
Gtr. 2: w/ Rhy. Fill 1, simile
Eb (C)
F (D)
Eb (C)
Yeah, ___ yeah. ___
(Yeah, ___
8va
13 15 15 15 15 15 15 15 15 15 15 17 17 17 17 17
10 12 12 12 12 12 12 12 12 12 12 14 14 14 14 14
17 18 18 18 18 18 18 18 18 20 20 20 20 20 20 20
14 15 15 15 15 15 15 15 15 17 17 17 17 17 17 17
8va
15 13 11 13 15 13 11 13 15 15 13 15 15 13 15 17
18 17 15 17 18 17 15 17 20 18 17 18 20 18 17 20
Outro-Chorus
Gtr. 2: w/ Rhy. Fig. 4, 6 times, simile
Gtr. 3: w/ Riff B, 6 times, simile
Gtr. 5 tacet
Bb (G)
Eb (C)
F (D)
Eb (C)
___ Straight up, what did you ___ hope to learn ___ a - bout here? ___
___)
8va
Gtr. 1
22 22 22 22 22 22 22 22 22 22 22 22 22 22 22 22
19 19 19 19 19 19 19 19 19 19 19 19 19 19 19 19
22 22 22 22 22 22 22 22 22 22 22 22 22 22 22 22
19 19 19 19 19 19 19 19 19 19 19 19 19 19 19 19
Gtr. 1 tacet
Bb (G)
Eb (C)
F (D)
Eb (C)
___ If I were some - one else ___ would this all ___ just fall
Bb (G)
Eb (C)
F (D)
Eb (C)
a - part? Strange, ___ where were you ___ when we start - ed this gig?

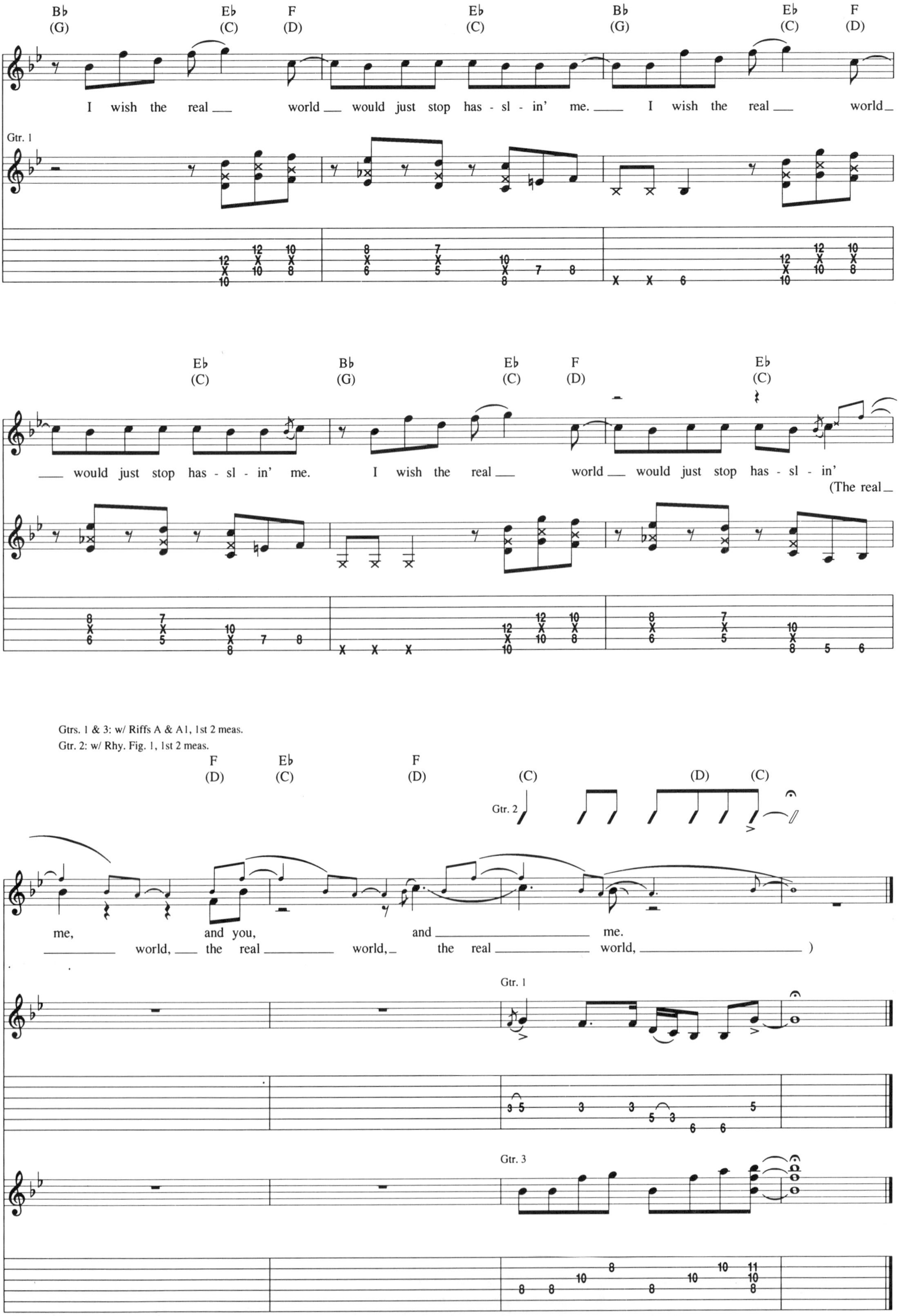
B♭ (G) E♭ (C) F (D) E♭ (C) B♭ (G) E♭ (C) F (D)
I wish the real world would just stop has - sl - in' me. I wish the real world
Gtr. 1
E♭ (C) B♭ (G) E♭ (C) F (D) E♭ (C)
would just stop has - sl - in' me. I wish the real world would just stop has - sl - in'
(The real
Gtrs. 1 & 3: w/ Riffs A & A1, 1st 2 meas.
Gtr. 2: w/ Rhy. Fig. 1, 1st 2 meas.
F (D) E♭ (C) F (D) (C) (D) (C)
Gtr. 2
me, and you, and me.
world, the real world, the real world,)
Gtr. 1
Gtr. 3

Long Day

Written by Rob Thomas

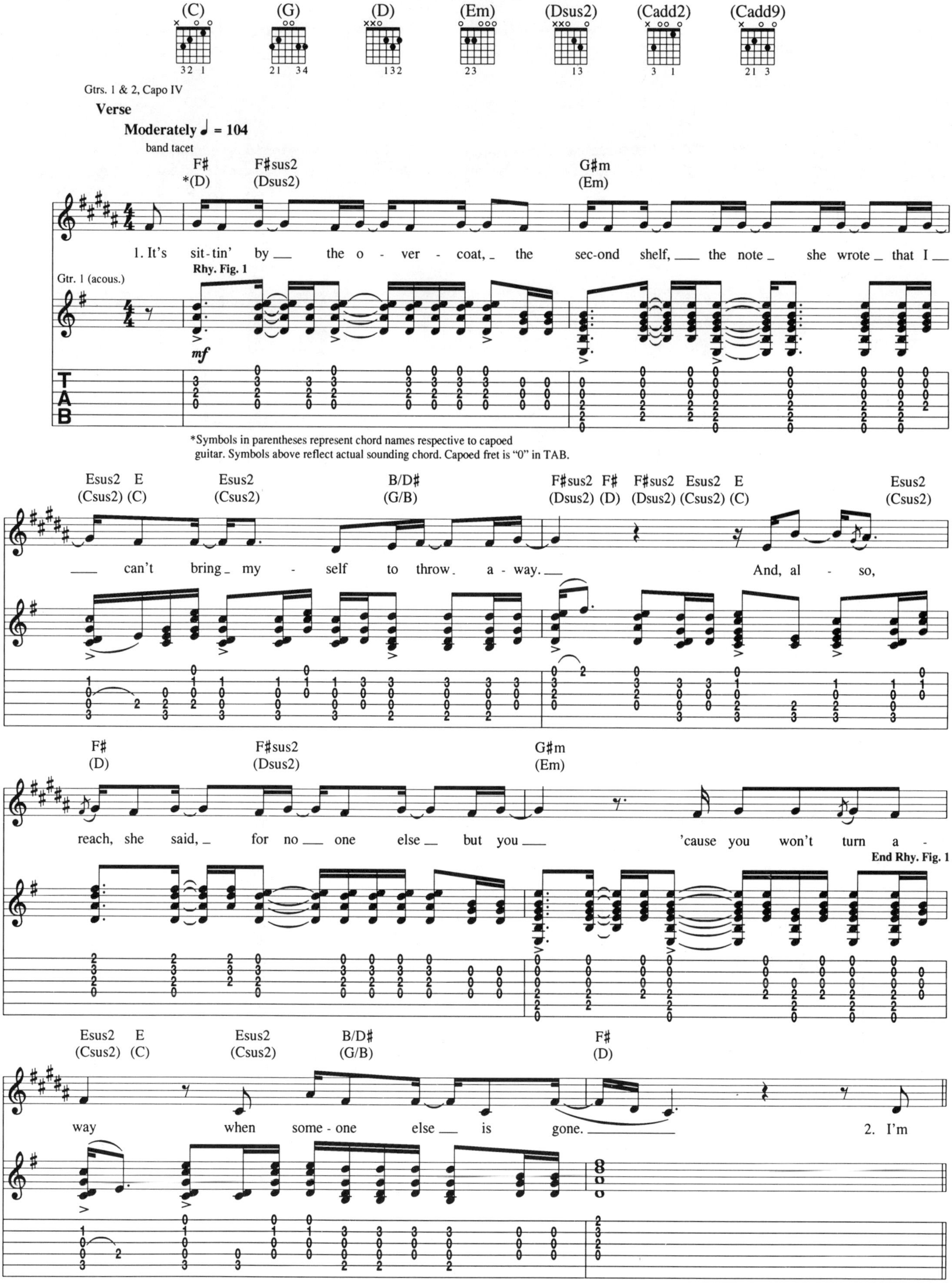

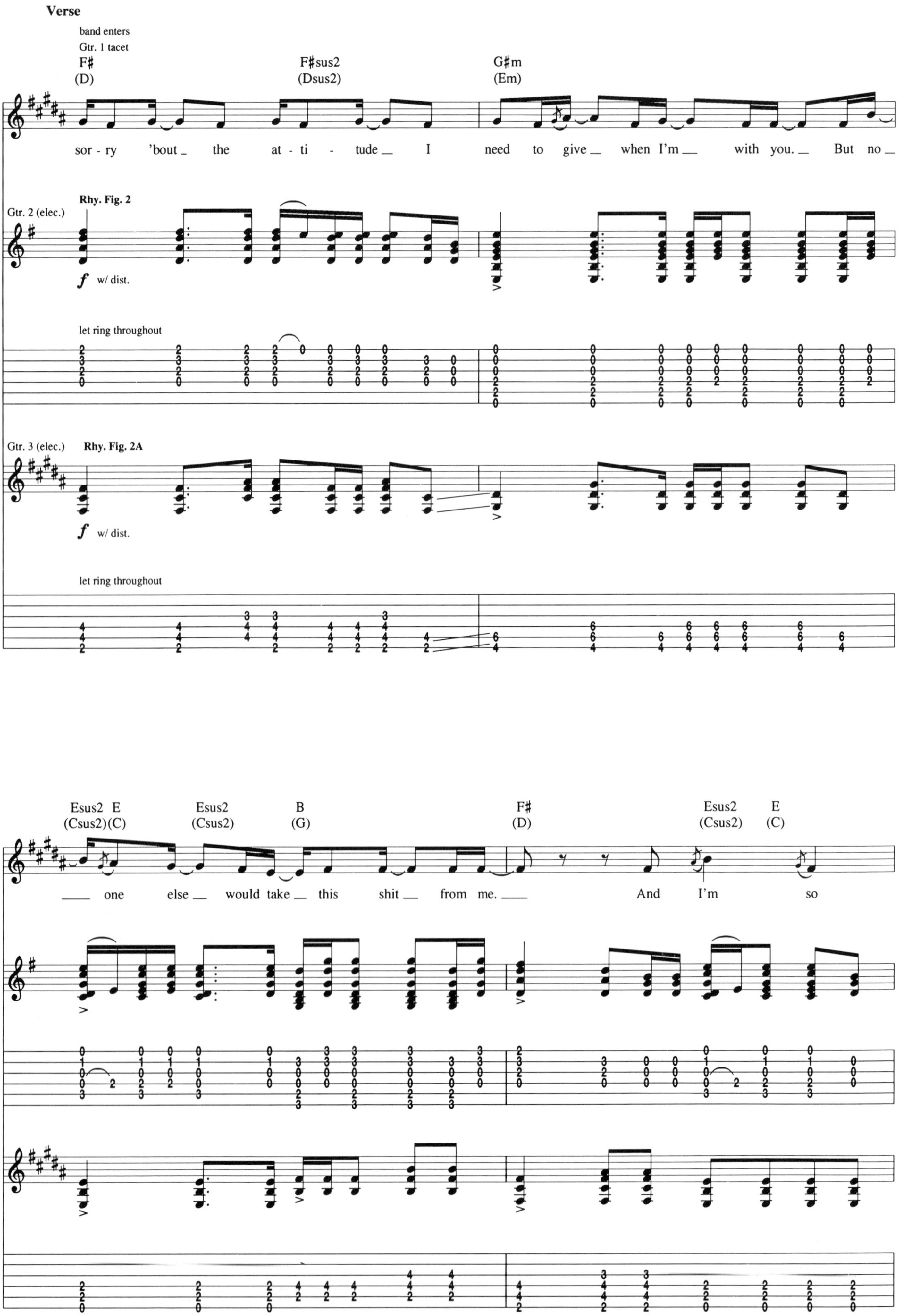
Verse
band enters
Gtr. 1 tacet
F♯ (D)
F♯sus2 (Dsus2)
G♯m (Em)
sor - ry 'bout _ the at - ti - tude _ I need to give _ when I'm _ with you. _ But no _
Gtr. 2 (elec.)
Rhy. Fig. 2
f w/ dist.
let ring throughout
Gtr. 3 (elec.)
Rhy. Fig. 2A
f w/ dist.
let ring throughout
Esus2 E (Csus2)(C)
Esus2 (Csus2)
B (G)
F♯ (D)
Esus2 (Csus2)
E (C)
_ one else _ would take _ this shit _ from me. _ And I'm so

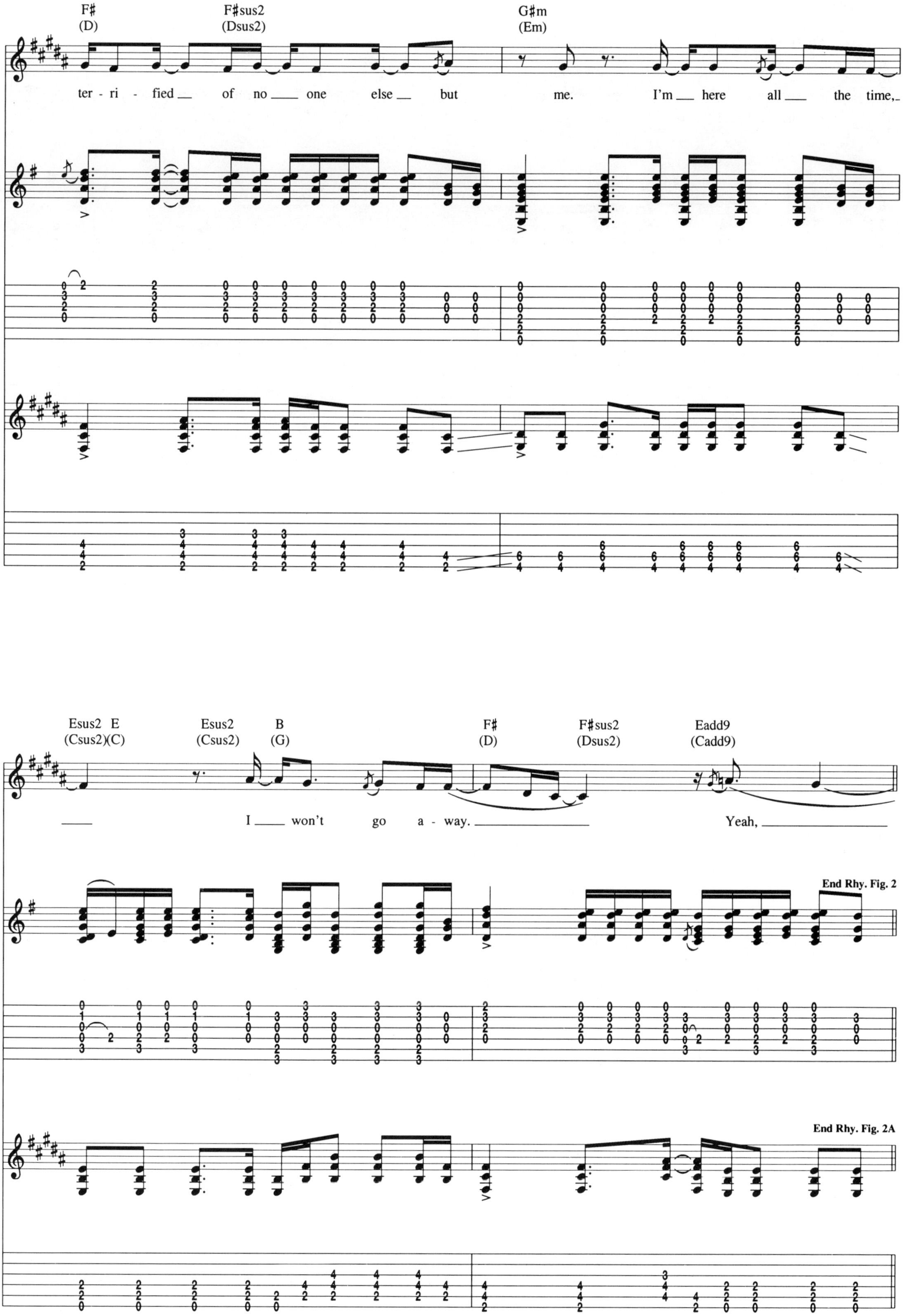
F♯ (D)
F♯sus2 (Dsus2)
G♯m (Em)
ter - ri - fied __ of no __ one else __ but me. I'm __ here all __ the time, _
Esus2 E (Csus2)(C)
Esus2 (Csus2)
B (G)
F♯ (D)
F♯sus2 (Dsus2)
Eadd9 (Cadd9)
__ I __ won't go a - way. __ Yeah, __
End Rhy. Fig. 2
End Rhy. Fig. 2A

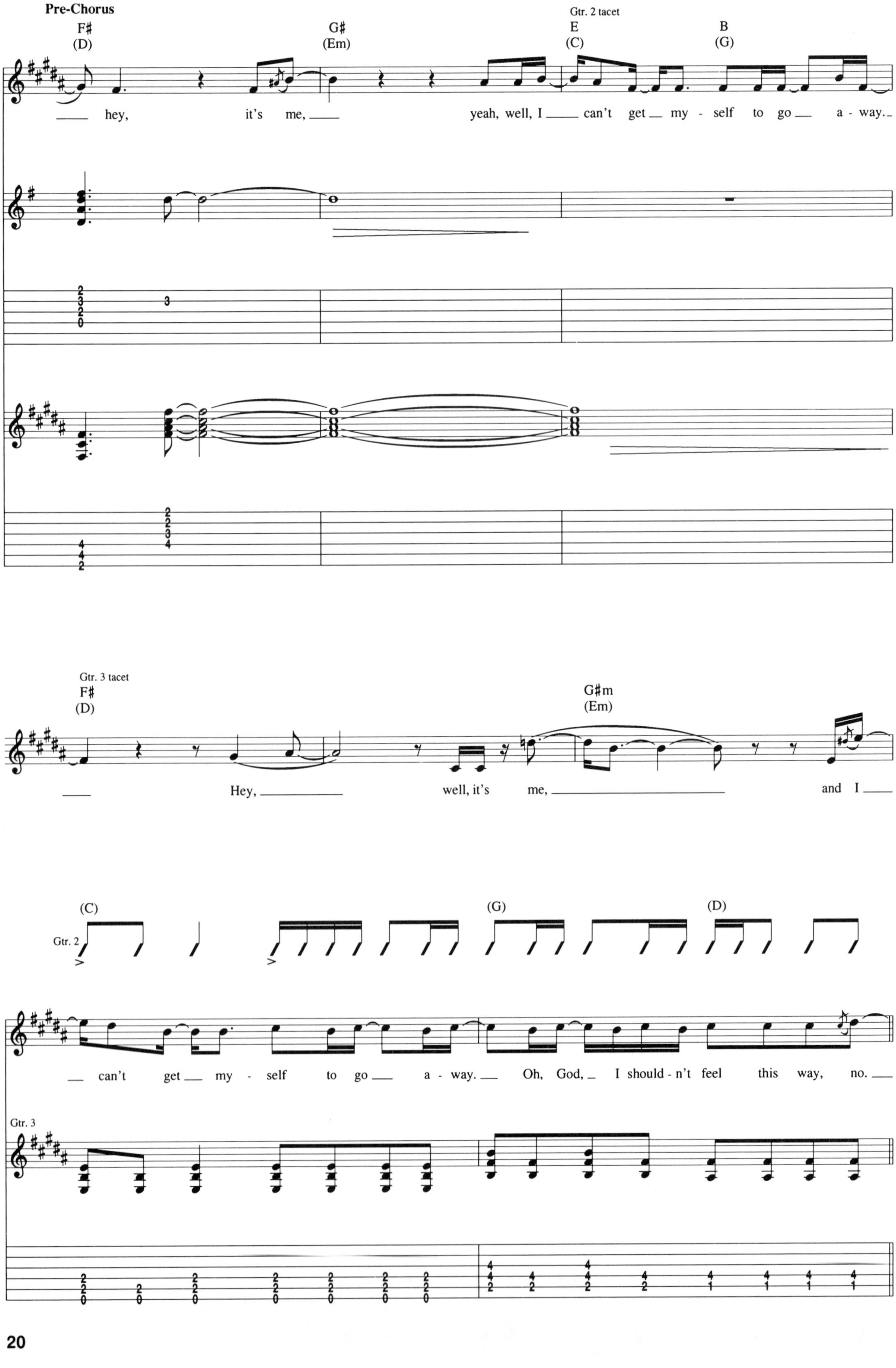
Pre-Chorus
Gtr. 2 tacet
F♯ (D)
G♯ (Em)
E (C)
B (G)
hey, it's me, yeah, well, I can't get my - self to go a - way.
Gtr. 3 tacet
F♯ (D)
G♯m (Em)
Hey, well, it's me, and I
(C)
(G)
(D)
Gtr. 2
can't get my - self to go a - way. Oh, God, I should - n't feel this way, no.
Gtr. 3

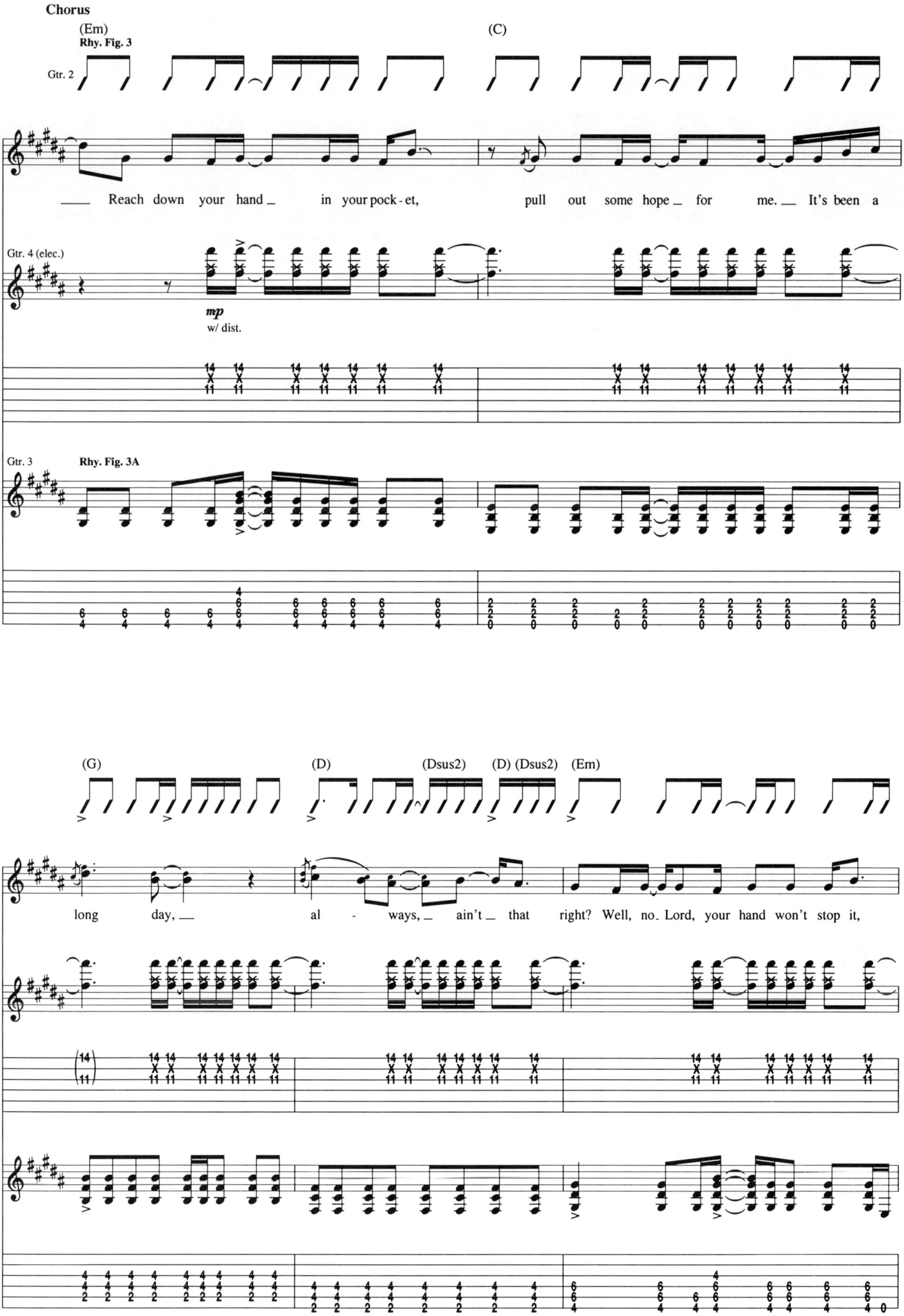
Chorus
(Em)
Rhy. Fig. 3
(C)
Gtr. 2
Reach down your hand in your pock-et, pull out some hope for me. It's been a
Gtr. 4 (elec.)
mp
w/ dist.
Gtr. 3
Rhy. Fig. 3A
(G)
(D)
(Dsus2)
(D) (Dsus2)
(Em)
long day, al - ways, ain't that right? Well, no. Lord, your hand won't stop it,

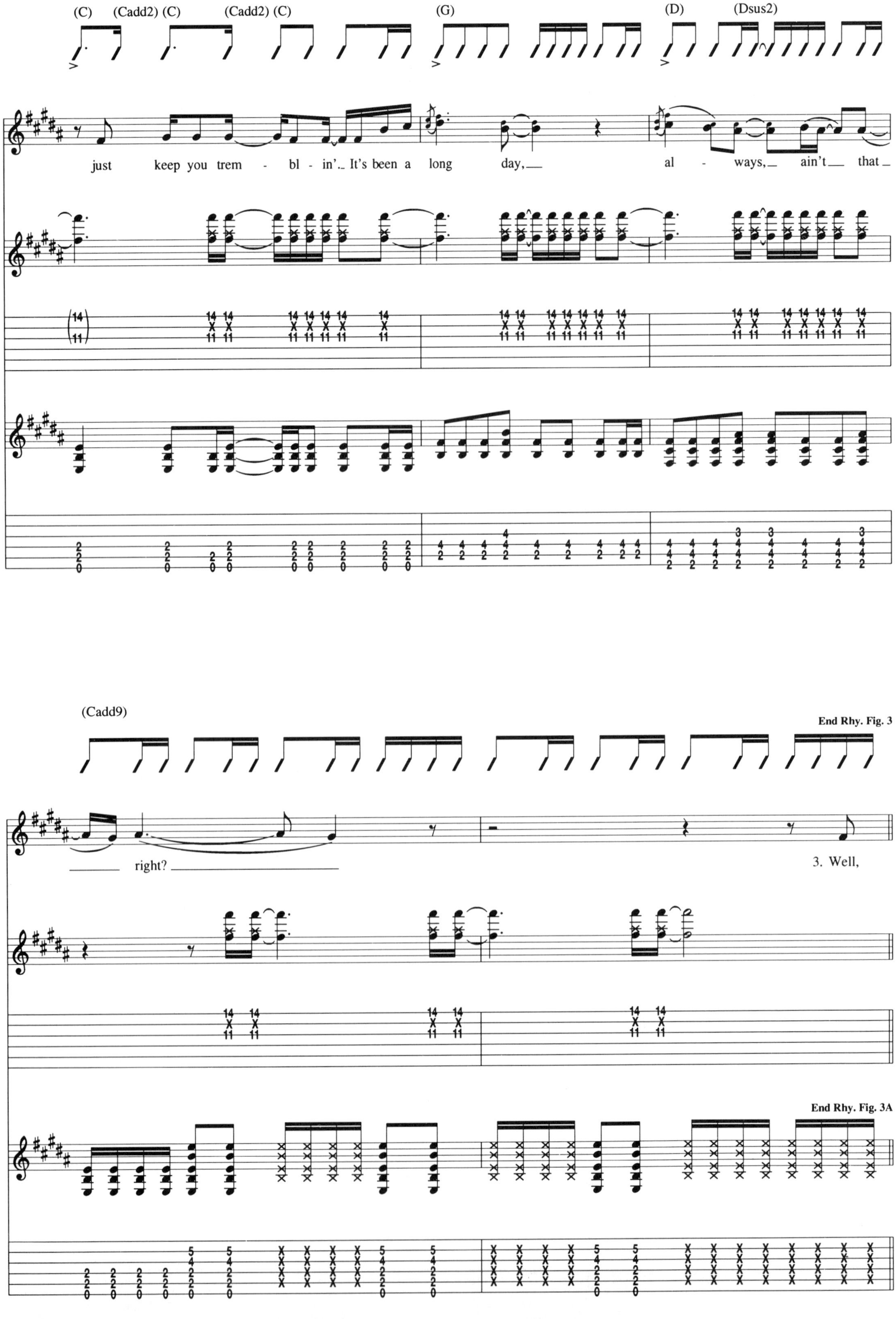
(C) (Cadd2) (C) (Cadd2) (C) (G) (D) (Dsus2)
just keep you trem - bl - in'. It's been a long day, al - ways, ain't that
(Cadd9)
End Rhy. Fig. 3
right?
3. Well,
End Rhy. Fig. 3A

Verse
Gtr. 2: w/ Rhy. Fig. 2, simile
Gtr. 4 tacet
F♯ (D) F♯sus2 (Dsus2) G♯m (Em)
I'm sur - prised if you be - lieve in an - y - thing that comes from me. I
Gtr. 3
Esus2 E (Csus2) (C) Esus2 (Csus2) B (G) F♯ (D) Esus2 (Csus2) E (C)
did - n't hear from you or from some - one else. And you're so
F♯ (D) F♯sus2 (Dsus2) G♯m (Em)
set in life, man, a pis - ser, they're wait - in'. Too damn bad you get so far so fast,
Esus2 E (Csus2) (C) Esus2 B (Csus2) (G) F♯ (D) F♯sus2 Eadd9 (Dsus2) (Cadd9)
so what, so long.

Chorus

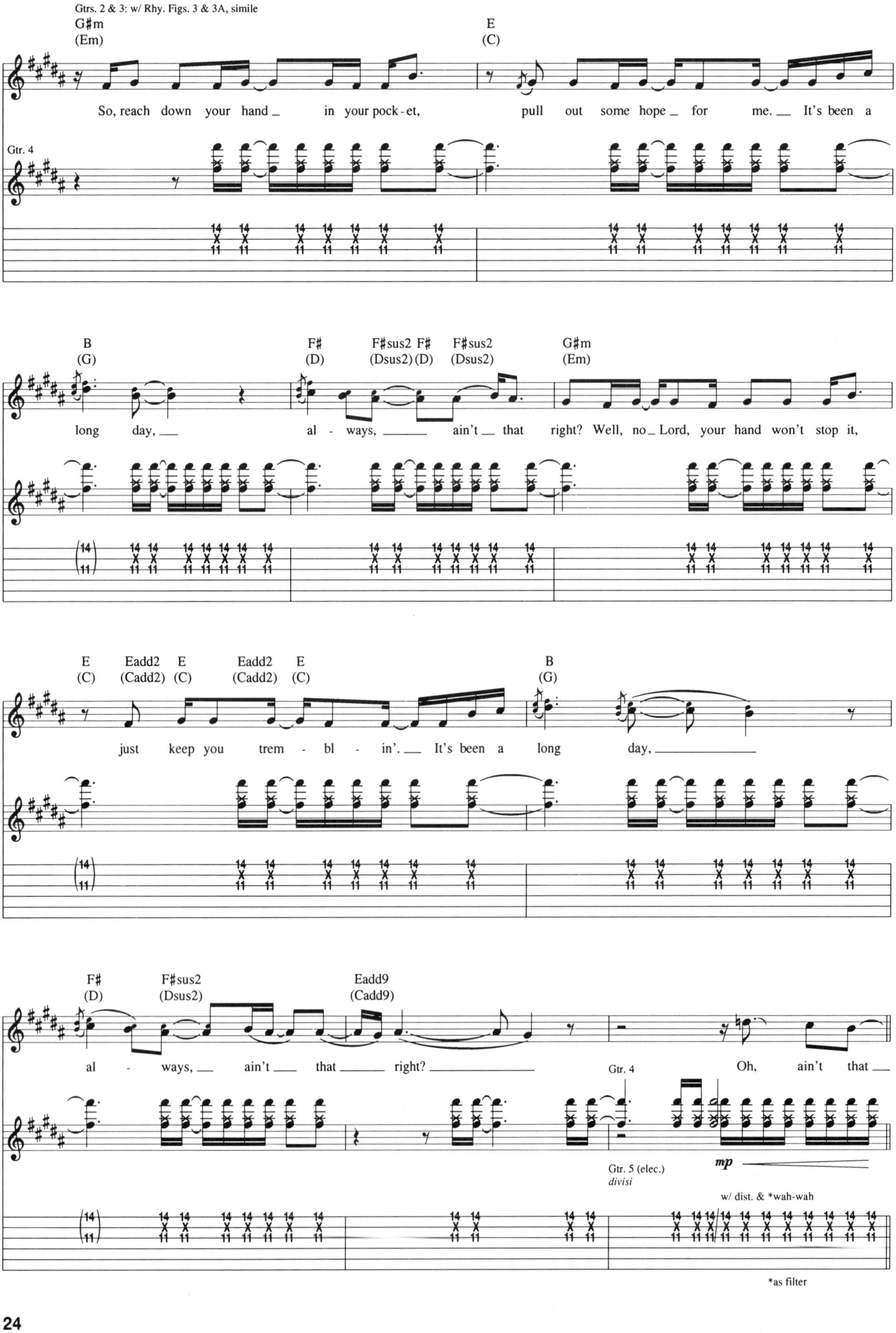
Gtrs. 2 & 3: w/ Rhy. Figs. 3 & 3A, simile
G♯m (Em)
E (C)
So, reach down your hand in your pock-et, pull out some hope for me. It's been a
Gtr. 4
B (G)
F♯ (D)
F♯sus2 (Dsus2)
F♯ (D)
F♯sus2 (Dsus2)
G♯m (Em)
long day, al - ways, ain't that right? Well, no Lord, your hand won't stop it,
E (C)
Eadd2 (Cadd2)
E (C)
Eadd2 (Cadd2)
E (C)
B (G)
just keep you trem - bl - in'. It's been a long day,
F♯ (D)
F♯sus2 (Dsus2)
Eadd9 (Cadd9)
al - ways, ain't that right?
Oh, ain't that
Gtr. 4
mp
Gtr. 5 (elec.)
divisi
w/ dist. & *wah-wah
*as filter

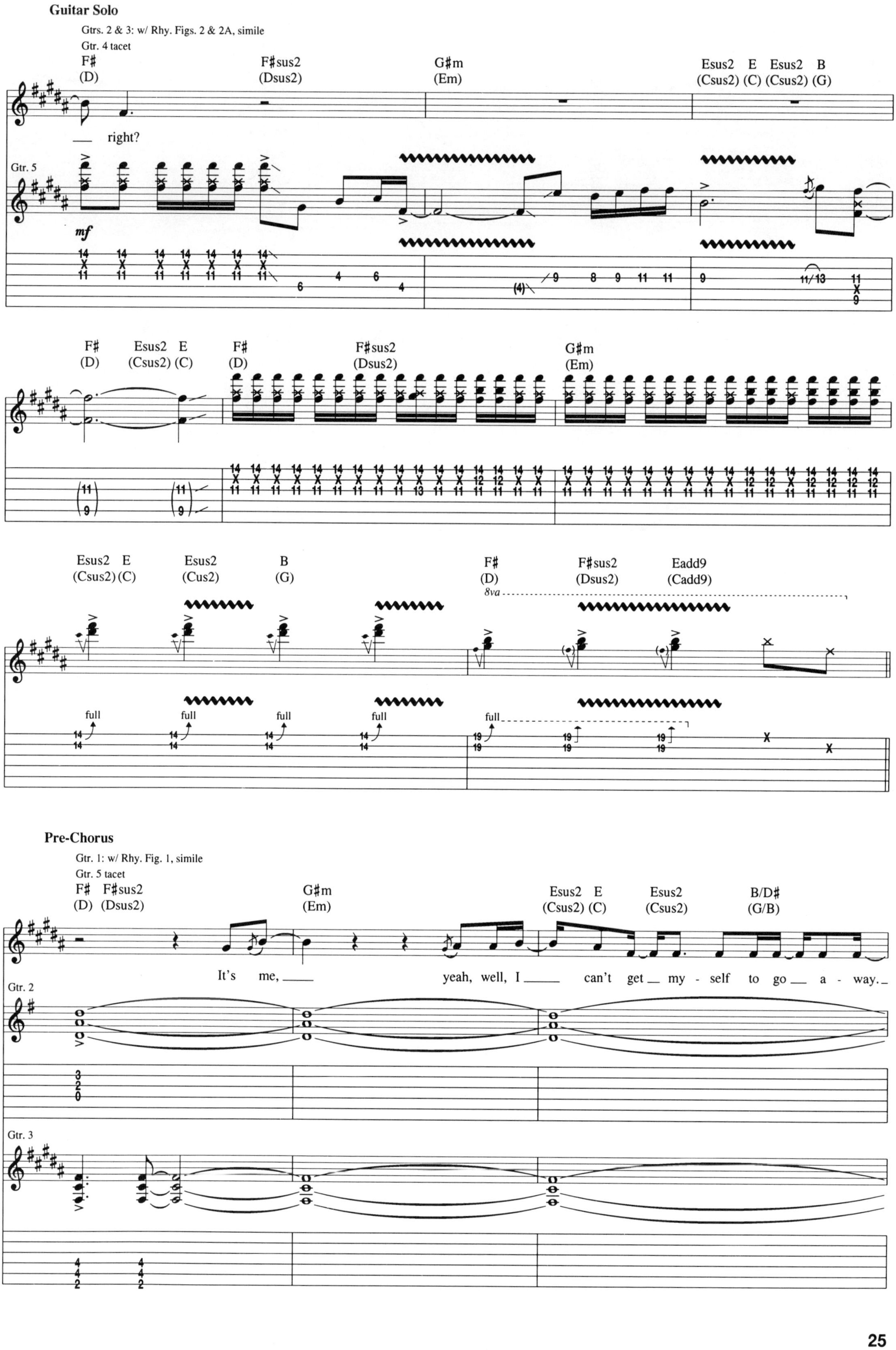
Guitar Solo
Gtrs. 2 & 3: w/ Rhy. Figs. 2 & 2A, simile
Gtr. 4 tacet
F♯ (D)
F♯sus2 (Dsus2)
G♯m (Em)
Esus2 E Esus2 B (Csus2) (C) (Csus2) (G)
right?
Gtr. 5
mf
F♯ (D)
Esus2 E (Csus2) (C)
F♯ (D)
F♯sus2 (Dsus2)
G♯m (Em)
Esus2 E (Csus2) (C)
Esus2 (Cus2)
B (G)
F♯ (D)
F♯sus2 (Dsus2)
Eadd9 (Cadd9)
8va
full
Pre-Chorus
Gtr. 1: w/ Rhy. Fig. 1, simile
Gtr. 5 tacet
F♯ F♯sus2 (D) (Dsus2)
G♯m (Em)
Esus2 E (Csus2) (C)
Esus2 (Csus2)
B/D♯ (G/B)
It's me, yeah, well, I can't get my - self to go a - way.
Gtr. 2
Gtr. 3

F♯sus2 F♯ F♯sus2 Esus2 E
(Dsus2) (D) (Dsus2) (Csus2) (C)
Esus2 F♯
(Csus2) (D)
F♯sus2
(Dsus2)
G♯m
(Em)
Hey, yeah, well, it's me, yeah, well, I
(C)
(G)
(D)
Gtr. 1
can't get my - self to go a - way. Oh, God I should - n't feel this way, no.
Gtr. 2
(cont. in slash)
Gtr. 3

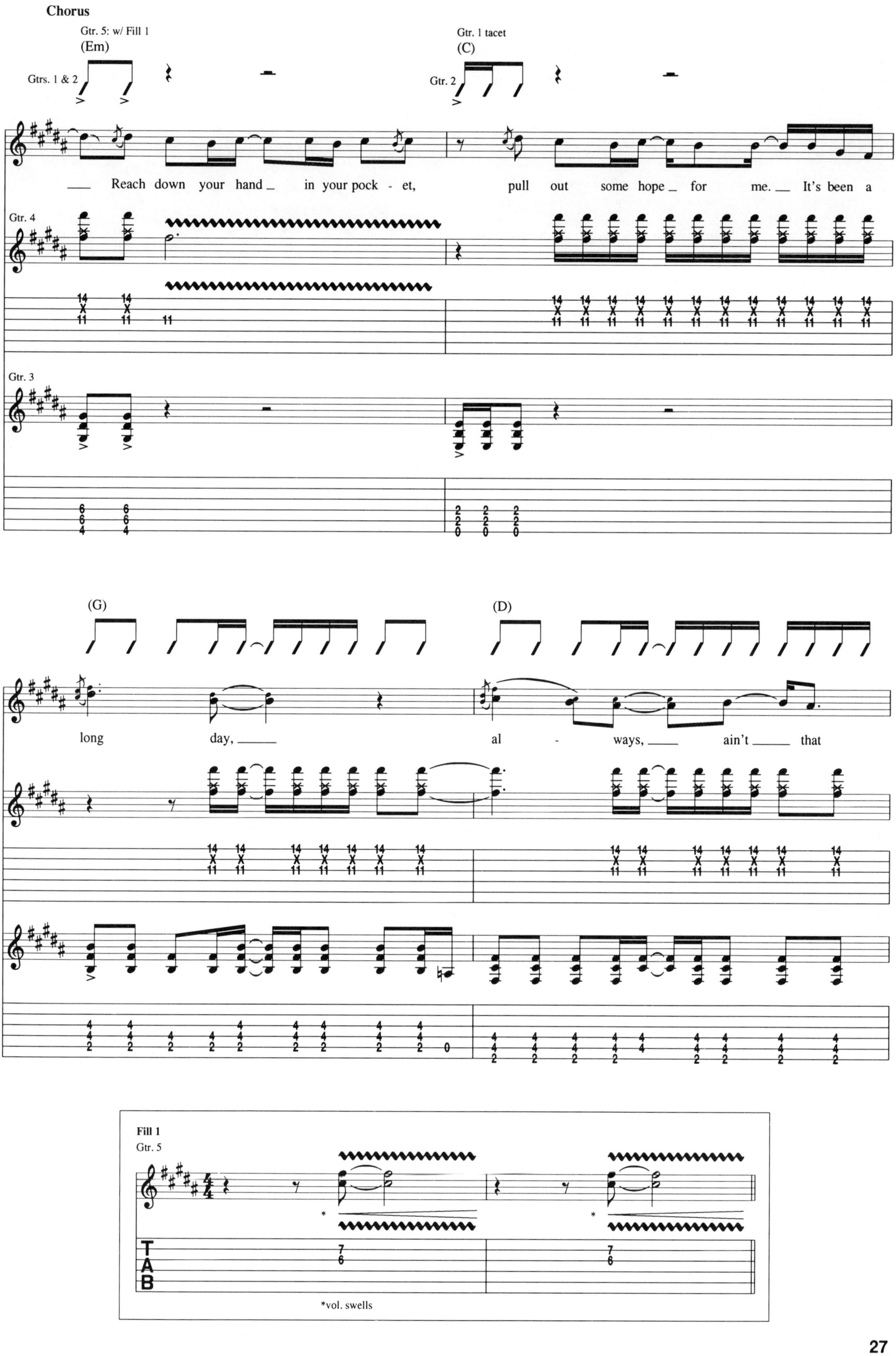
Chorus
Gtr. 5: w/ Fill 1
(Em)
Gtrs. 1 & 2
Gtr. 1 tacet
(C)
Gtr. 2
Reach down your hand in your pock - et, pull out some hope for me. It's been a
Gtr. 4
Gtr. 3
(G)
(D)
long day, al - ways, ain't that
Fill 1
Gtr. 5
*vol. swells

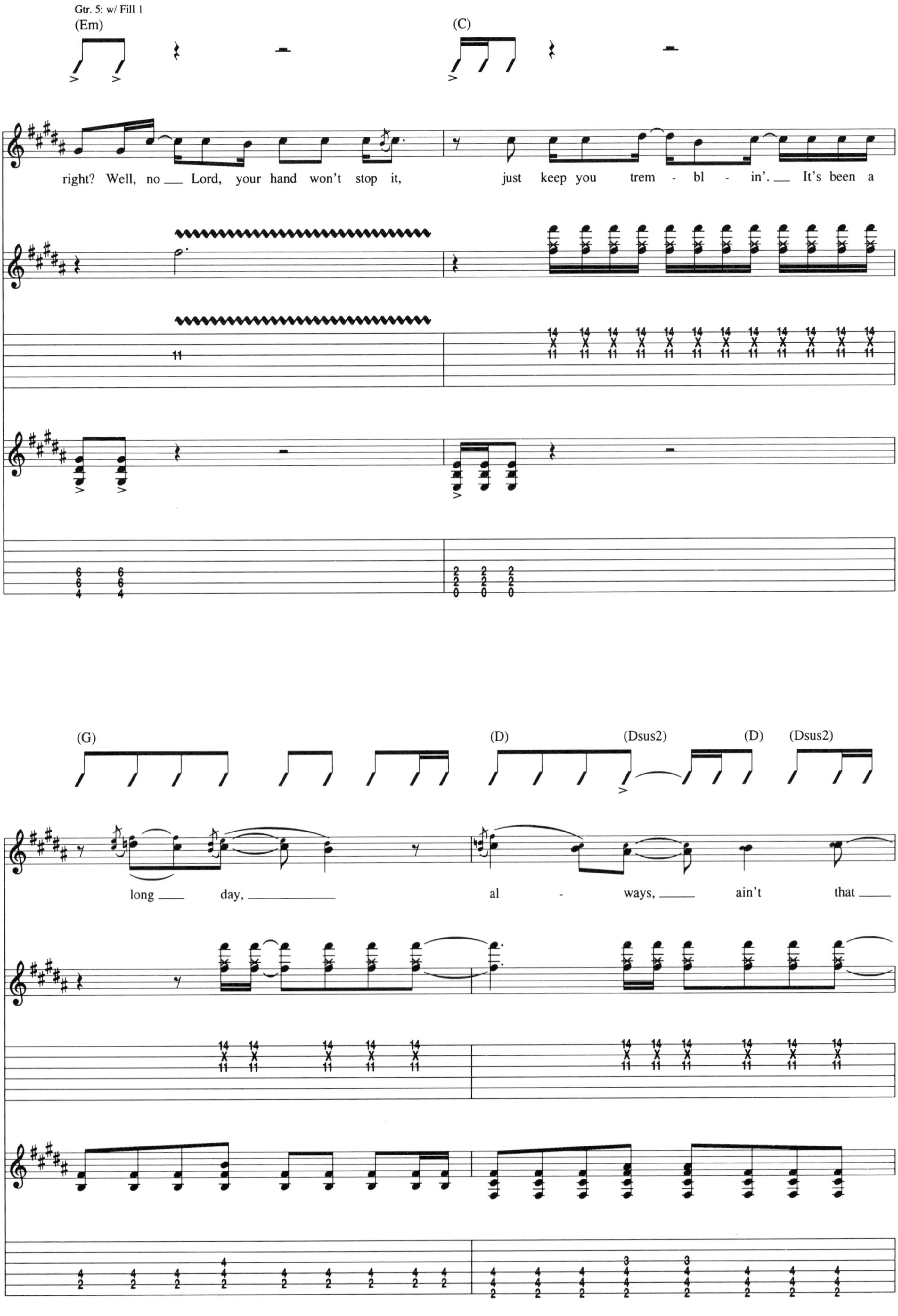
Gtr. 5: w/ Fill 1
(Em)
(C)
right? Well, no Lord, your hand won't stop it, just keep you trem - bl - in'. It's been a
(G)
(D)
(Dsus2)
(D)
(Dsus2)
long day, al - ways, ain't that

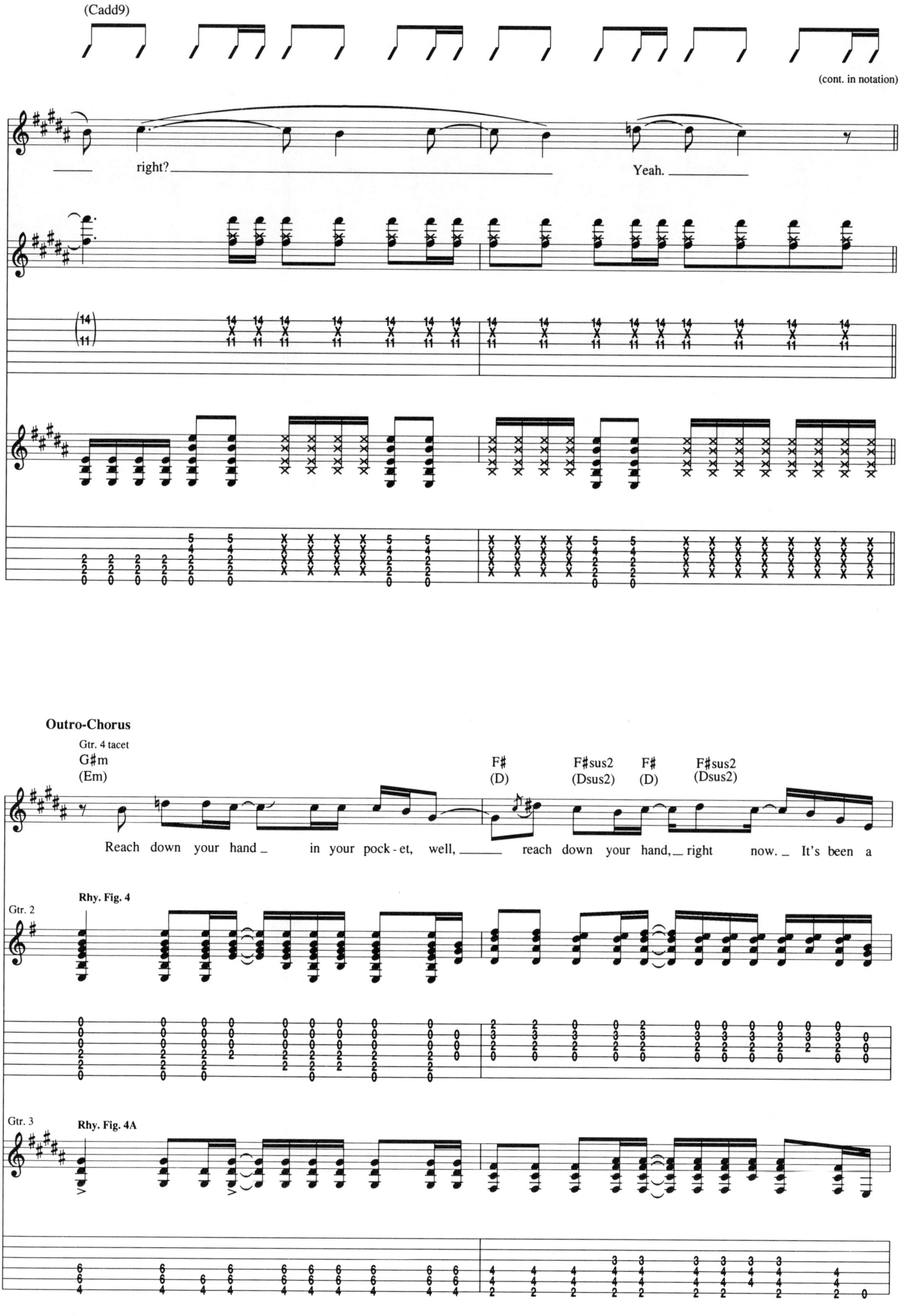

(Cadd9)
(cont. in notation)
right?
Yeah.
Outro-Chorus
Gtr. 4 tacet
G♯m
(Em)
F♯
(D)
F♯sus2
(Dsus2)
F♯
(D)
F♯sus2
(Dsus2)
Reach down your hand in your pock-et, well, reach down your hand, right now. It's been a
Rhy. Fig. 4
Gtr. 2
Gtr. 3
Rhy. Fig. 4A

Gtr. 5: w/ Fill 1
E
(C)
long day, al - ways, ain't that
End Rhy. Fig. 4
End Rhy. Fig. 4A
Gtrs. 2 & 3: w/ Rhy. Figs. 4 & 4A, 2 1/2 times, simile
G♯m
(Em)
F♯
(D)
F♯sus2
(Dsus2)
right? Reach down your hand in your pock - et, well, reach down your hand, right now. It's been a
Gtr. 5: w/ Fill 1, 4 times
long day, al - ways, ain't that right? Oh, ain't that
right? Well, ain't that right, right, right, oh, child? Right, right, right, oh, right, right, oh, child,
(Right, right, right, right, right, oh,
ah, ah. So, come on.
child.)
Gtr. 2
Gtr. 3

3am

Lyrics by Rob Thomas
Music by Rob Thomas, Brian Yale, John Leslie Goff and John Joseph Stanley

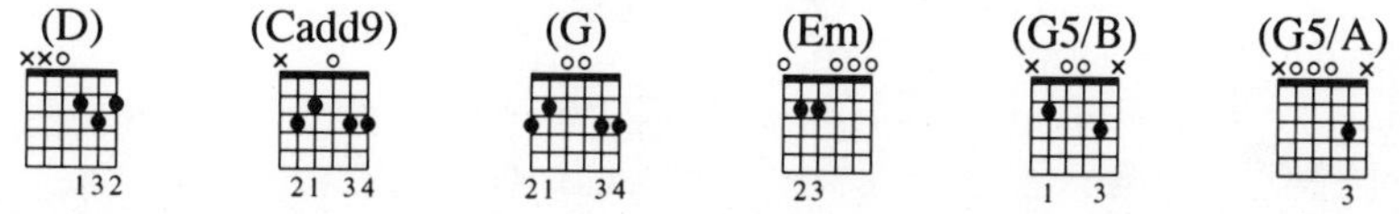

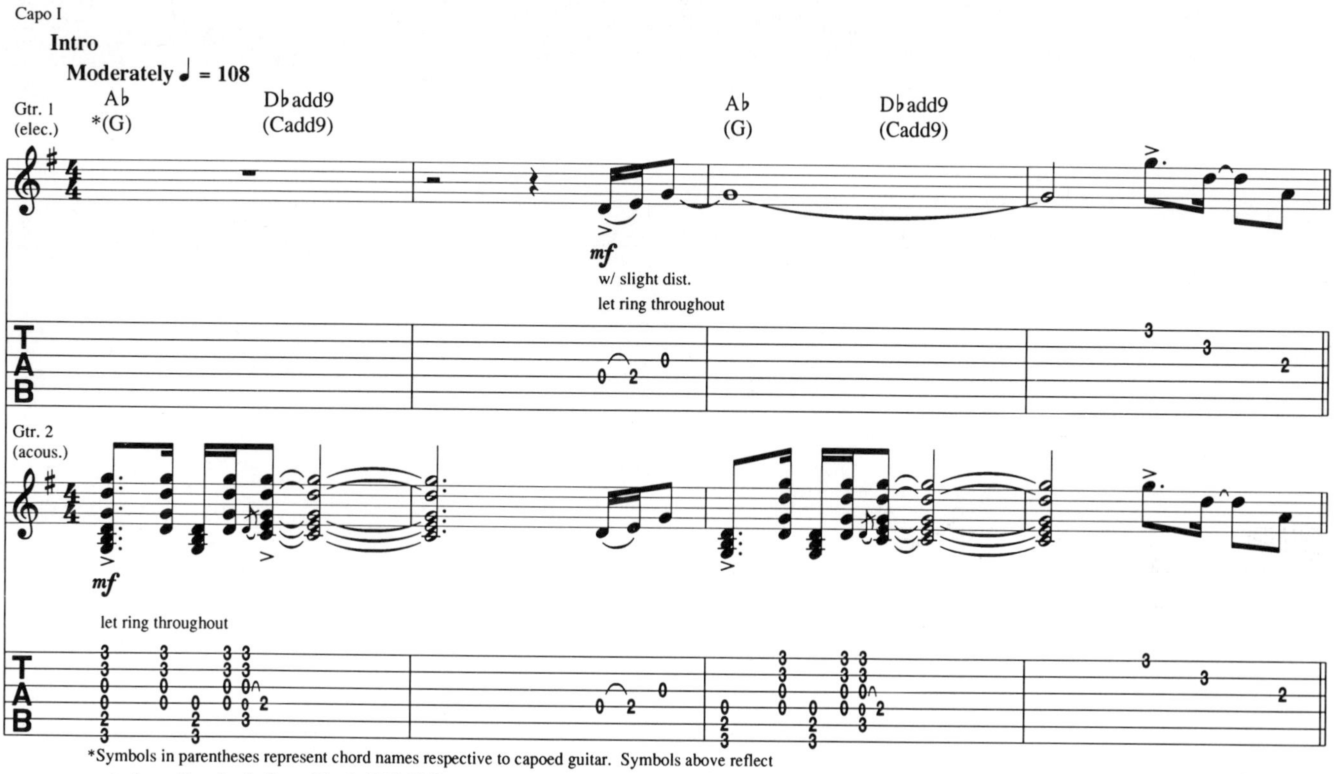

*Symbols in parentheses represent chord names respective to capoed guitar. Symbols above reflect actual sounding chord. Capoed fret is "0" in TAB.

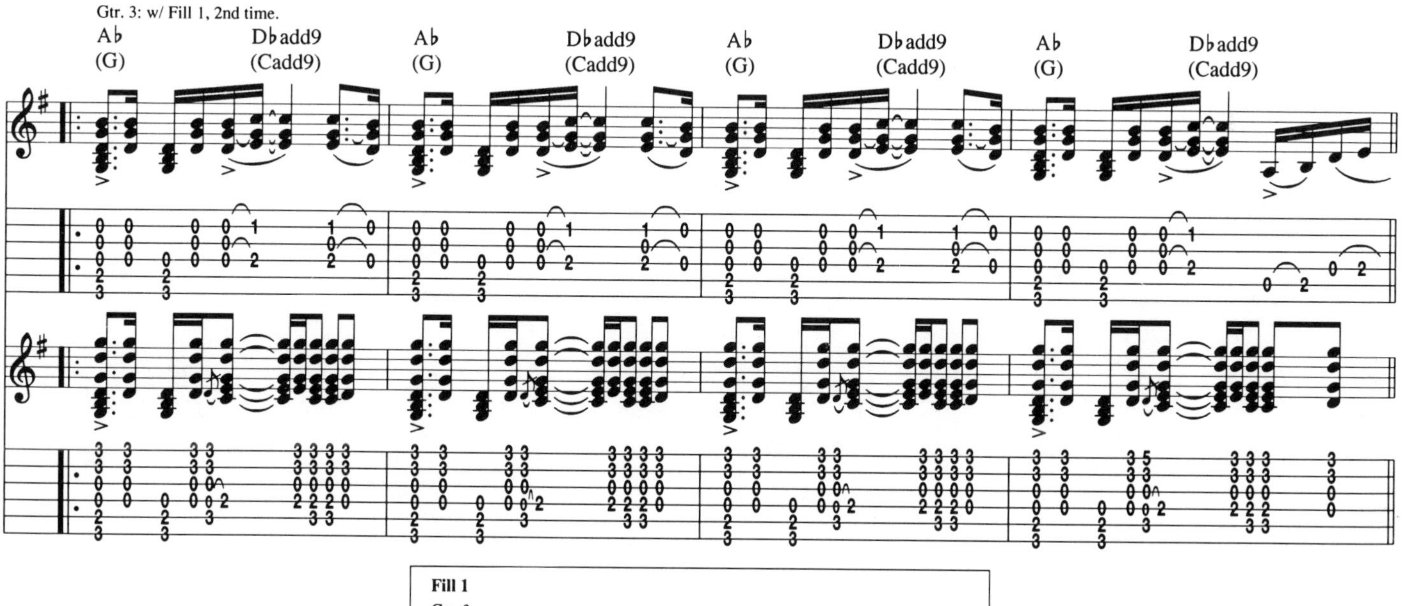

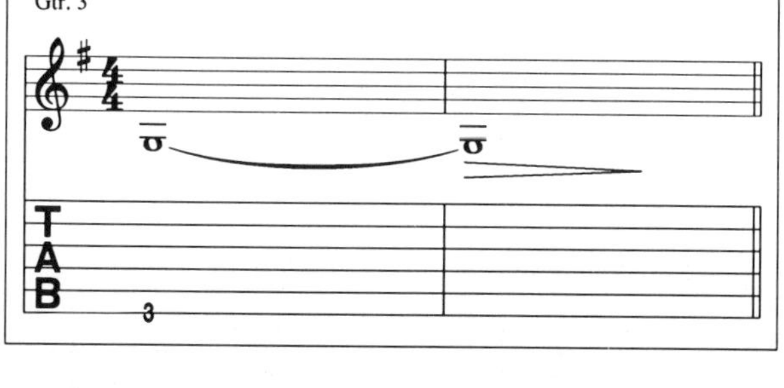

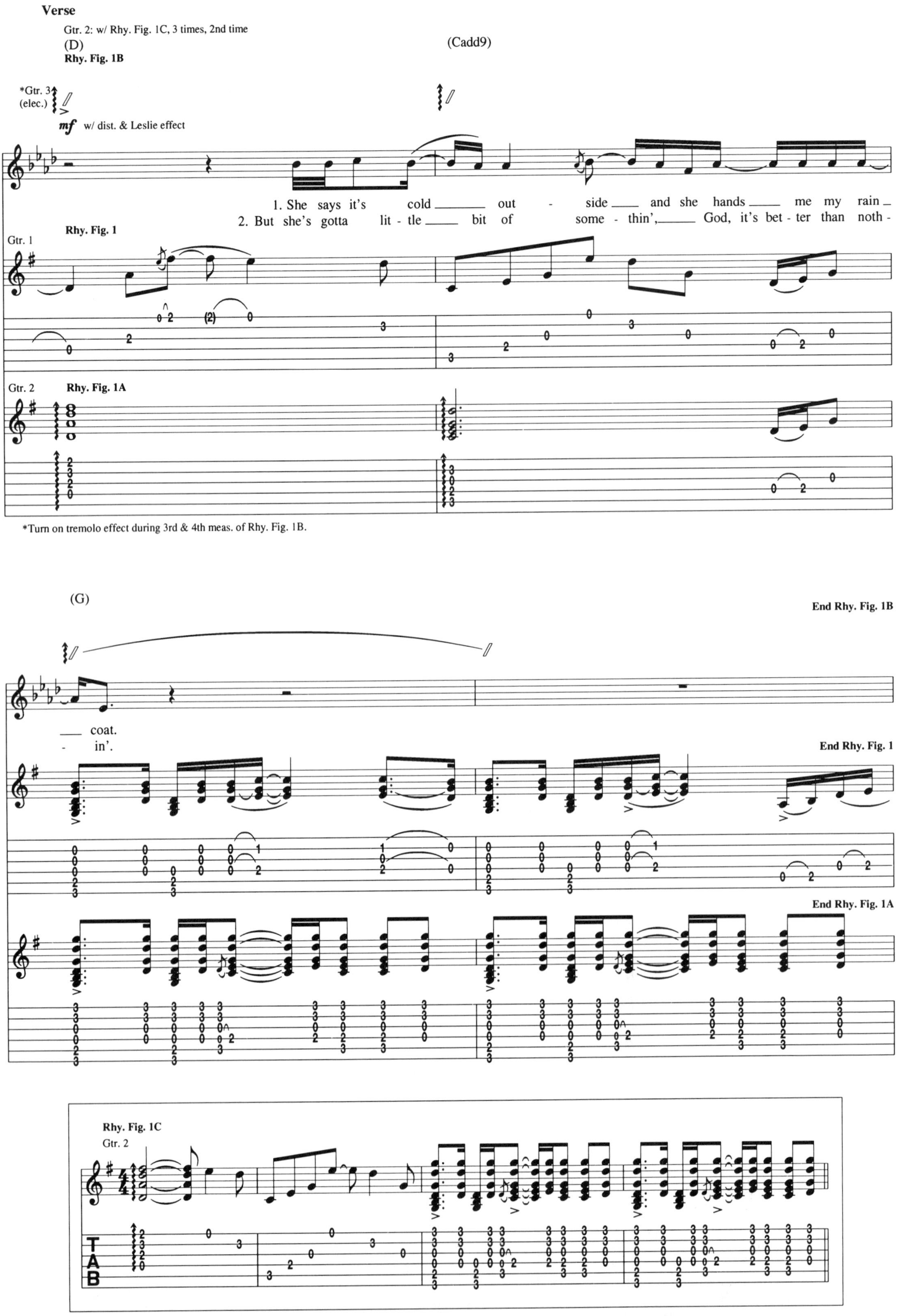
Verse
Gtr. 2: w/ Rhy. Fig. 1C, 3 times, 2nd time
(D)
Rhy. Fig. 1B
(Cadd9)
*Gtr. 3
(elec.)
mf w/ dist. & Leslie effect
1. She says it's cold out - side and she hands me my rain -
2. But she's gotta lit - tle bit of some - thin', God, it's bet - ter than noth -
Rhy. Fig. 1
Gtr. 1
Gtr. 2
Rhy. Fig. 1A
*Turn on tremolo effect during 3rd & 4th meas. of Rhy. Fig. 1B.
(G)
End Rhy. Fig. 1B
coat.
in'.
End Rhy. Fig. 1
End Rhy. Fig. 1A
Rhy. Fig. 1C
Gtr. 2
T
A
B

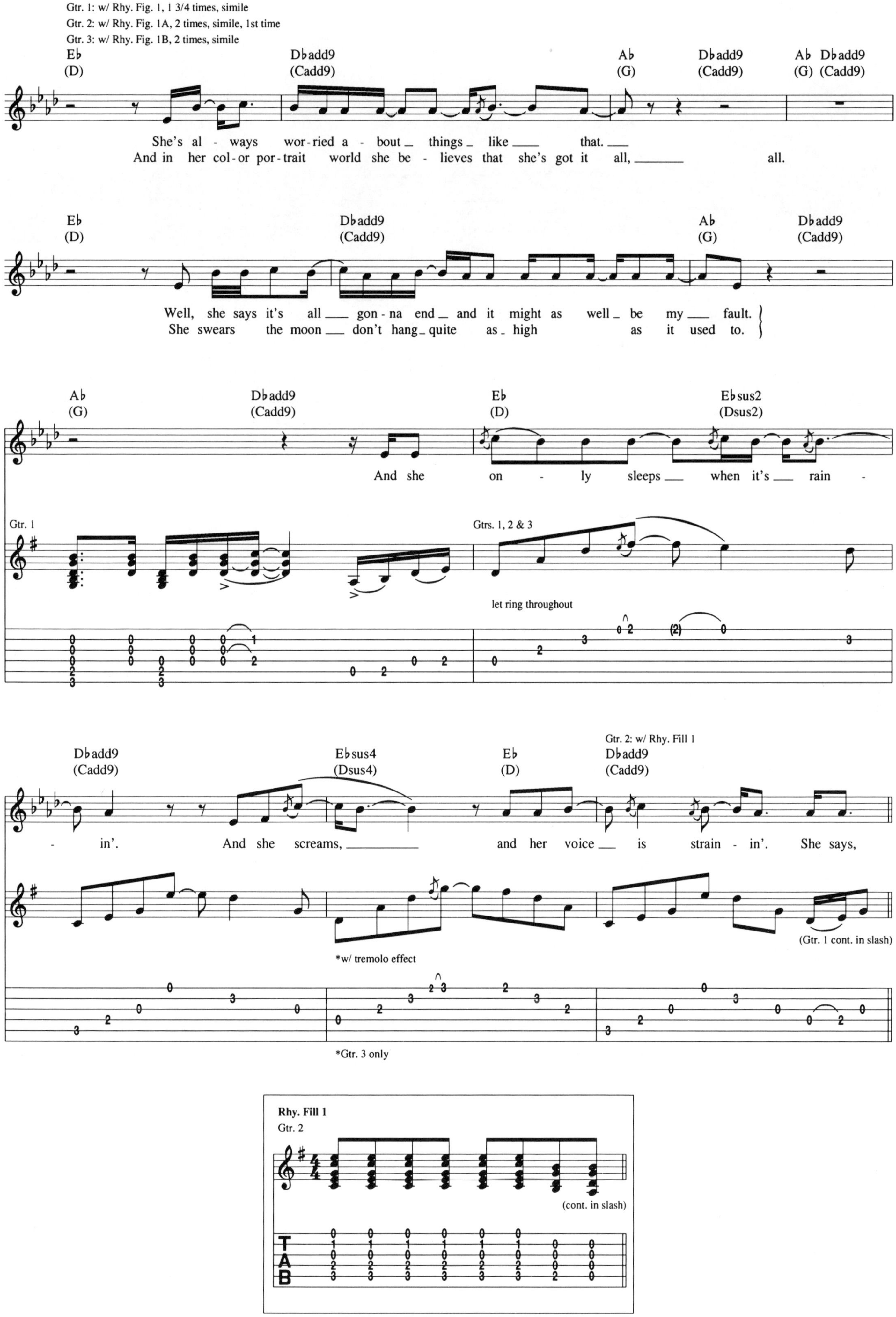
Gtr. 1: w/ Rhy. Fig. 1, 1 3/4 times, simile
Gtr. 2: w/ Rhy. Fig. 1A, 2 times, simile, 1st time
Gtr. 3: w/ Rhy. Fig. 1B, 2 times, simile
Eb (D) Dbadd9 (Cadd9) Ab (G) Dbadd9 (Cadd9) Ab Dbadd9 (G) (Cadd9)
She's al - ways wor-ried a - bout things like that.
And in her col-or por-trait world she be - lieves that she's got it all, all.
Eb (D) Dbadd9 (Cadd9) Ab (G) Dbadd9 (Cadd9)
Well, she says it's all gon-na end and it might as well be my fault.
She swears the moon don't hang quite as high as it used to.
Ab (G) Dbadd9 (Cadd9) Eb (D) Ebsus2 (Dsus2)
And she on - ly sleeps when it's rain -
Gtr. 1
Gtrs. 1, 2 & 3
let ring throughout
Dbadd9 (Cadd9) Ebsus4 (Dsus4) Eb (D)
Gtr. 2: w/ Rhy. Fill 1
Dbadd9 (Cadd9)
- in'. And she screams, and her voice is strain - in'. She says,
(Gtr. 1 cont. in slash)
*w/ tremolo effect
*Gtr. 3 only
Rhy. Fill 1
Gtr. 2
(cont. in slash)
T
A
B

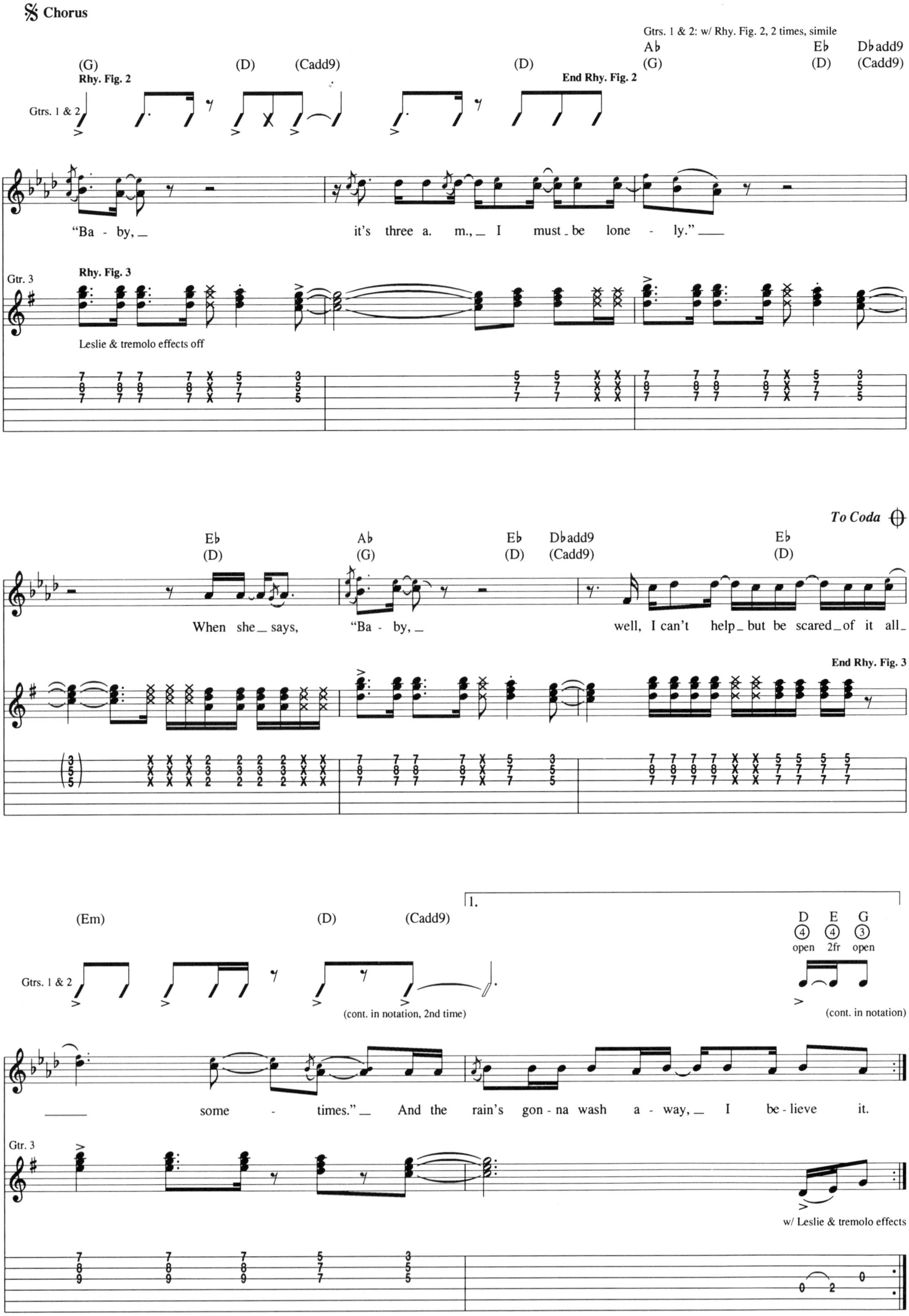

Chorus
Gtrs. 1 & 2: w/ Rhy. Fig. 2, 2 times, simile
(G) (D) (Cadd9) (D)
Ab (G) Eb (D) Dbadd9 (Cadd9)
Rhy. Fig. 2
End Rhy. Fig. 2
Gtrs. 1 & 2
"Ba - by, it's three a. m., I must be lone - ly."
Gtr. 3
Rhy. Fig. 3
Leslie & tremolo effects off
To Coda
Eb (D) Ab (G) Eb (D) Dbadd9 (Cadd9) Eb (D)
When she says, "Ba - by, well, I can't help but be scared of it all
End Rhy. Fig. 3
(Em) (D) (Cadd9)
1.
D E G
4 4 3
open 2fr open
Gtrs. 1 & 2
(cont. in notation, 2nd time)
(cont. in notation)
some - times." And the rain's gon - na wash a - way, I be - lieve it.
Gtr. 3
w/ Leslie & tremolo effects

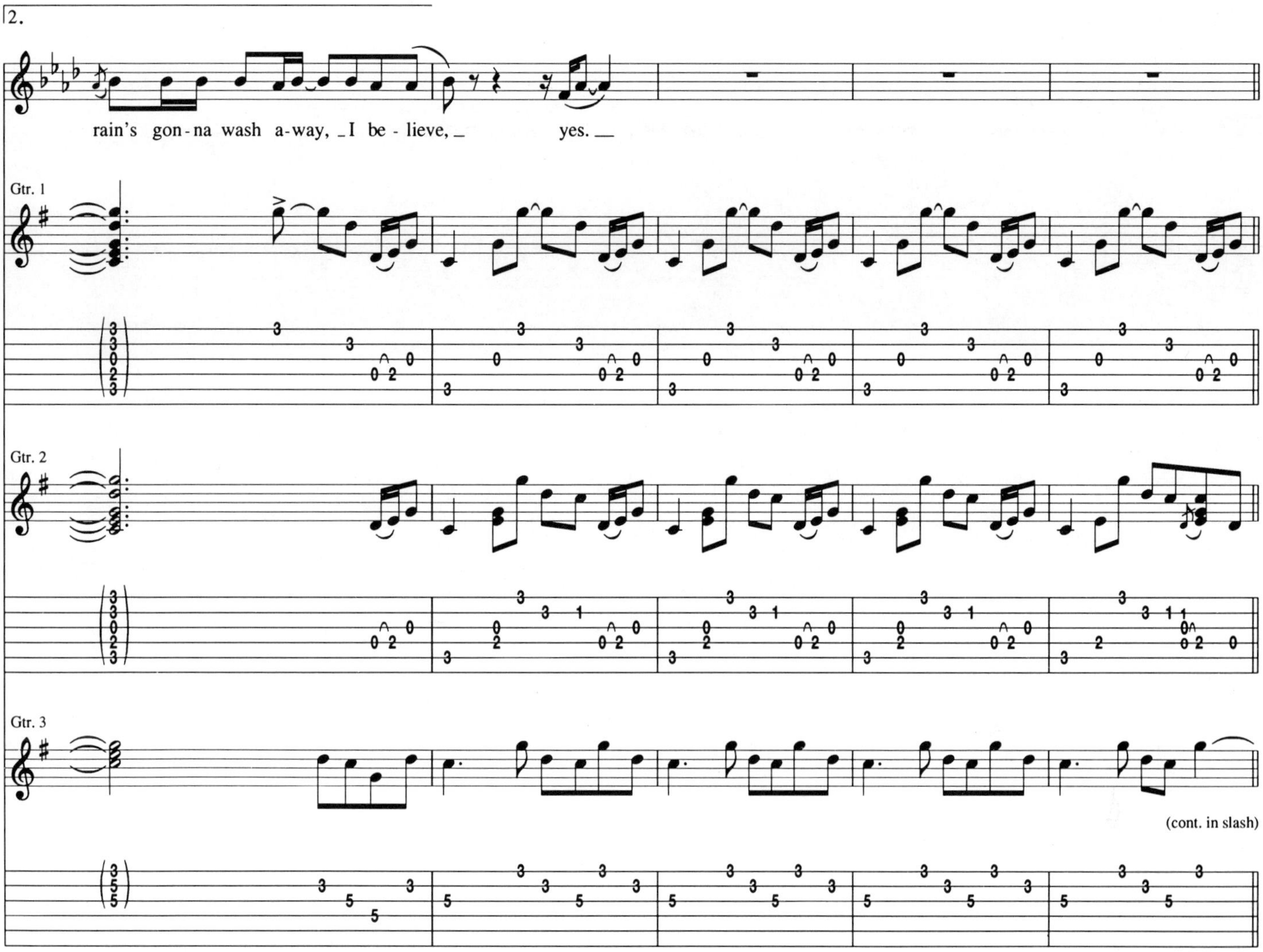
2.
rain's gon-na wash a-way, _I be - lieve, _ yes. _
Gtr. 1
Gtr. 2
Gtr. 3
(cont. in slash)

Interlude

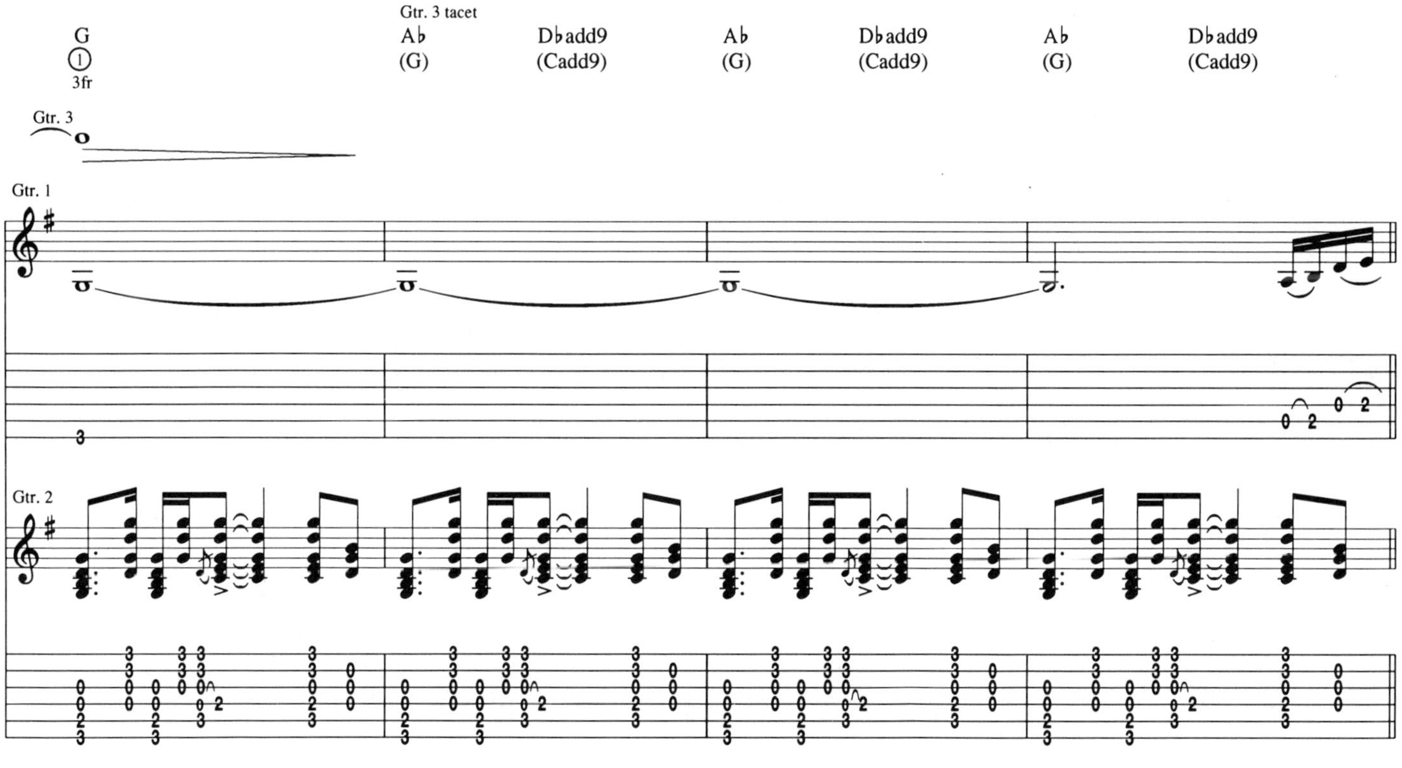
Gtr. 3 tacet
G
3fr
A♭ (G)
D♭add9 (Cadd9)
A♭ (G)
D♭add9 (Cadd9)
A♭ (G)
D♭add9 (Cadd9)
Gtr. 3
Gtr. 1
Gtr. 2

Verse
Gtrs. 2 & 3: w/ Rhy. Figs. 1A & 1B, 3 times, simile
E♭ (D)
D♭add9 (Cadd9)
A♭ (G)
D♭add9 (Cadd9)
3. Well, she be - lieves _ that life _ is made up of all _ that you're used _ to.
Gtr. 1
A♭ (G)
D♭add9 (Cadd9)
E♭ (D)
D♭add9 (Cadd9)
And the clock on the wall _____ has _ been stuck at three _ for
A♭ (G)
D♭add9 (Cadd9)
A♭ (G)
D♭add9 (Cadd9)
E♭ (D)
days ___ and days. ___
She thinks that hap -
Harm.
D♭add9 (Cadd9)
A♭ (G)
D♭add9 (Cadd9)
A♭ (G)
D♭add9 (Cadd9)
- pi - ness _ is a mat _ that sits _ on her door - way, _____ yeah.
But
Harm.

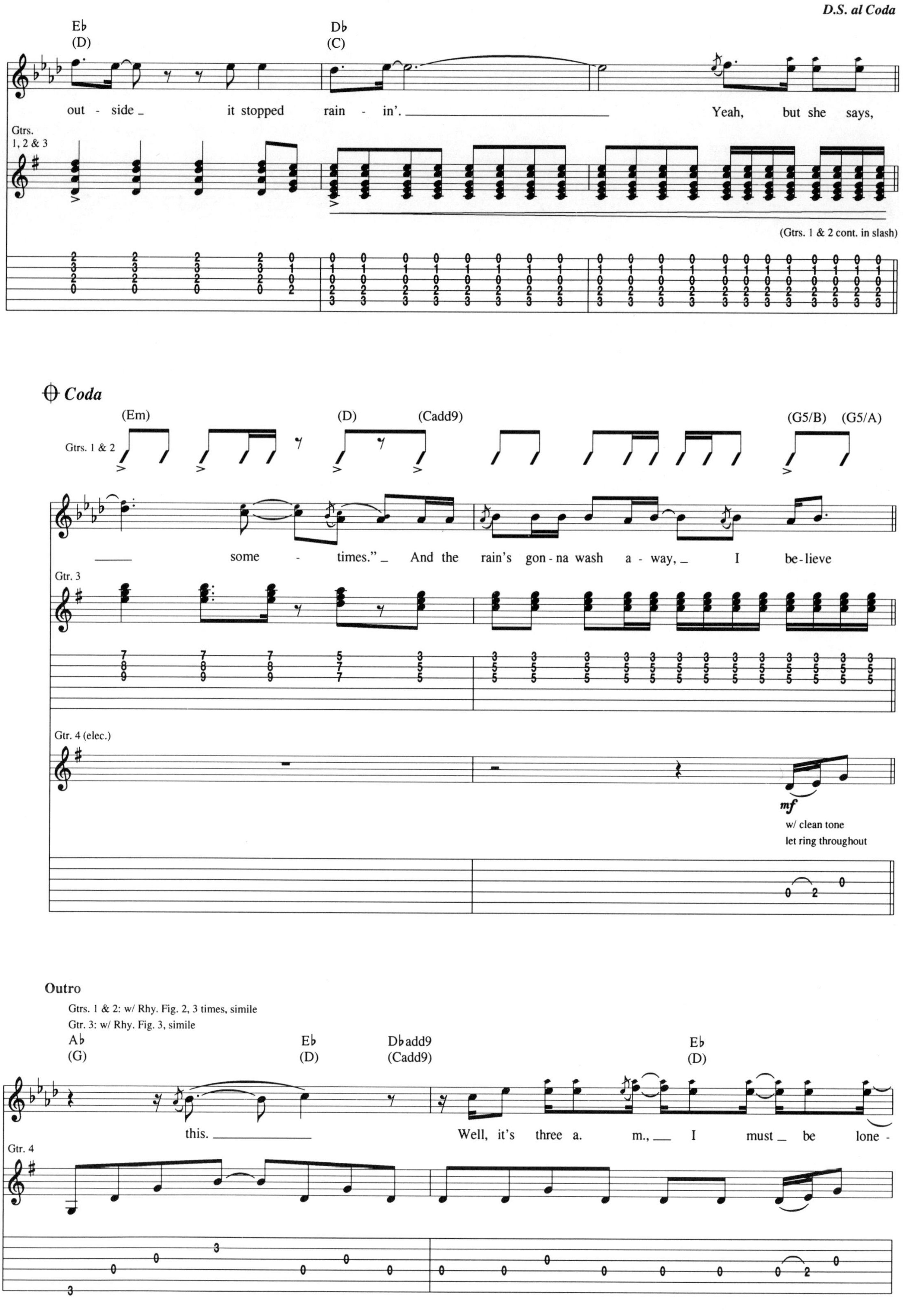
D.S. al Coda
E♭ (D)
D♭ (C)
out - side it stopped rain - in'.
Yeah, but she says,
Gtrs. 1, 2 & 3
(Gtrs. 1 & 2 cont. in slash)
Coda
(Em) (D) (Cadd9) (G5/B) (G5/A)
Gtrs. 1 & 2
some - times." And the rain's gon - na wash a - way, I be - lieve
Gtr. 3
Gtr. 4 (elec.)
mf
w/ clean tone
let ring throughout
Outro
Gtrs. 1 & 2: w/ Rhy. Fig. 2, 3 times, simile
Gtr. 3: w/ Rhy. Fig. 3, simile
A♭ (G)
E♭ (D)
D♭add9 (Cadd9)
E♭ (D)
this.
Well, it's three a. m., I must be lone -
Gtr. 4

A♭ (G) E♭ (D) D♭add9 (Cadd9) E♭ (D)
- ly. When - ev - er she says,
(Well, I must feel lone - ly.)
A♭ (G) E♭ (D) D♭add9 (Cadd9) E♭ (D)
"Ba - by." Well, I can't help but be scared of it all
(Em) (D) (Cadd9)
Gtrs. 1 & 2
some - times.
Gtr. 3
Gtr. 4

Push

Written by Rob Thomas and Matt Serletic

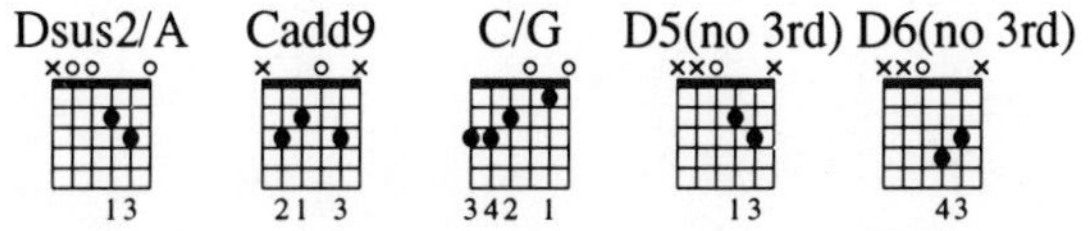

Tune Down 1/2 Step:
①=E♭ ④=D♭
②=B♭ ⑤=A♭
③=G♭ ⑥=E♭

Gtr. 2: Nashville Tuning: Bottom 4 strings tuned up 1 octave

G5 D/F♯ Em C
Well, I feel like some-thing's gon - na give, and I'm a lit - tle bit an - gry.
Pre-Chorus
Dsus2/A Cadd9
Gtr. 3 (dist.)
mf
Well, this ain't o - ver, no, not here,
Oh, well, don't just stand there, say nice things to me
Gtr. 4 (dist.)
mf let ring
Gtrs. 1 & 2
Dsus2/A
not while I still need you a - round. You don't owe
'Cause I've been cheat - ed, I've been wronged. And you, you don't know
let ring

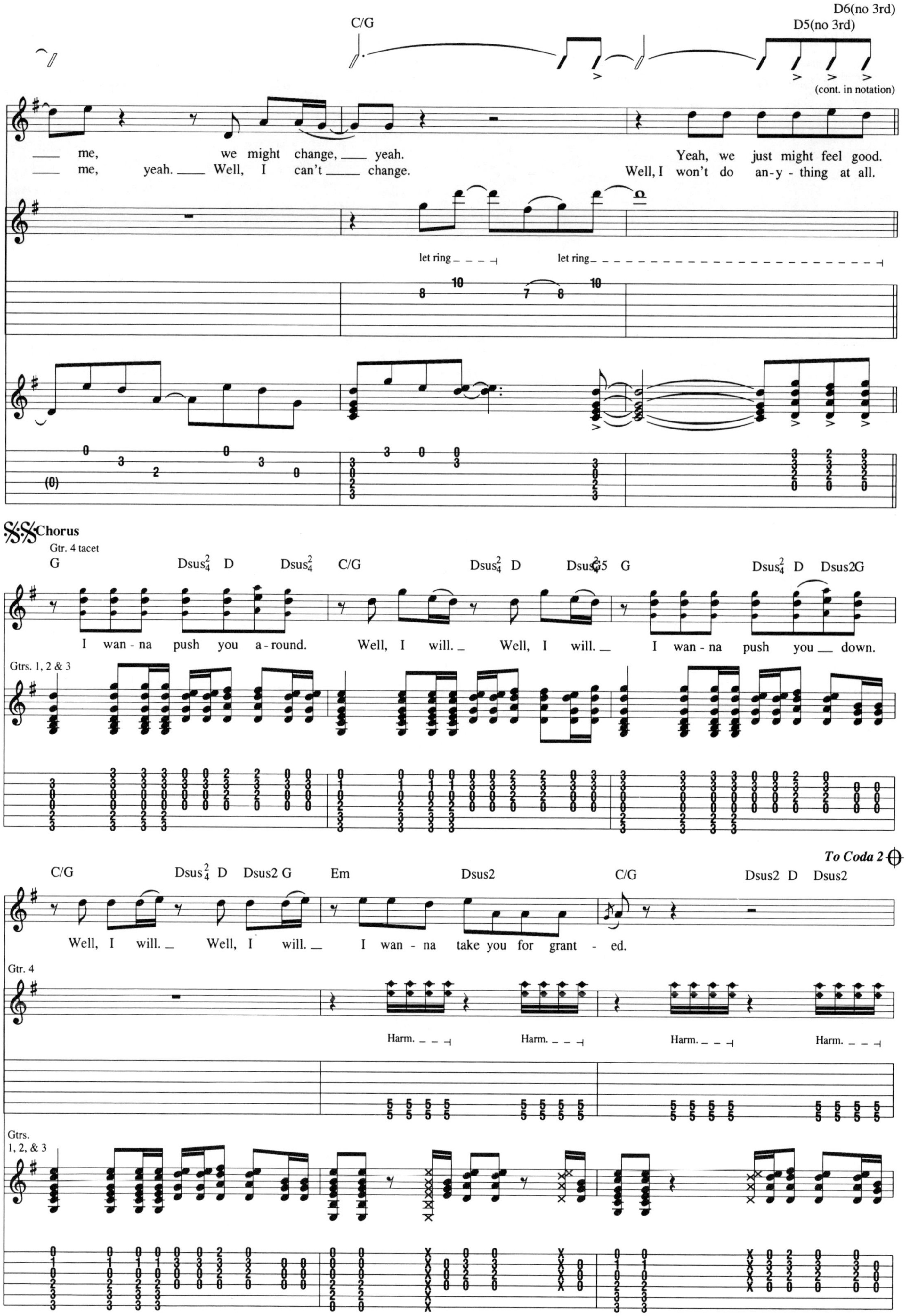
D6(no 3rd)
C/G
D5(no 3rd)
(cont. in notation)
me, we might change, yeah. Yeah, we just might feel good.
me, yeah. Well, I can't change. Well, I won't do an-y-thing at all.
let ring
let ring
Chorus
Gtr. 4 tacet
G Dsus4 D Dsus4 C/G Dsus4 D Dsus4 G5 G Dsus4 D Dsus2 G
I wan-na push you a-round. Well, I will. Well, I will. I wan-na push you down.
Gtrs. 1, 2 & 3
C/G Dsus4 D Dsus2 G Em Dsus2 C/G Dsus2 D Dsus2
To Coda 2
Well, I will. Well, I will. I wan-na take you for grant-ed.
Gtr. 4
Harm.
Harm.
Harm.
Harm.
Gtrs. 1, 2, & 3

To Coda 1
Em
Dsus2
C/G
D
Well, I wan - na take you for grant - ed. I, I will, I will.
Gtr. 4
Rhy. Fill 1
End Rhy. Fill 1
Harm.
Harm.
Harm.
Gtr. 5 (dist.)
mf
let ring
let ring
Gtrs. 1, 2 & 3
Guitar Solo
Gtrs. 1,2 & 3: w/ Rhy. Fig 1
Gtr. 4 tacet
G
Dsus4/F♯
Em
C
G
Dsus4/F♯
Em
C
I will.
2. She said
Gtr. 5
let ring

Verse
Gtrs. 1 & 2: w/ Rhy. Fig. 2, 2 times
G5 D/F# Em C
I don't know why you ev - er would lie to me. Like I'm a lit - tle un - trust - ing when
Gtr. 5
Gtr. 4 Riff A
w/ clean tone
Gtr. 5 tacet
G5 D/F# Em C
I think that the truth is gon - na hurt ya. And
Gtr. 4
End Riff A
Gtr. 4: w/ Riff A
G5 D/F# Em C
I don't know why you could - n't just stay with me. You could - n't stand to be near me
G5 D/F# Em C
when my face don't seem to want to shine cuz it's a lit - tle bit dirt - y.
D.S. al Coda 1
Coda 1
Gtr. 4: w/ Rhy. Fill 1
C/G D Dsus2 D
ed. I, I will, I will.
Bridge
Em Dsus2/F#
Oh, but don't bowl me o - ver,
Gtrs. 1, 2 & 3

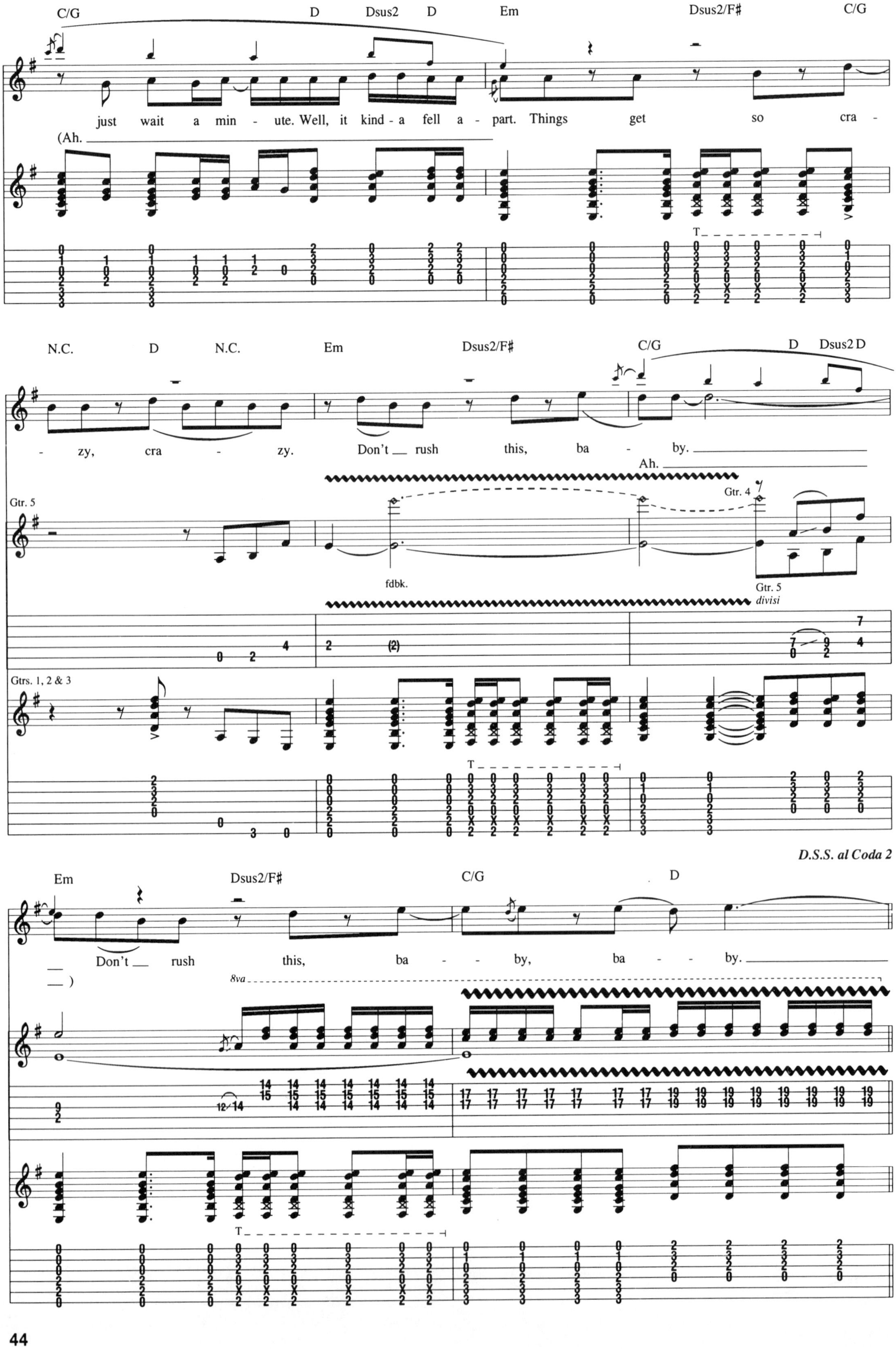
C/G D Dsus2 D Em Dsus2/F♯ C/G
just wait a min - ute. Well, it kind - a fell a - part. Things get so cra -
(Ah.
T
N.C. D N.C. Em Dsus2/F♯ C/G D Dsus2 D
- zy, cra - zy. Don't rush this, ba - by.
Ah.
Gtr. 5
fdbk.
Gtr. 4
Gtr. 5
divisi
Gtrs. 1, 2 & 3
T
D.S.S. al Coda 2
Em Dsus2/F♯ C/G D
Don't rush this, ba - by, ba - by.
)
8va
T

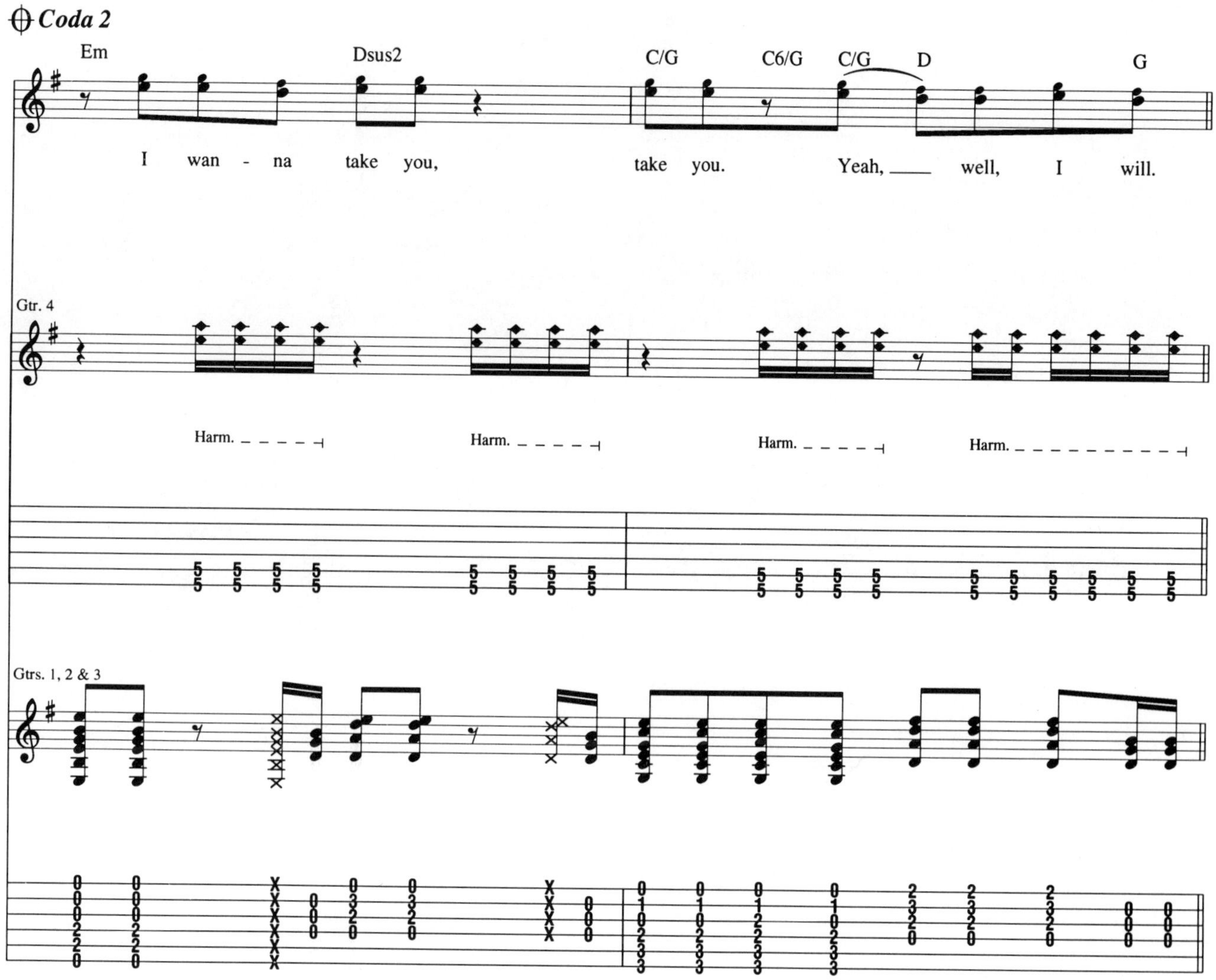
Coda 2
Em
Dsus2
C/G
C6/G
C/G
D
G
I wan - na take you, take you. Yeah, well, I will.
Gtr. 4
Harm.
Harm.
Harm.
Harm.
Gtrs. 1, 2 & 3

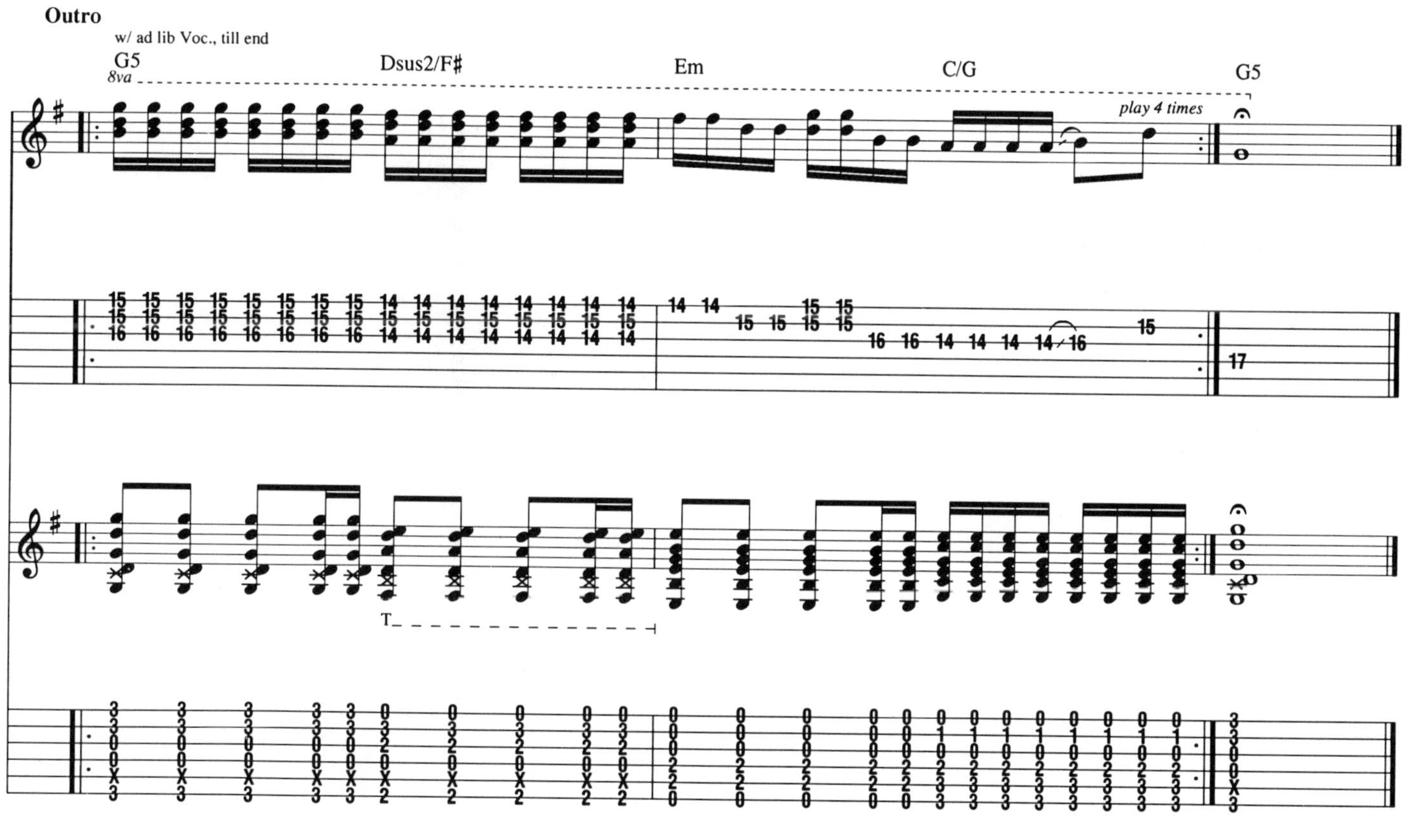
Outro
w/ ad lib Voc., till end
G5
Dsus2/F#
Em
C/G
G5
8va
play 4 times
T

Girl Like That

Written by Rob Thomas

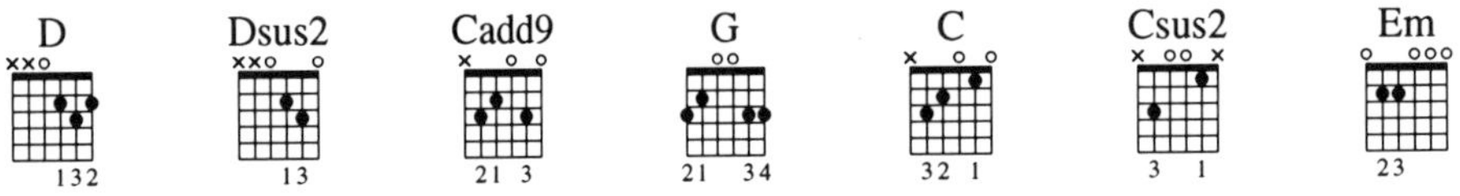

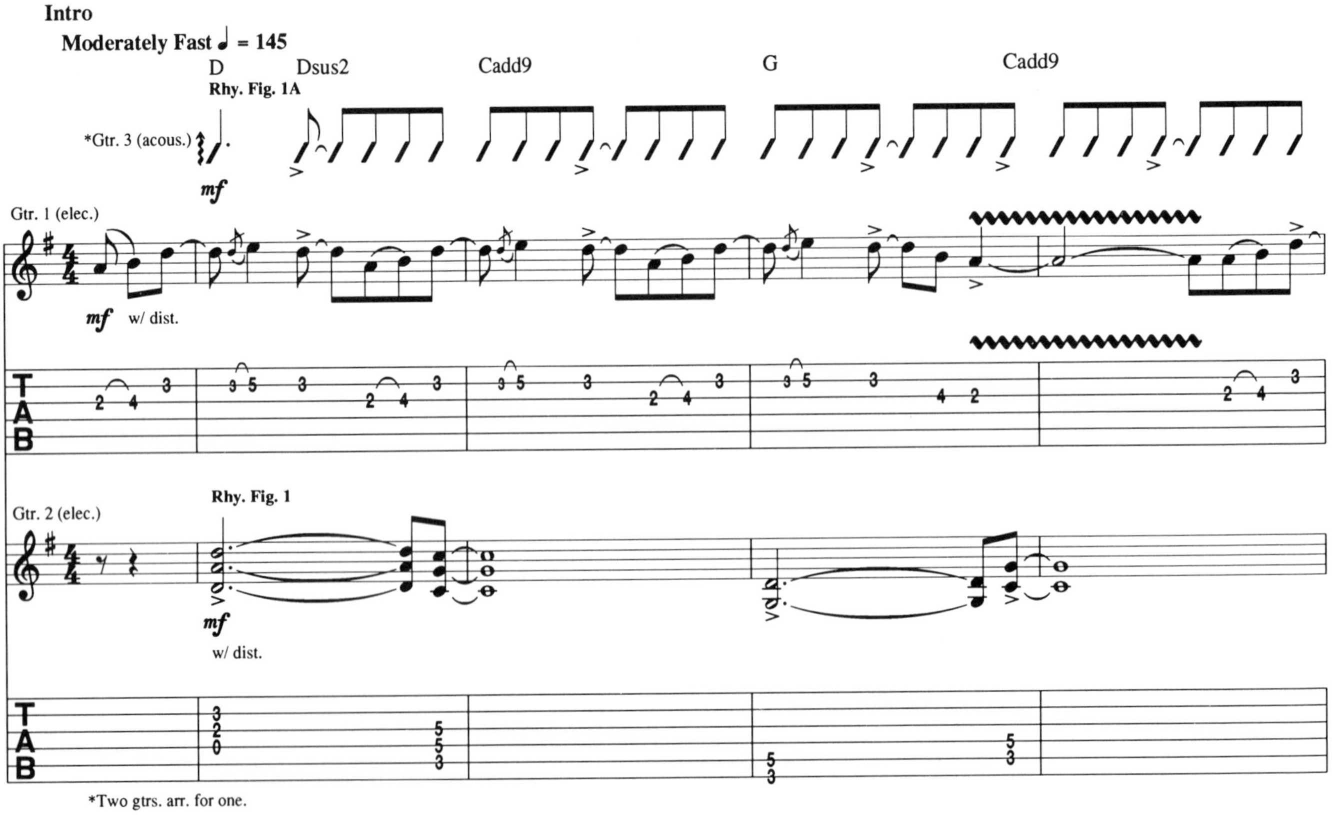

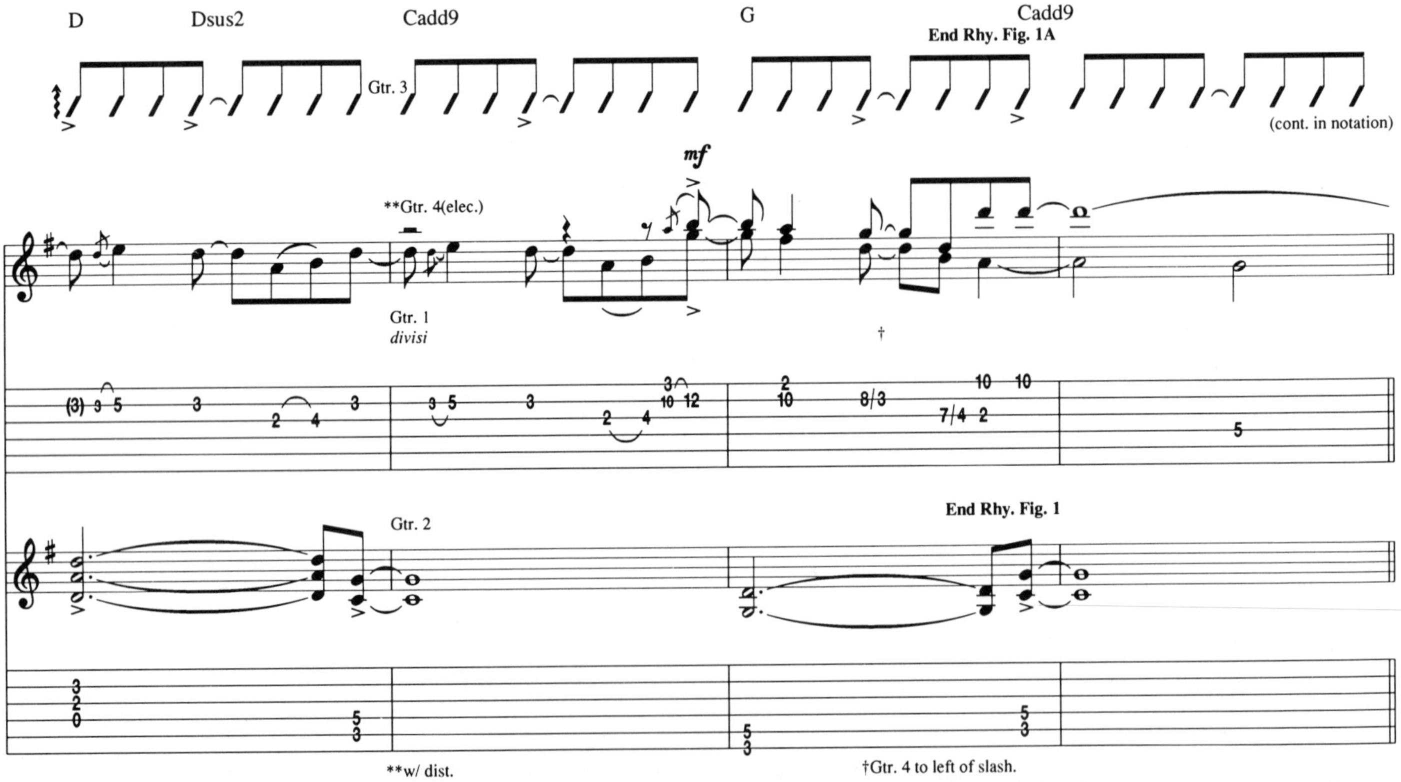

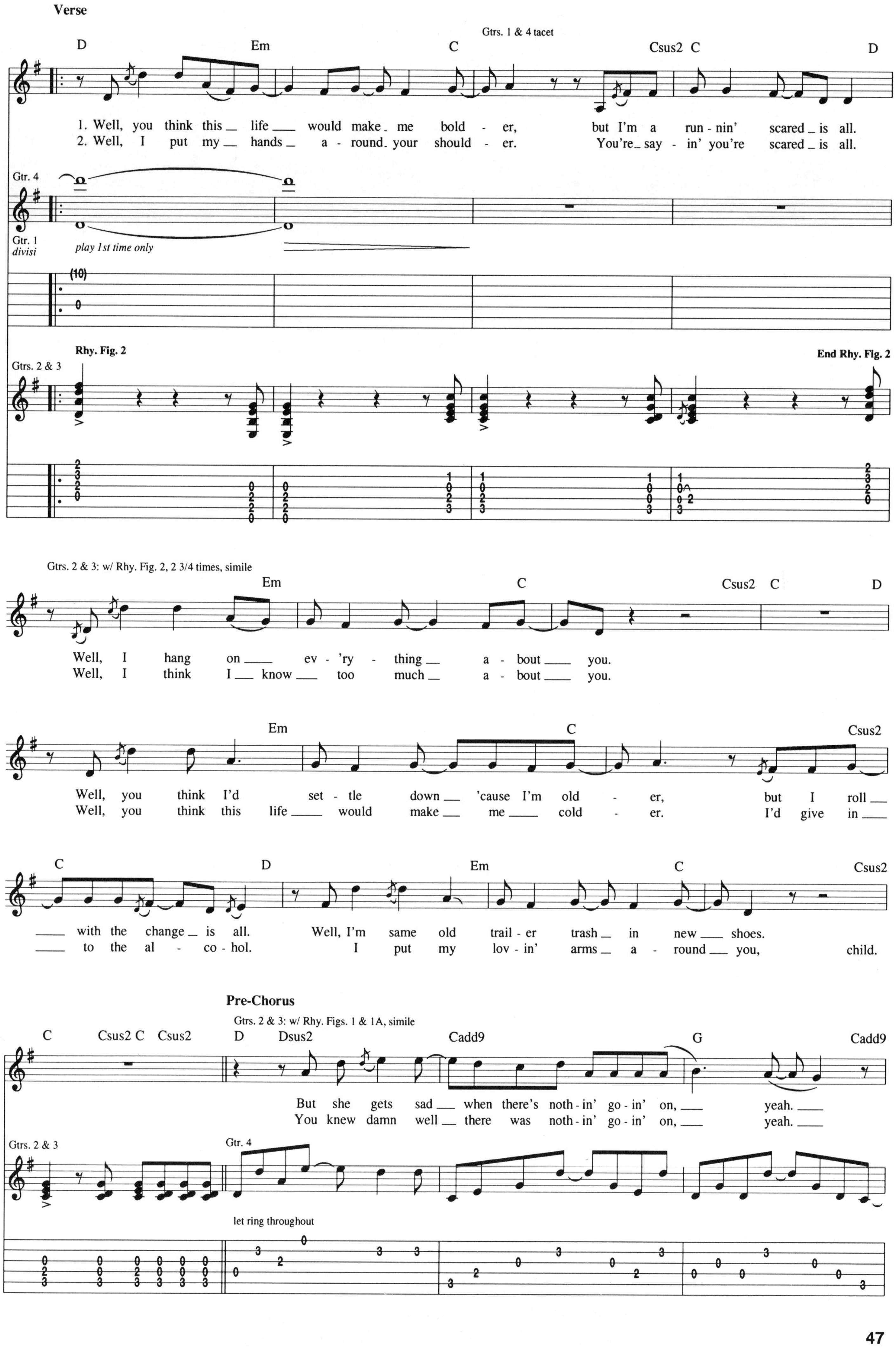
Verse
Gtrs. 1 & 4 tacet
D Em C Csus2 C D
1. Well, you think this life would make me bolder, but I'm a runnin' scared is all.
2. Well, I put my hands around your shoulder. You're sayin' you're scared is all.
Gtr. 4
Gtr. 1 divisi
play 1st time only
Rhy. Fig. 2
End Rhy. Fig. 2
Gtrs. 2 & 3
Gtrs. 2 & 3: w/ Rhy. Fig. 2, 2 3/4 times, simile
Em C Csus2 C D
Well, I hang on ev'ry thing about you.
Well, I think I know too much about you.
Em C Csus2
Well, you think I'd settle down 'cause I'm older, but I roll
Well, you think this life would make me colder. I'd give in
C D Em C Csus2
with the change is all. Well, I'm same old trailer trash in new shoes.
to the alcohol. I put my lovin' arms around you, child.
Pre-Chorus
Gtrs. 2 & 3: w/ Rhy. Figs. 1 & 1A, simile
C Csus2 C Csus2 D Dsus2 Cadd9 G Cadd9
But she gets sad when there's nothin' goin' on, yeah.
You knew damn well there was nothin' goin' on, yeah.
Gtrs. 2 & 3
Gtr. 4
let ring throughout

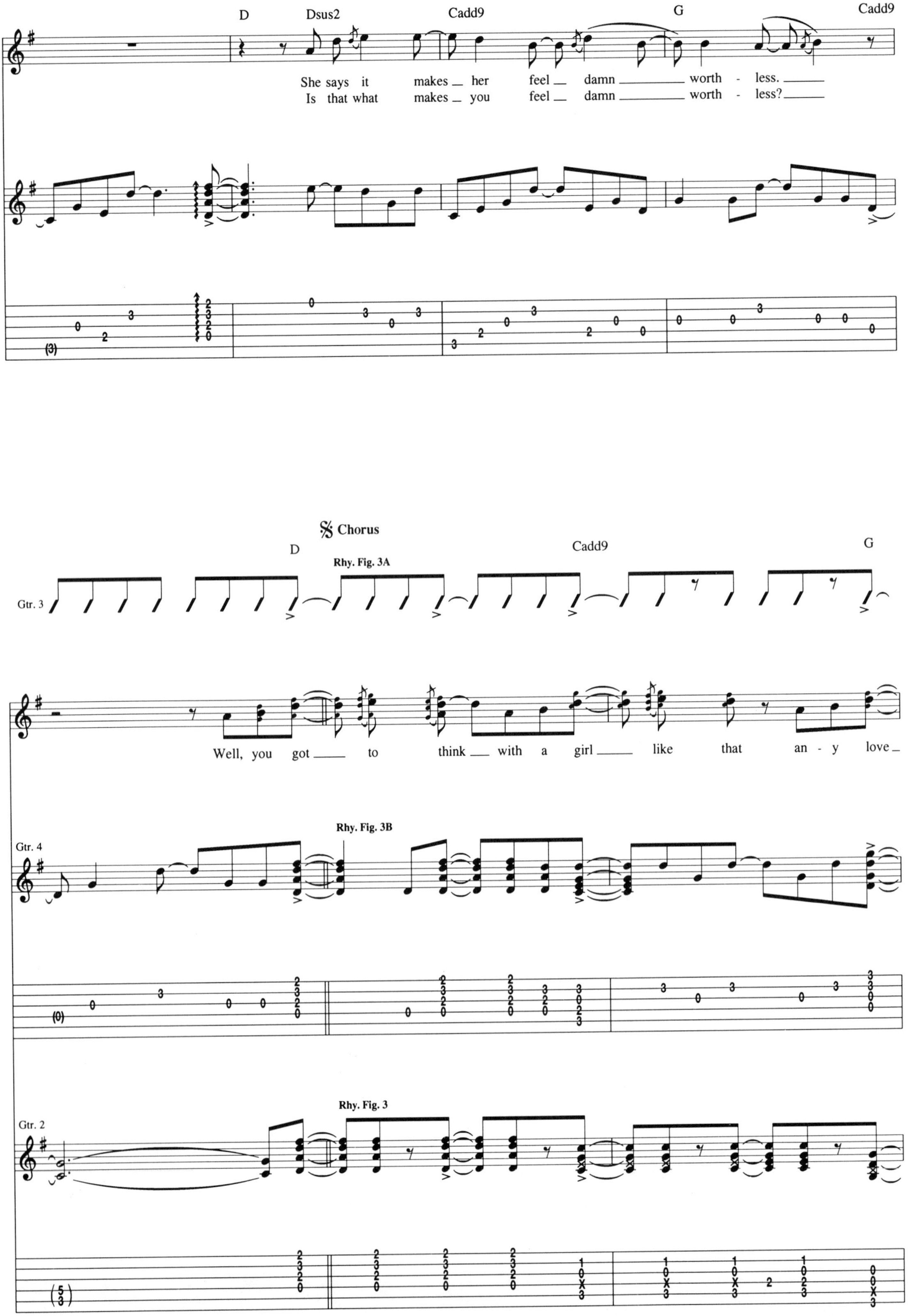
D
Dsus2
Cadd9
G
Cadd9
She says it makes her feel damn worth - less.
Is that what makes you feel damn worth - less?
Chorus
D
Cadd9
G
Rhy. Fig. 3A
Gtr. 3
Well, you got to think with a girl like that an - y love
Gtr. 4
Rhy. Fig. 3B
Gtr. 2
Rhy. Fig. 3

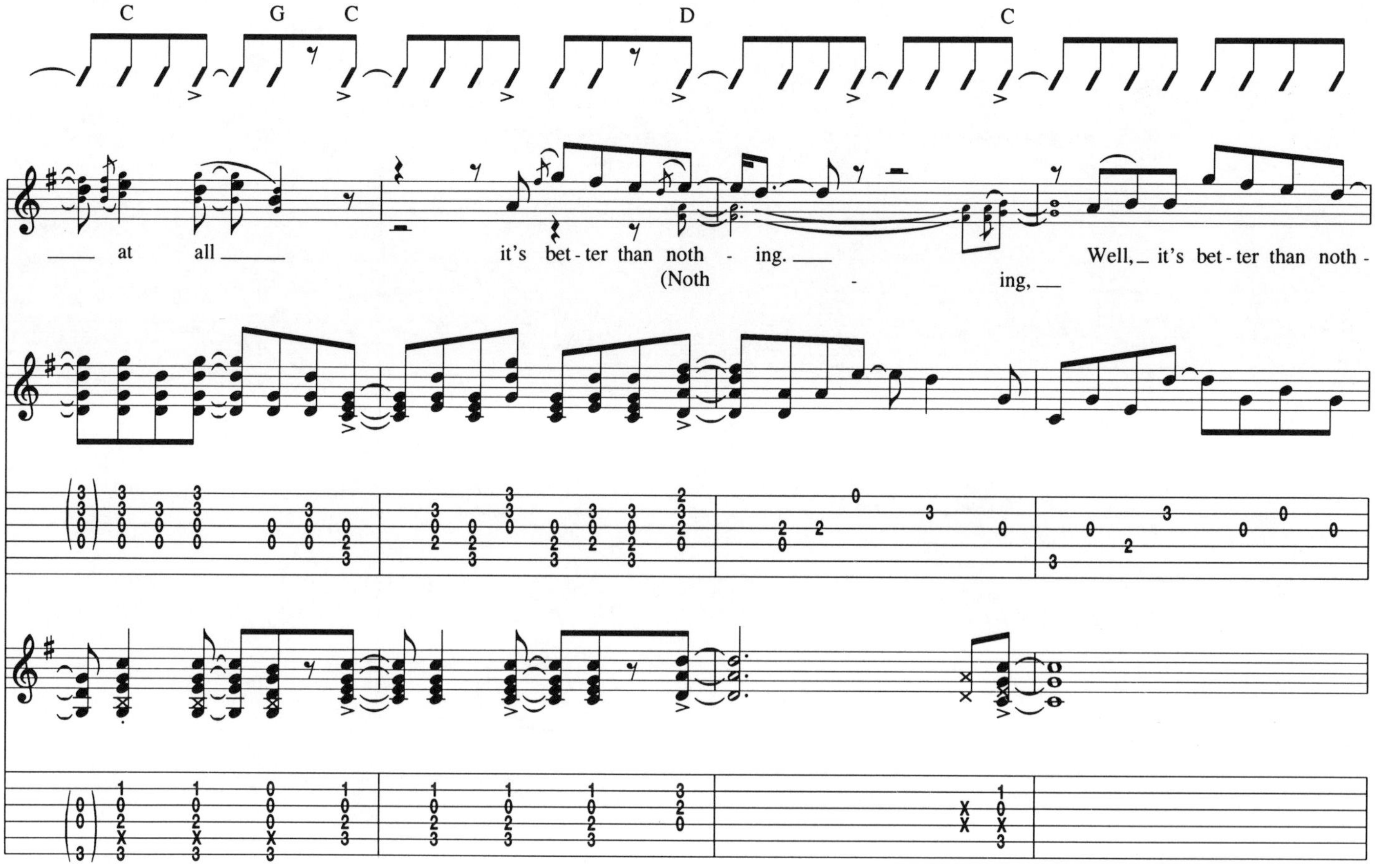
C G C D C
at all
it's bet-ter than noth - ing.
Well, it's bet-ter than noth -
(Noth - ing,

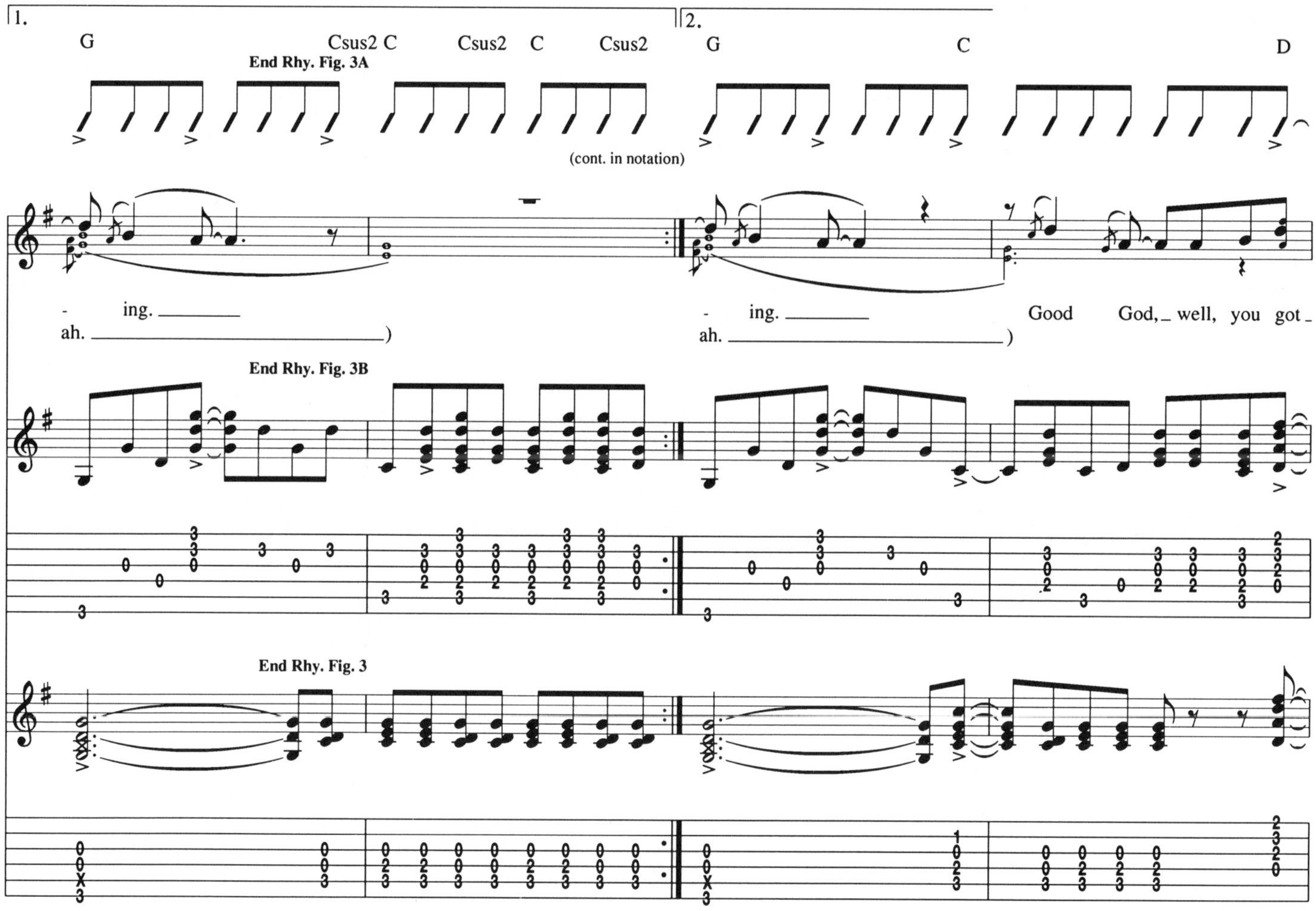
1.
2.
G Csus2 C Csus2 C Csus2
G C D
End Rhy. Fig. 3A
(cont. in notation)
- ing.
ah.)
- ing.
Good God, well, you got
ah.)
End Rhy. Fig. 3B
End Rhy. Fig. 3

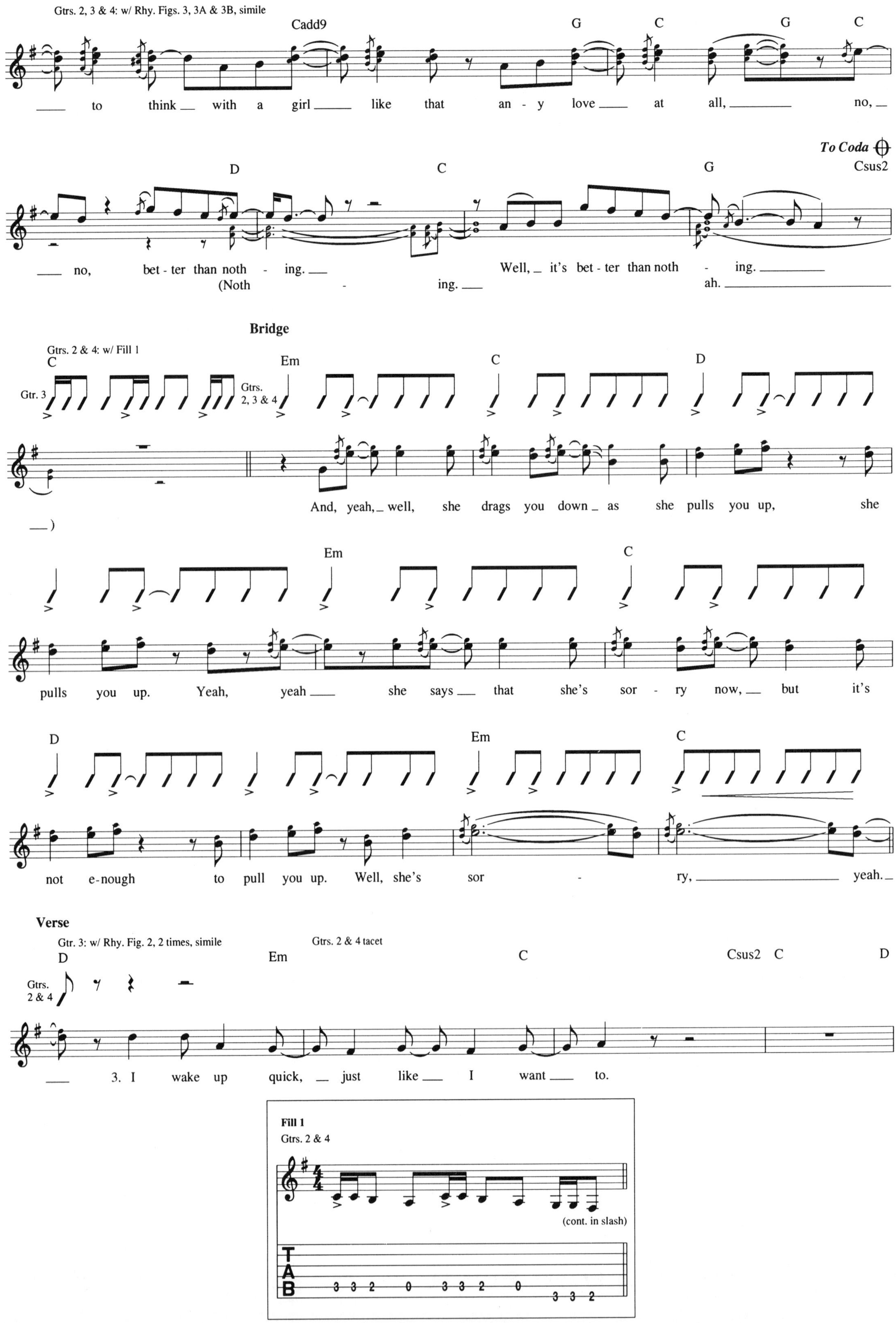

Gtrs. 2, 3 & 4: w/ Rhy. Figs. 3, 3A & 3B, simile
Cadd9 G C G C
to think with a girl like that an - y love at all, no,
To Coda
D C G Csus2
no, bet - ter than noth - ing. Well, it's bet - ter than noth - ing.
(Noth - ing. ah.
Bridge
Gtrs. 2 & 4: w/ Fill 1
C Em C D
Gtr. 3
Gtrs. 2, 3 & 4
And, yeah, well, she drags you down as she pulls you up, she
)
Em C
pulls you up. Yeah, yeah she says that she's sor - ry now, but it's
D Em C
not e-nough to pull you up. Well, she's sor - ry, yeah.
Verse
Gtr. 3: w/ Rhy. Fig. 2, 2 times, simile
Gtrs. 2 & 4 tacet
D Em C Csus2 C D
Gtrs. 2 & 4
3. I wake up quick, just like I want to.
Fill 1
Gtrs. 2 & 4
(cont. in slash)
T
A
B
3 3 2 0 3 3 2 0 3 3 2

Em C Csus2 D
Gtr. 2
(cont. in notation)
Yeah, but I stay out much too late.
D Dsus2 Em C Cadd9
Gtrs. 3 & 4
You think this life can get a bit un - kind, but she stays down
Gtr. 2
let ring
C Cadd9 D Em
'til the worth is gone and pulls you up, she pulls you up, yeah, she
let ring
D.S. al Coda
(take 2nd ending)
C Cadd9 C Cadd9
(Gtr. 4 cont. in notation)
pulls you up and o - ver, o - ver. You got

𝄌 *Coda*

Outro-Chorus

Back 2 Good

Written by Rob Thomas and Matt Serletic

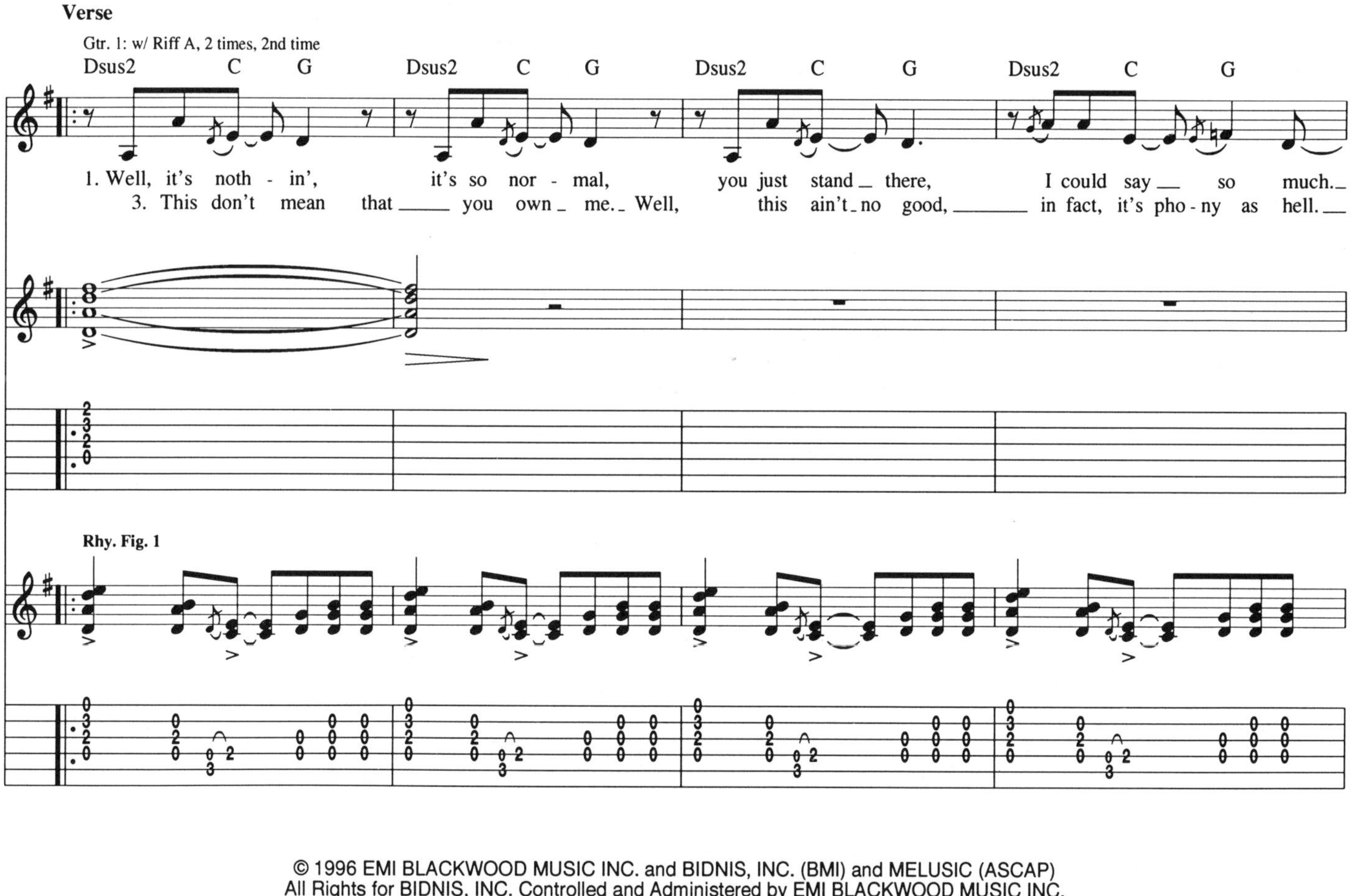

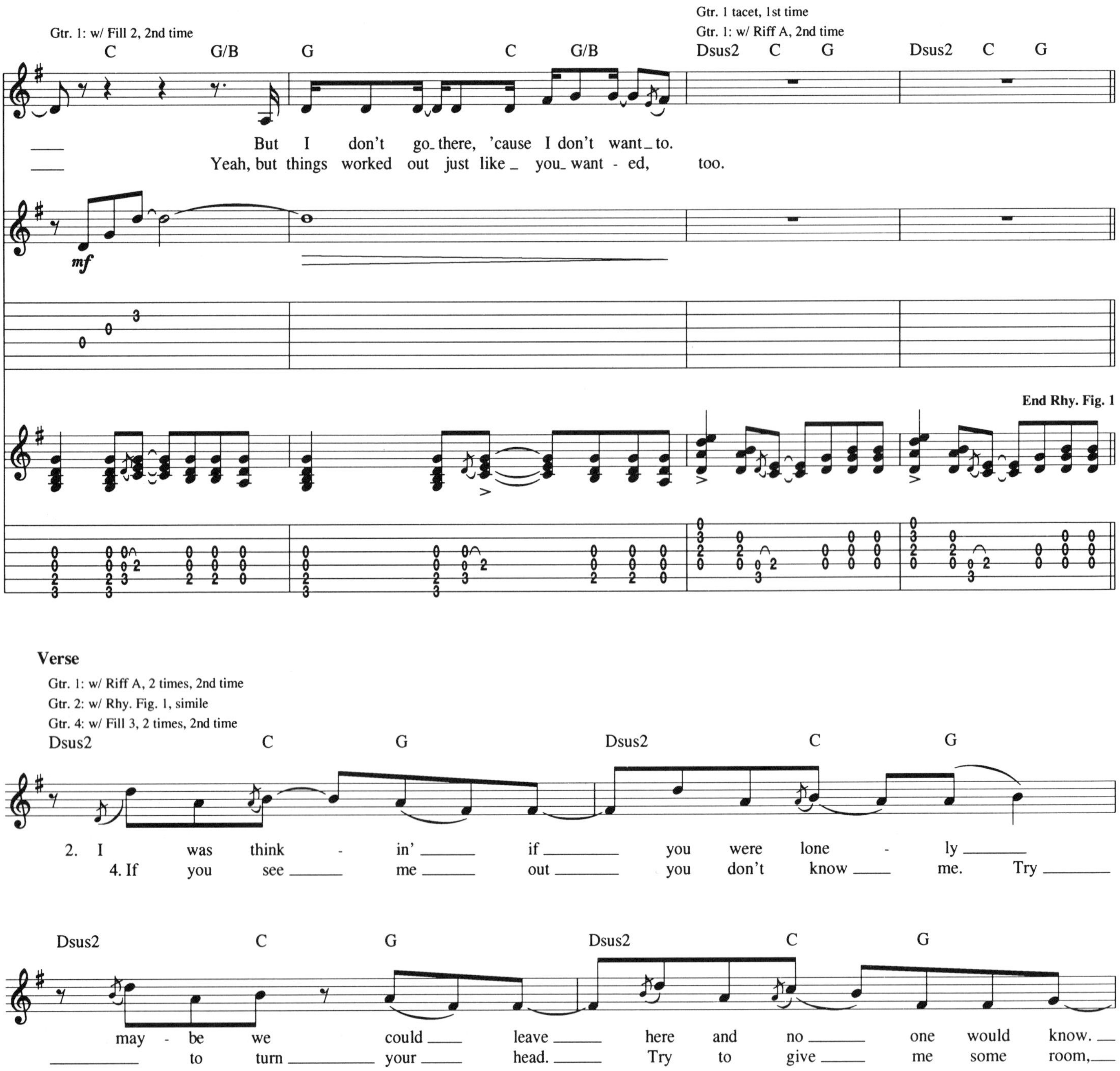
Gtr. 1: w/ Fill 2, 2nd time
Gtr. 1 tacet, 1st time
Gtr. 1: w/ Riff A, 2nd time
C G/B G C G/B Dsus2 C G Dsus2 C G
But I don't go_ there, 'cause I don't want_ to.
Yeah, but things worked out just like_ you_ want - ed, too.
mf
End Rhy. Fig. 1
Verse
Gtr. 1: w/ Riff A, 2 times, 2nd time
Gtr. 2: w/ Rhy. Fig. 1, simile
Gtr. 4: w/ Fill 3, 2 times, 2nd time
Dsus2 C G Dsus2 C G
2. I was think - in' if you were lone - ly
4. If you see me out you don't know me. Try
Dsus2 C G Dsus2 C G
may - be we could leave here and no one would know.
to turn your head. Try to give me some room,

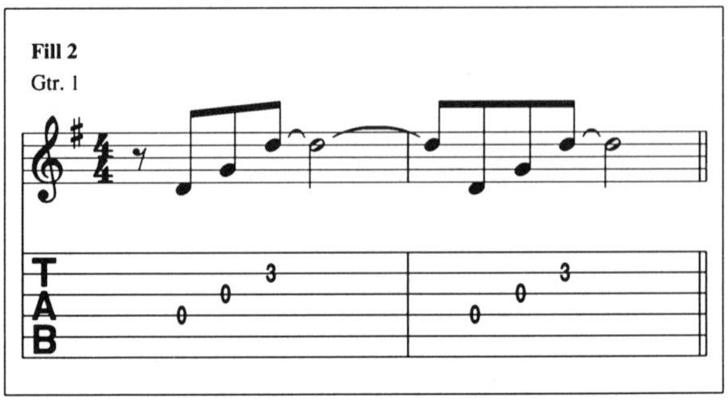
Fill 2
Gtr. 1
TAB

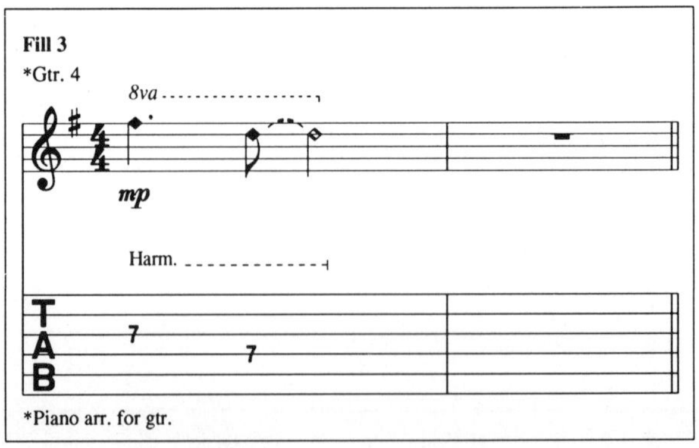
Fill 3
*Gtr. 4
8va
mp
Harm.
TAB
*Piano arr. for gtr.

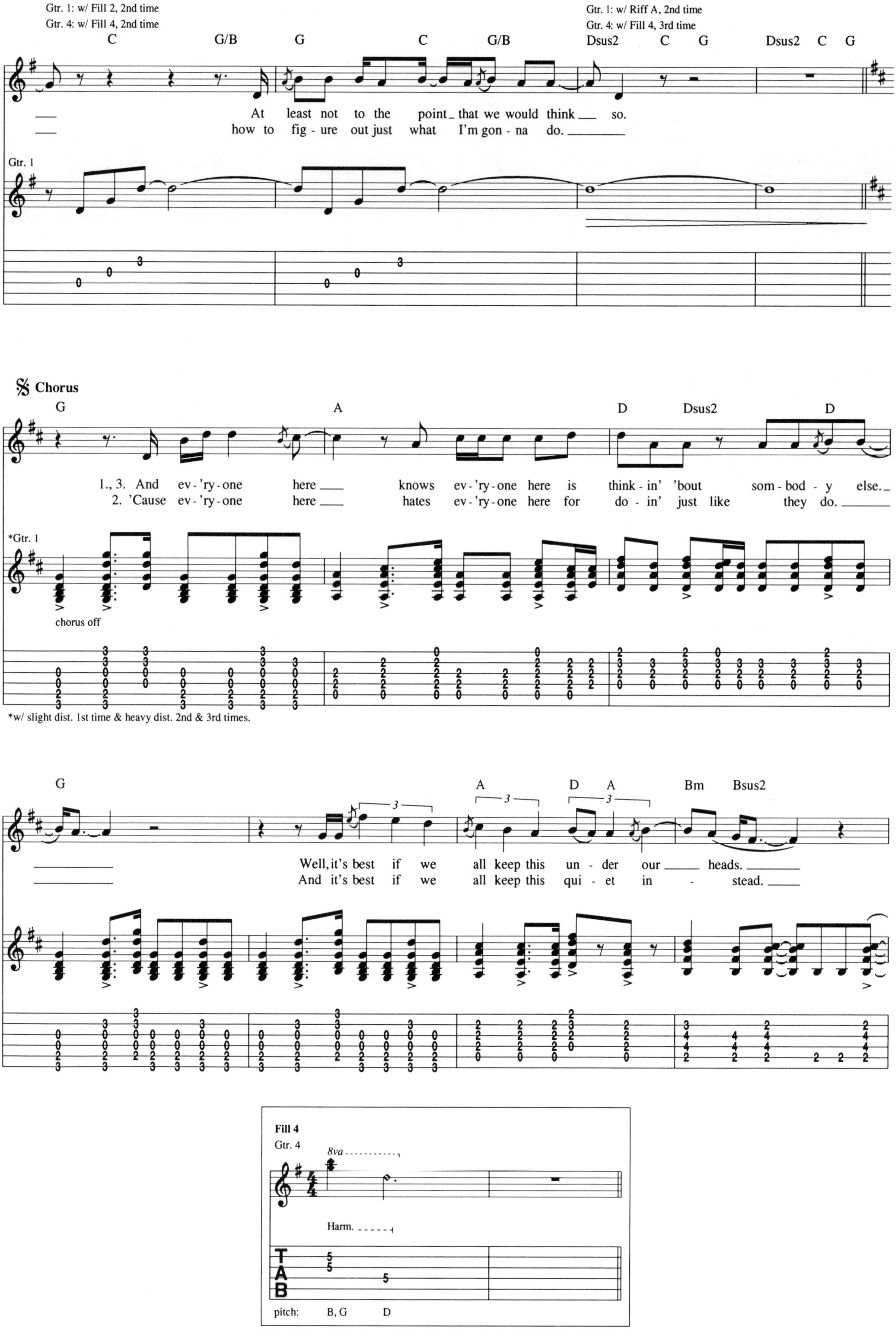

Gtr. 1: w/ Fill 2, 2nd time
Gtr. 4: w/ Fill 4, 2nd time
Gtr. 1: w/ Riff A, 2nd time
Gtr. 4: w/ Fill 4, 3rd time
C G/B G C G/B Dsus2 C G Dsus2 C G
At least not to the point that we would think so.
how to fig - ure out just what I'm gon - na do.
Gtr. 1
Chorus
G A D Dsus2 D
1., 3. And ev - 'ry - one here knows ev - 'ry - one here is think - in' 'bout som - bod - y else.
2. 'Cause ev - 'ry - one here hates ev - 'ry - one here for do - in' just like they do.
*Gtr. 1
chorus off
*w/ slight dist. 1st time & heavy dist. 2nd & 3rd times.
G A D A Bm Bsus2
Well, it's best if we all keep this un - der our heads.
And it's best if we all keep this qui - et in - stead.
Fill 4
Gtr. 4
8va
Harm.
pitch: B, G D

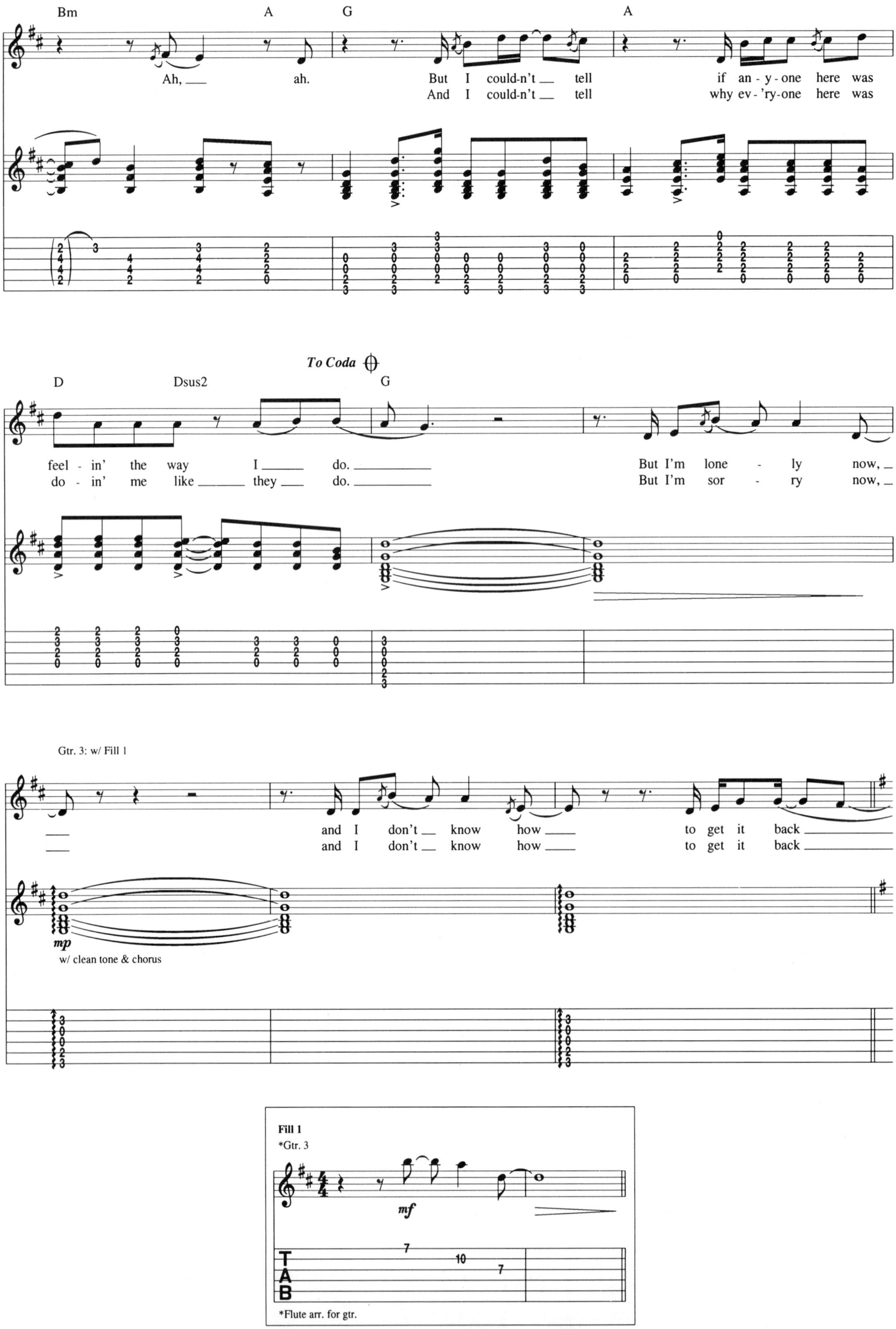
Bm A G A
Ah, ah. But I could-n't tell if an - y - one here was
And I could-n't tell why ev - 'ry-one here was
To Coda
D Dsus2 G
feel - in' the way I do. But I'm lone - ly now,
do - in' me like they do. But I'm sor - ry now,
Gtr. 3: w/ Fill 1
and I don't know how to get it back
and I don't know how to get it back
mp
w/ clean tone & chorus
Fill 1
*Gtr. 3
mf
TAB
*Flute arr. for gtr.

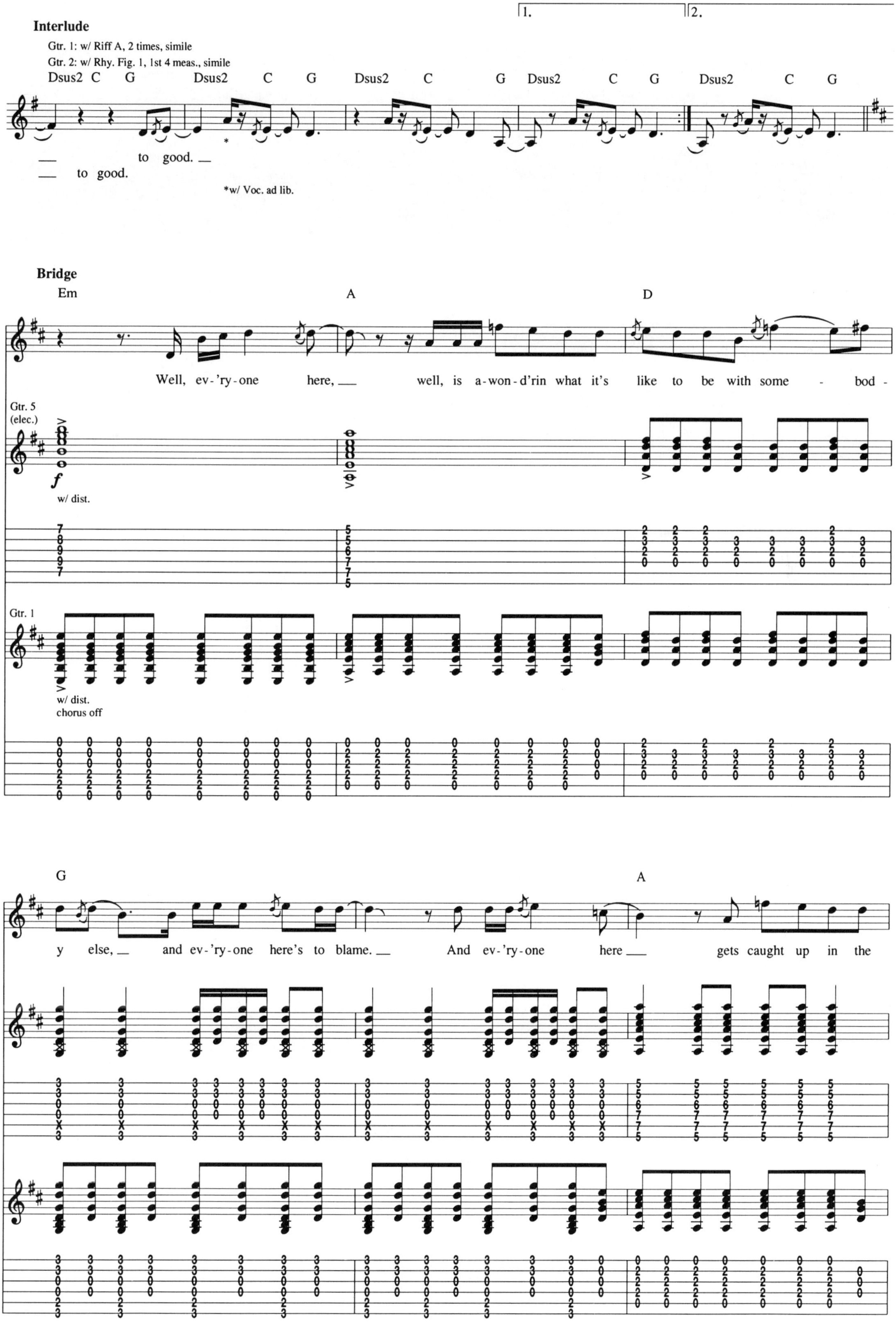
1.
2.
Interlude
Gtr. 1: w/ Riff A, 2 times, simile
Gtr. 2: w/ Rhy. Fig. 1, 1st 4 meas., simile
Dsus2 C G Dsus2 C G Dsus2 C G Dsus2 C G Dsus2 C G
__ to good. __
__ to good.
*w/ Voc. ad lib.
Bridge
Em A D
Well, ev-'ry-one here, __ well, is a-won-d'rin what it's like to be with some - bod -
Gtr. 5 (elec.)
f
w/ dist.
Gtr. 1
w/ dist.
chorus off
G A
y else, __ and ev-'ry-one here's to blame. __ And ev-'ry-one here __ gets caught up in the

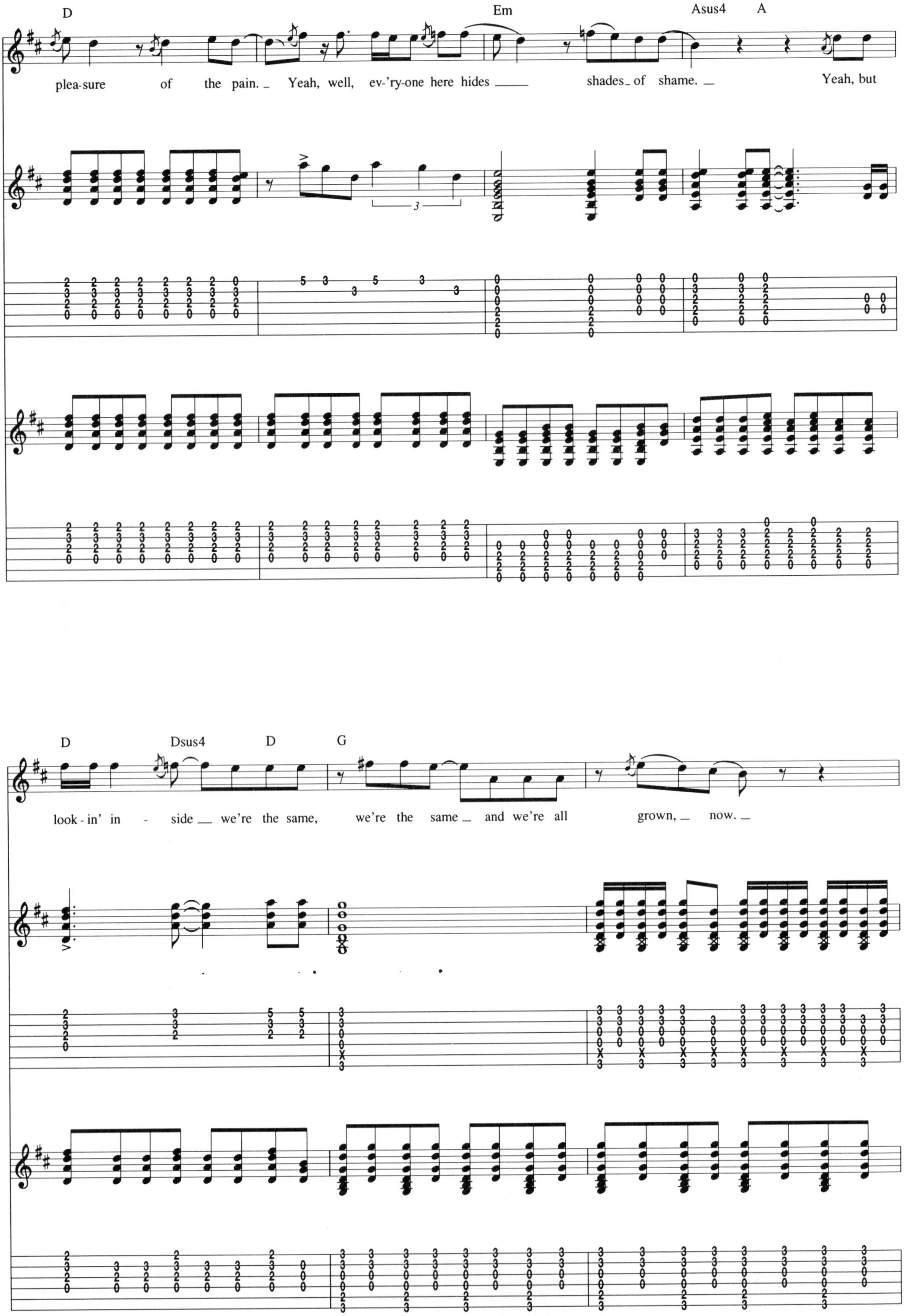
D
Em
Asus4
A
plea-sure of the pain. Yeah, well, ev-'ry-one here hides shades of shame. Yeah, but
D
Dsus4
D
G
look-in' in - side we're the same, we're the same and we're all grown, now.

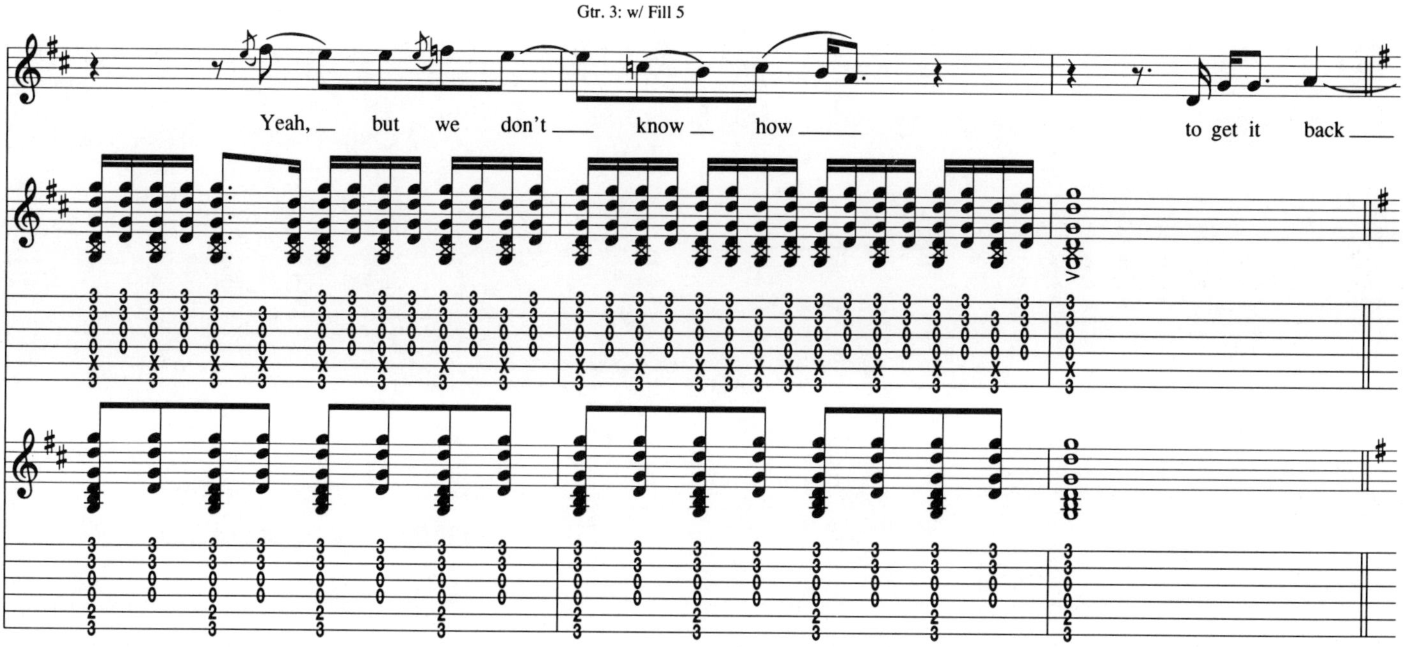

D.S. al Coda

Interlude

Gtr. 1: w/ Riff A, 2 times, simile
Gtr. 2: w/ Rhy. Fig. 1, 1st 4 meas., simile
Gtr. 5 tacet

*w/ Voc. ad lib.

Coda

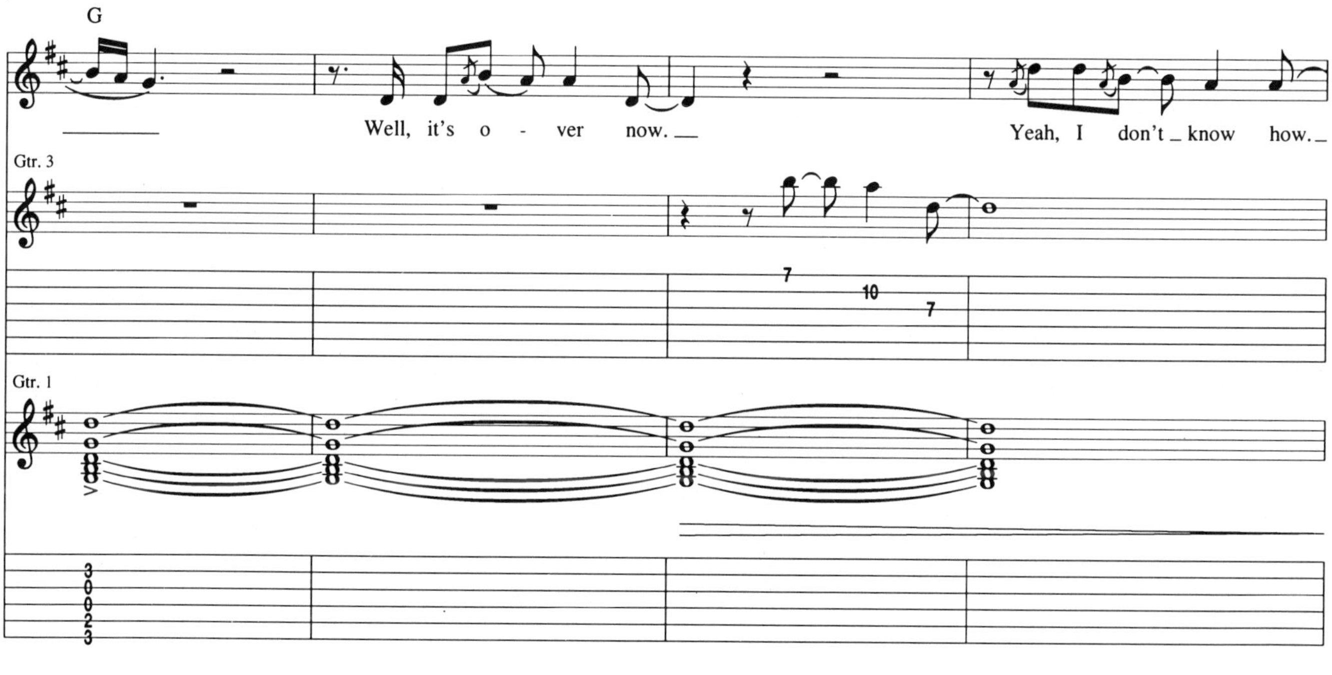

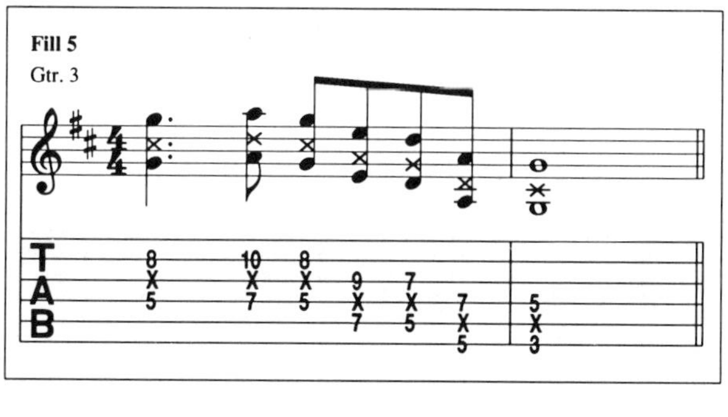

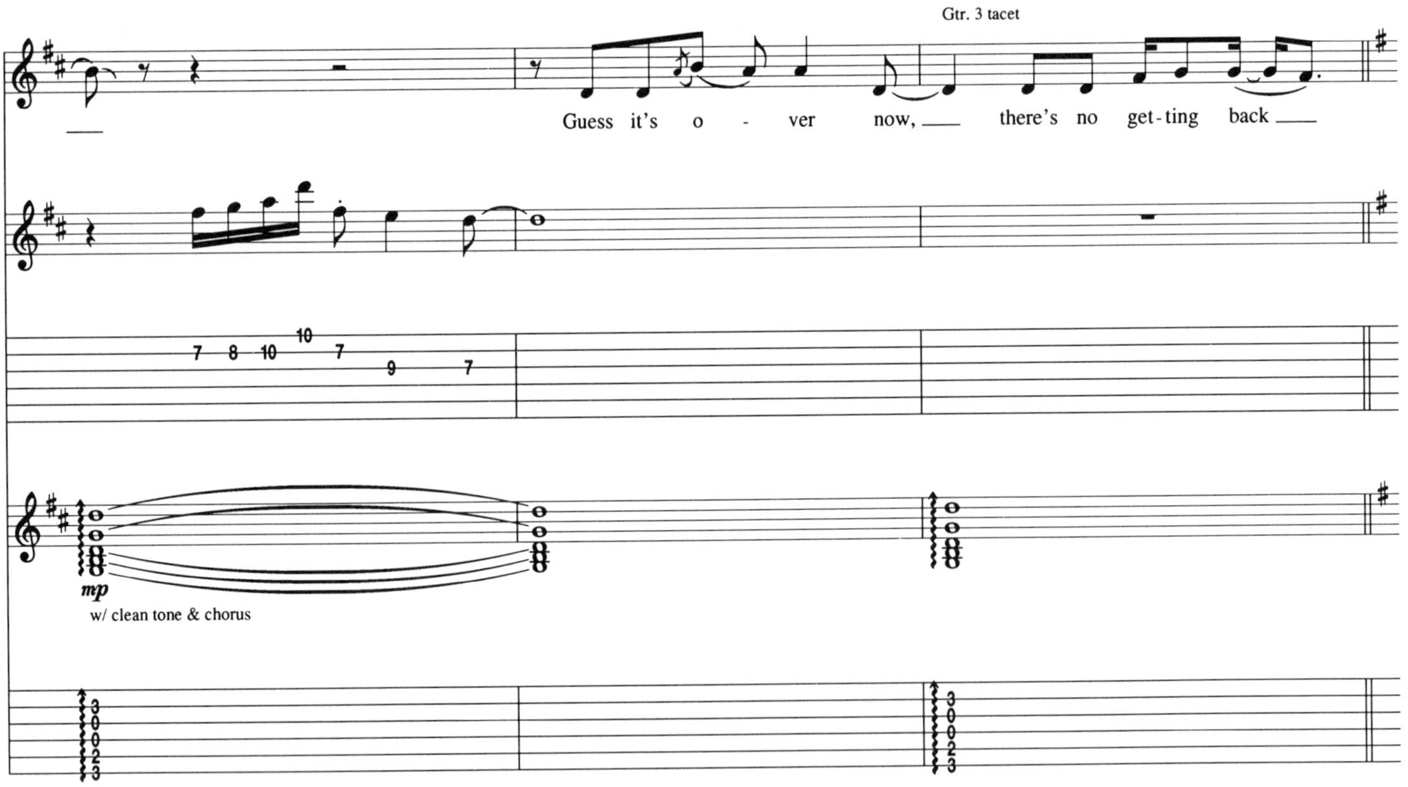
Gtr. 3 tacet
Guess it's o - ver now, there's no get-ting back
mp
w/ clean tone & chorus

Outro

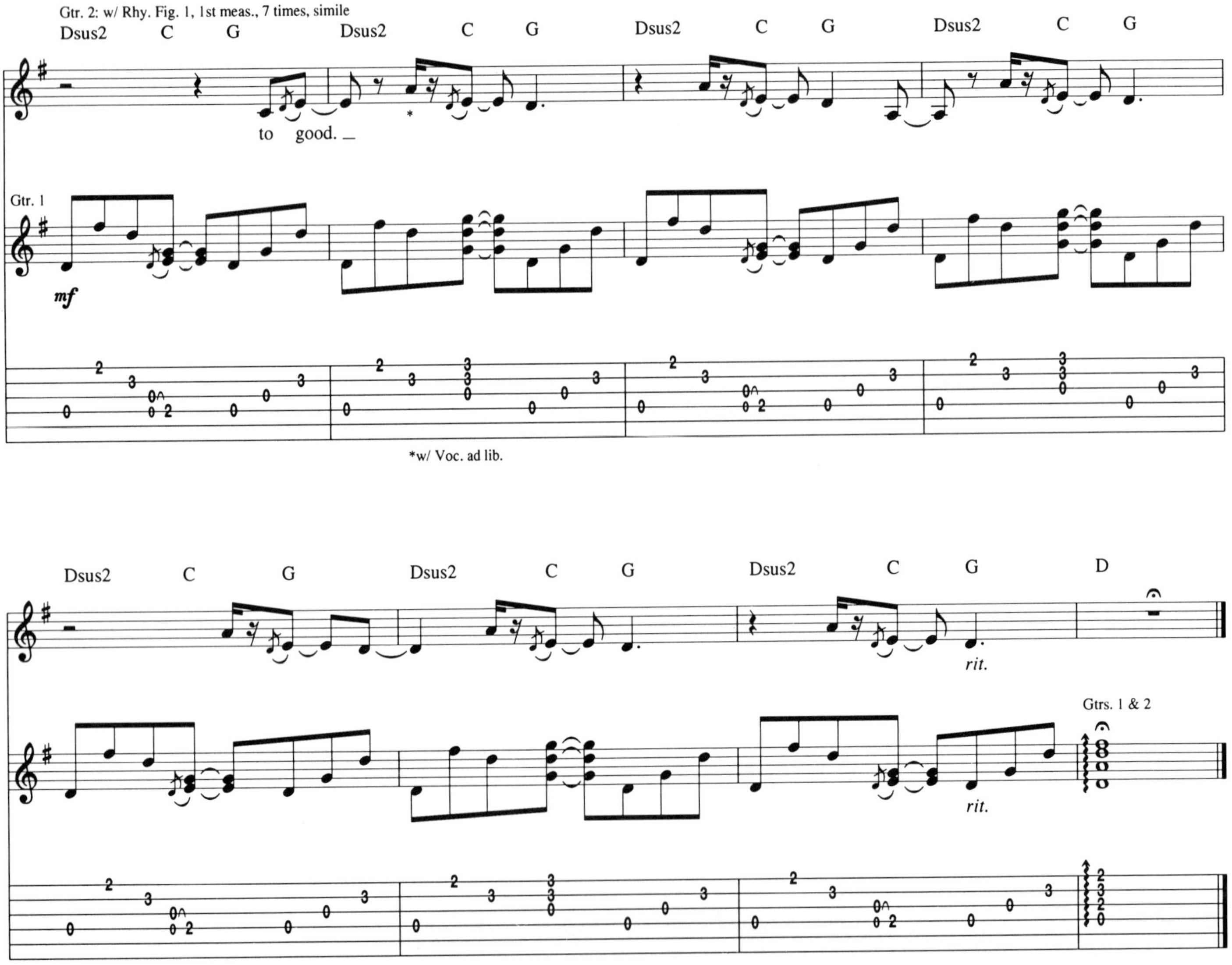
Gtr. 2: w/ Rhy. Fig. 1, 1st meas., 7 times, simile
Dsus2 C G Dsus2 C G Dsus2 C G Dsus2 C G
to good.
Gtr. 1
mf
*w/ Voc. ad lib.
Dsus2 C G Dsus2 C G Dsus2 C G D
rit.
Gtrs. 1 & 2
rit.

Damn

Written by Rob Thomas

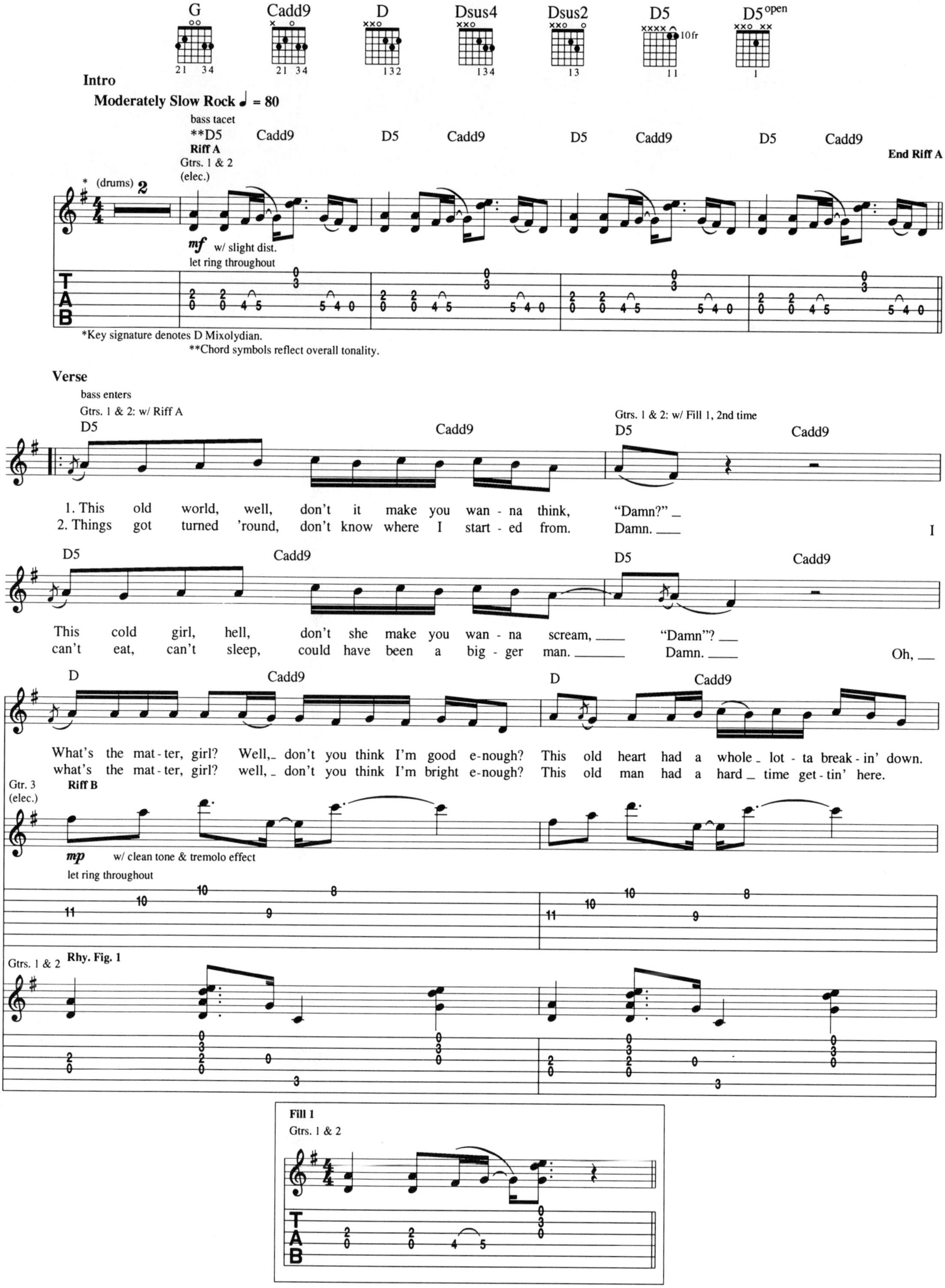

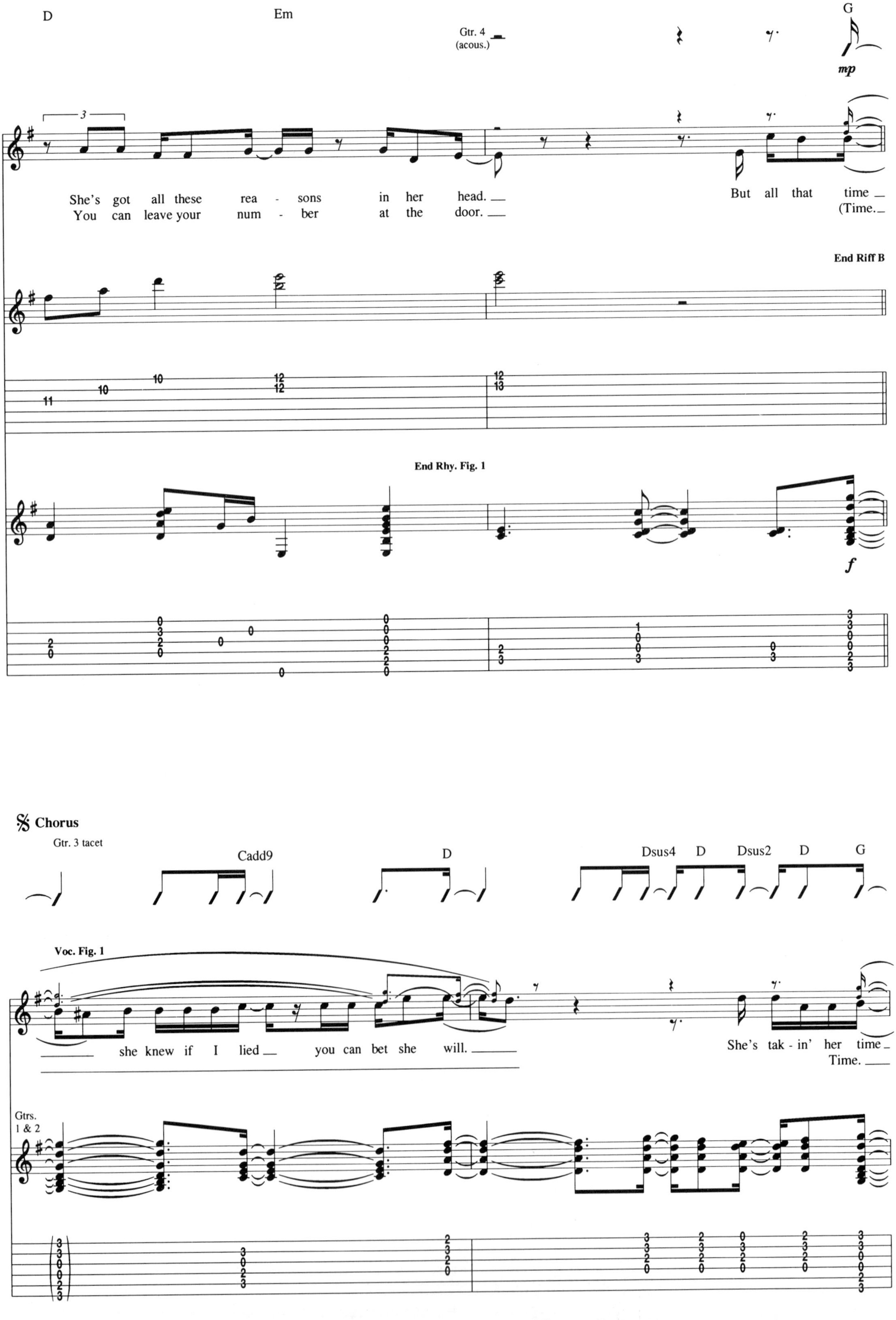
D
Em
G
Gtr. 4 (acous.)
mp
She's got all these rea - sons in her head. But all that time
You can leave your num - ber at the door. (Time.
End Riff B
End Rhy. Fig. 1
f
Chorus
Gtr. 3 tacet
Cadd9
D
Dsus4 D Dsus2 D G
Voc. Fig. 1
she knew if I lied you can bet she will. She's tak - in' her time
Time.
Gtrs. 1 & 2

1.
To Coda
Gtr. 5: w/ Fill 2, 2nd time
Cadd9
D
D5
End Voc. Fig. 1
'til I thought I would die and I can't sit still.
2.
Bridge
Double-Time Feel
Gtr. 4 tacet
G5
C5
D5
Oh, there's noth-ing at all.
Yeah, there's noth-ing at all.
Gtr. 5
Riff C
Gtrs. 1 & 2
Rhy. Fig. 2

Fill 2
Gtr. 5 (elec.)
mf
w/ dist.
T
A
B

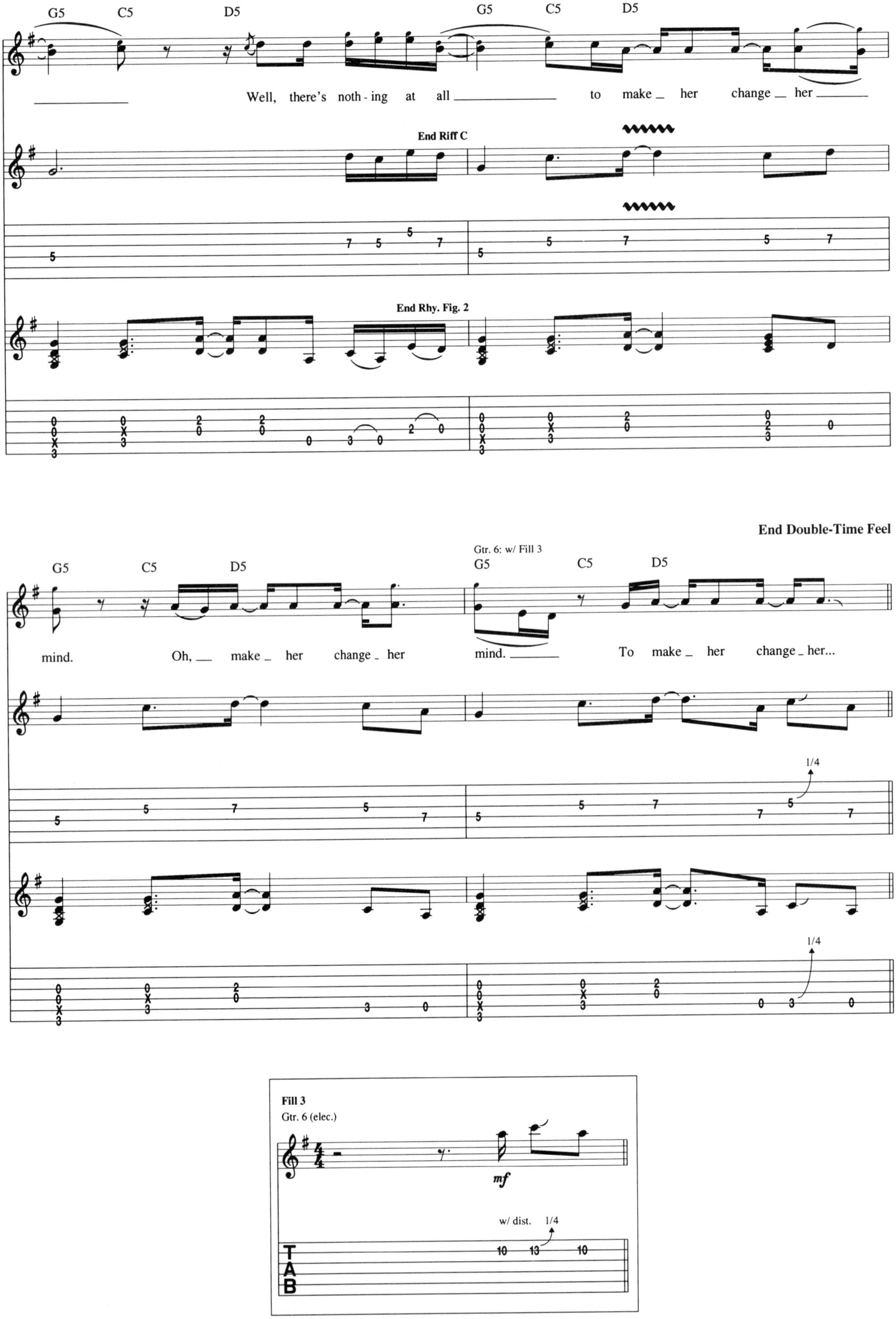
G5 C5 D5 G5 C5 D5
Well, there's noth - ing at all to make her change her
End Riff C
End Rhy. Fig. 2
5 7 5 5 7 5 5 7 5 7
0 0 0 3 0 X 3 2 0 2 0 0 3 0 2 0
0 0 0 X 3 0 X 3 2 0 0 2 3 0
End Double-Time Feel
Gtr. 6: w/ Fill 3
G5 C5 D5 G5 C5 D5
mind. Oh, make her change her mind. To make her change her...
1/4
5 5 7 5 7 5 5 7 7 5 7
0 0 0 X 3 0 X 3 2 0 3 0 0 0 0 X 3 0 X 3 2 0 0 3 0
1/4
Fill 3
Gtr. 6 (elec.)
mf
w/ dist. 1/4
T
A
B
10 13 10

Guitar Solo
Gtr. 5 tacet
Gtr. 7 (elec.)
D5 Cadd9 D5 Cadd9 G C
f
w/ dist.
1/2
Gtrs. 1 & 2
Rhy. Fig. 3
End Rhy. Fig. 3
Gtrs. 1 & 2: w/ Rhy. Fig. 3
D5 Cadd9 D5 Cadd9 G C
Gtr. 7
Verse
D5 Cadd9 D5 Cadd9
3. This old house been qui - et since you went a - way. Damn. A
Gtr. 7
Gtr. 1
Gtr. 2

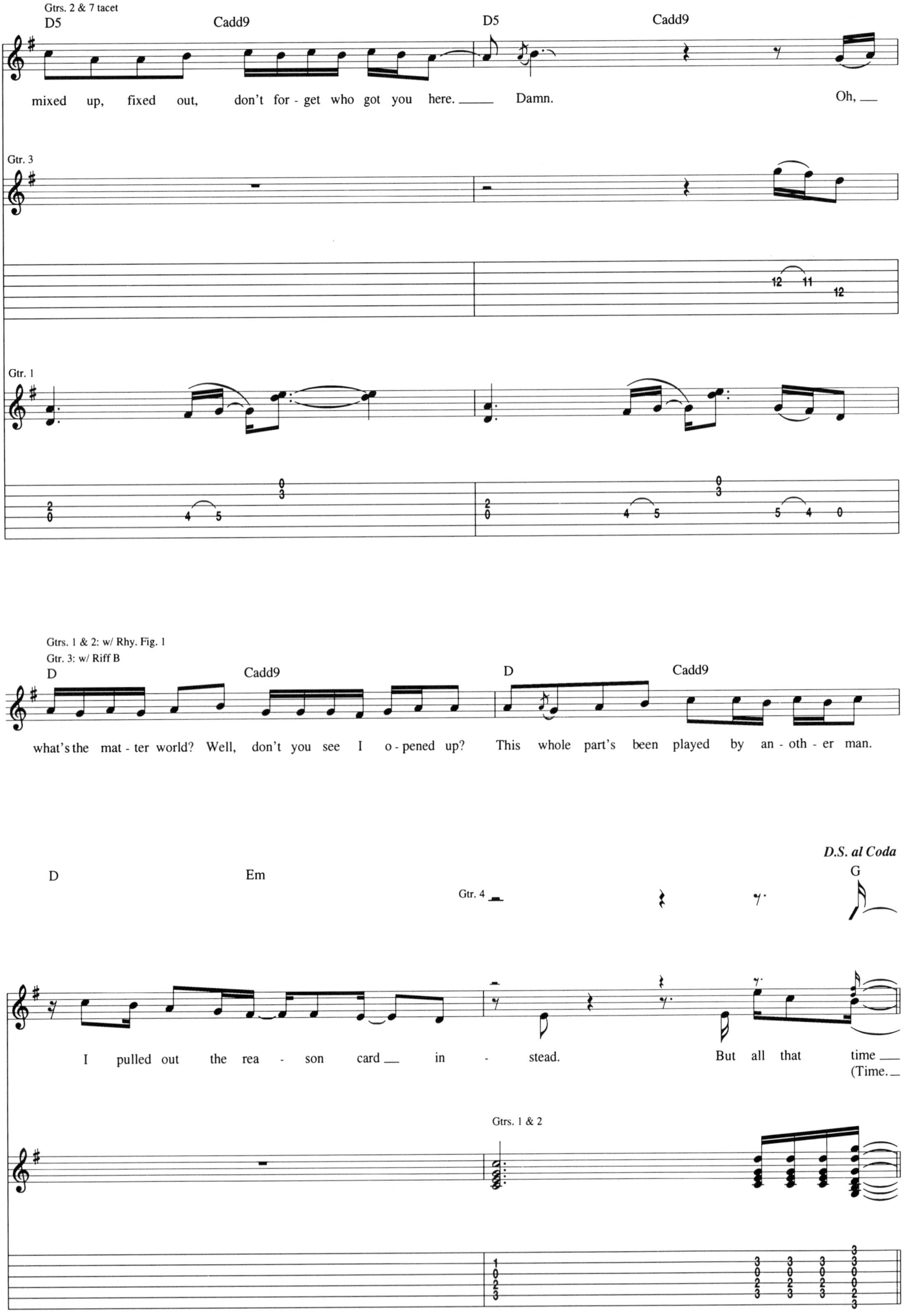
Gtrs. 2 & 7 tacet
D5 Cadd9 D5 Cadd9
mixed up, fixed out, don't for - get who got you here. Damn. Oh,
Gtr. 3
Gtr. 1
Gtrs. 1 & 2: w/ Rhy. Fig. 1
Gtr. 3: w/ Riff B
D Cadd9 D Cadd9
what's the mat - ter world? Well, don't you see I o - pened up? This whole part's been played by an - oth - er man.
D.S. al Coda
D Em G
Gtr. 4
I pulled out the rea - son card in - stead. But all that time
(Time.
Gtrs. 1 & 2

Coda
Dsus2 D Dsus4 D Dsus2 G
She says she can find
Time.
Bkgd. Voc.: w/ Voc. Fig. 1
Cadd9 D Dsus4 D Dsus2 D G
the things that make up a life. Well, I can bet she will, ah, ha. She says stay be - hind.
Cadd9 D D5open
I could stay here all night, I could stay here un - til, un - til there's noth - ing at all.

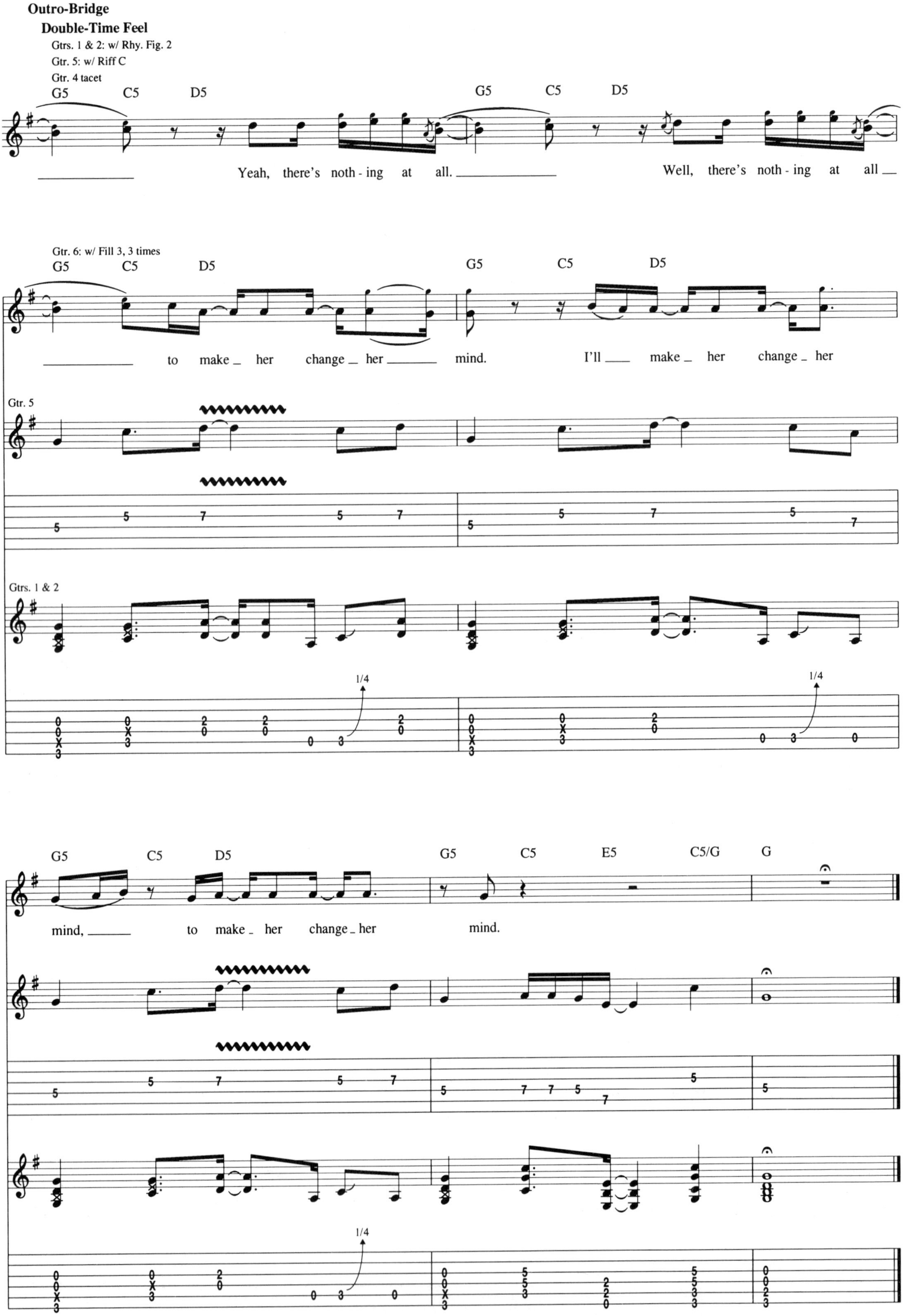
Outro-Bridge
Double-Time Feel
Gtrs. 1 & 2: w/ Rhy. Fig. 2
Gtr. 5: w/ Riff C
Gtr. 4 tacet
G5 C5 D5 G5 C5 D5
Yeah, there's noth - ing at all.
Well, there's noth - ing at all
Gtr. 6: w/ Fill 3, 3 times
G5 C5 D5 G5 C5 D5
to make her change her mind.
I'll make her change her
Gtr. 5
Gtrs. 1 & 2
1/4
G5 C5 D5 G5 C5 E5 C5/G G
mind, to make her change her mind.

Argue

Written by Rob Thomas

*Chord symbols reflect overall tonality.

Gtr. 1: w/ Rhy. Fig. 1, simile
Gtr. 2: w/ Rhy. Fig. 1A, 1st 3 meas., simile
D5 C5 G5 D/G Em7/G
Gtr. 2: w/ Rhy. Fill 1
Em7 Cadd9 D/C
But she takes what she gets, and she nev - er did flinch, no.
- fense. So go on and wreck me. Fun - ny how I car - ry on and not be tak - en

Pre-Chorus
Dadd9 Asus2 Cadd9 G
So, o - ver and o - ver, well, an - y - one with an - y mind would think that's all she
o - ver. I will not roll o - ver on an - y - one 'cause an - y - one would stand up on my
me. So, o - ver and o - ver, well, an - y - one, yeah, an - y - one.
Gtr. 1
let ring
let ring
(cont. in slash)
Gtr. 2
let ring
let ring

Rhy. Fill 1
Gtr. 2
T
A
B

Chorus
D5 E5 C G D5 E5 C G
Rhy. Fig. 2
End Rhy. Fig. 2
Gtr. 1
gets.
side.
If _ you want, you _ can get _ to know me _ well. We get a - long, - so _ we should - n't ar - gue, yeah.
Gtr. 2
Rhy. Fig. 2A
End Rhy. Fig. 2A
Gtr. 3
(elec.)
Rhy. Fig. 2B
End Rhy. Fig. 2B
mf
w/ dist.
*Lead Voc. doubled one octave lower for next 8 meas.
To Coda
Gtrs. 1, 2 & 3: w/ Rhy. Figs. 2, 2A & 2B
D5 E5 C G D5 E5 C G
And I don't - know, yeah, _ said I _ don't know, - know. All _ these feel - in's _ cloud up _ my rea - son - in'.
D5 G5 C5 D5 G5 C5
Yeah, _ they cloud up _ my rea - son - in'. _
Gtr. 3
Gtr. 1
divisi
let ring throughout
Gtr. 2

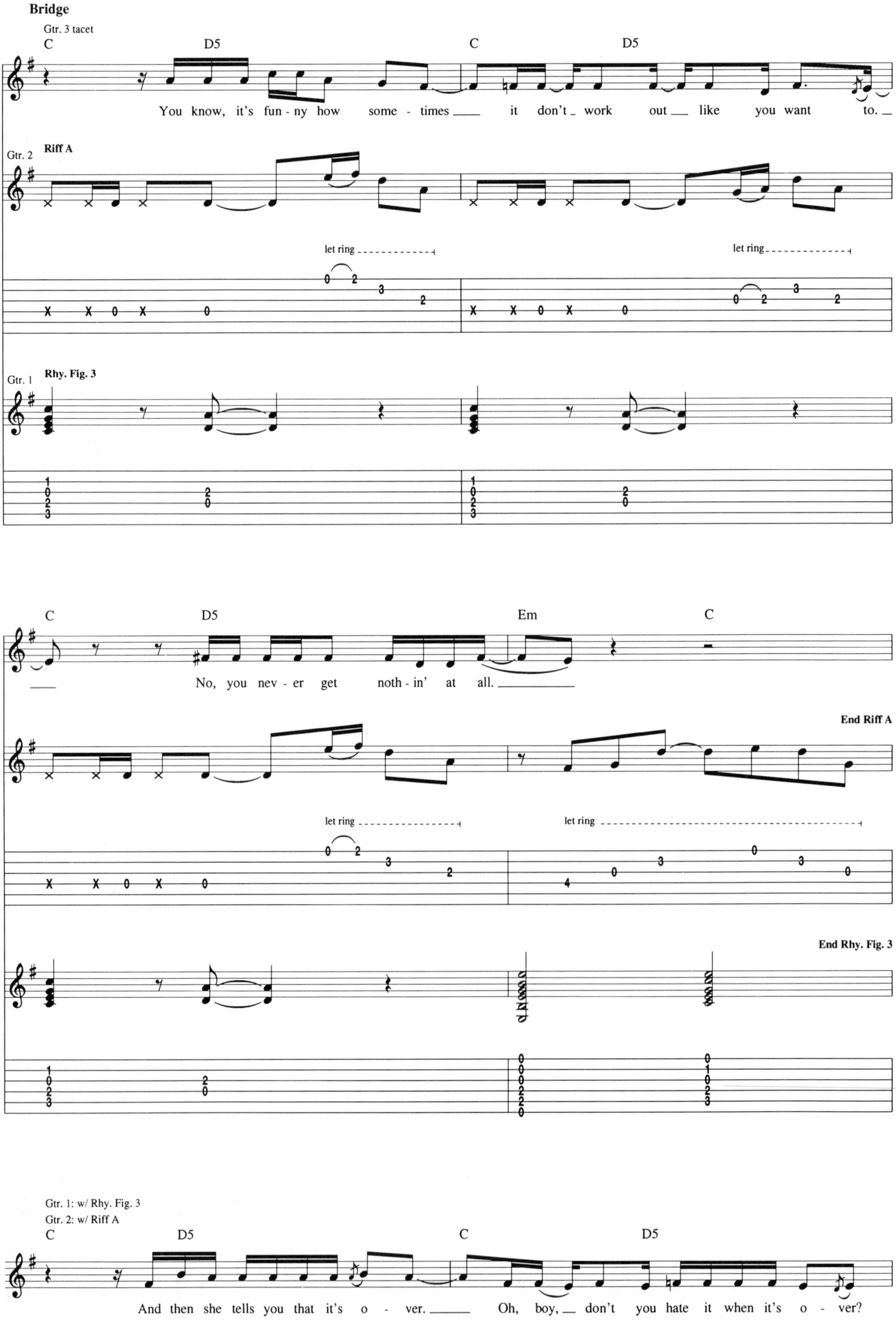
Bridge
Gtr. 3 tacet
C D5 C D5
You know, it's fun - ny how some - times ___ it don't _ work out ___ like you want to. ___
Gtr. 2 Riff A
let ring
Gtr. 1 Rhy. Fig. 3
C D5 Em C
___ No, you nev - er get noth - in' at all. ___
End Riff A
let ring
End Rhy. Fig. 3
Gtr. 1: w/ Rhy. Fig. 3
Gtr. 2: w/ Riff A
C D5 C D5
And then she tells you that it's o - ver. ___ Oh, boy, __ don't you hate it when it's o - ver?

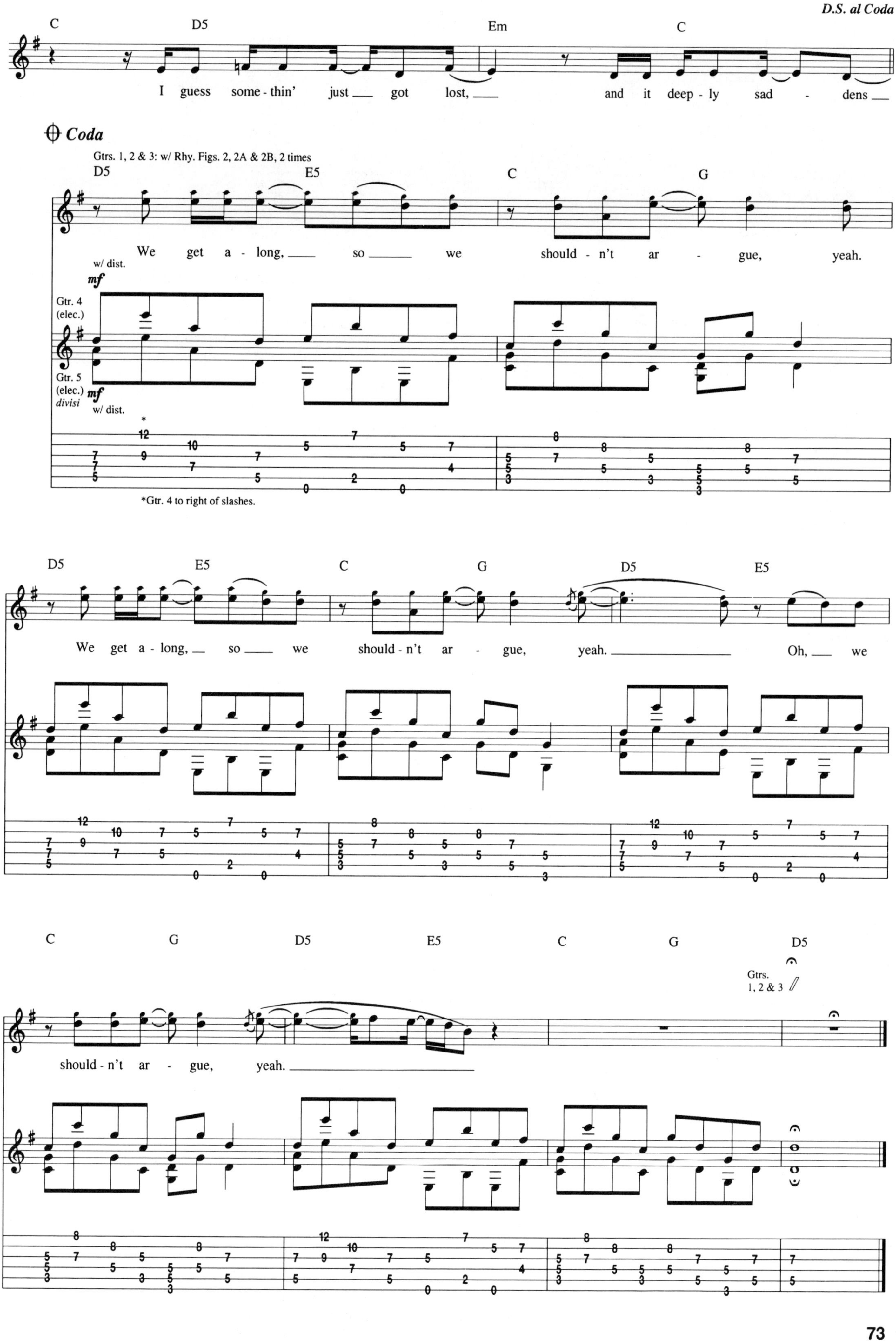
D.S. al Coda
C D5 Em C
I guess some - thin' just got lost, and it deep - ly sad - dens
Coda
Gtrs. 1, 2 & 3: w/ Rhy. Figs. 2, 2A & 2B, 2 times
D5 E5 C G
We get a - long, so we should - n't ar - gue, yeah.
w/ dist.
mf
Gtr. 4 (elec.)
Gtr. 5 (elec.) divisi
mf
w/ dist.
*Gtr. 4 to right of slashes.
D5 E5 C G D5 E5
We get a - long, so we should - n't ar - gue, yeah. Oh, we
C G D5 E5 C G D5
Gtrs. 1, 2 & 3
should - n't ar - gue, yeah.

Kody

Written by Rob Thomas

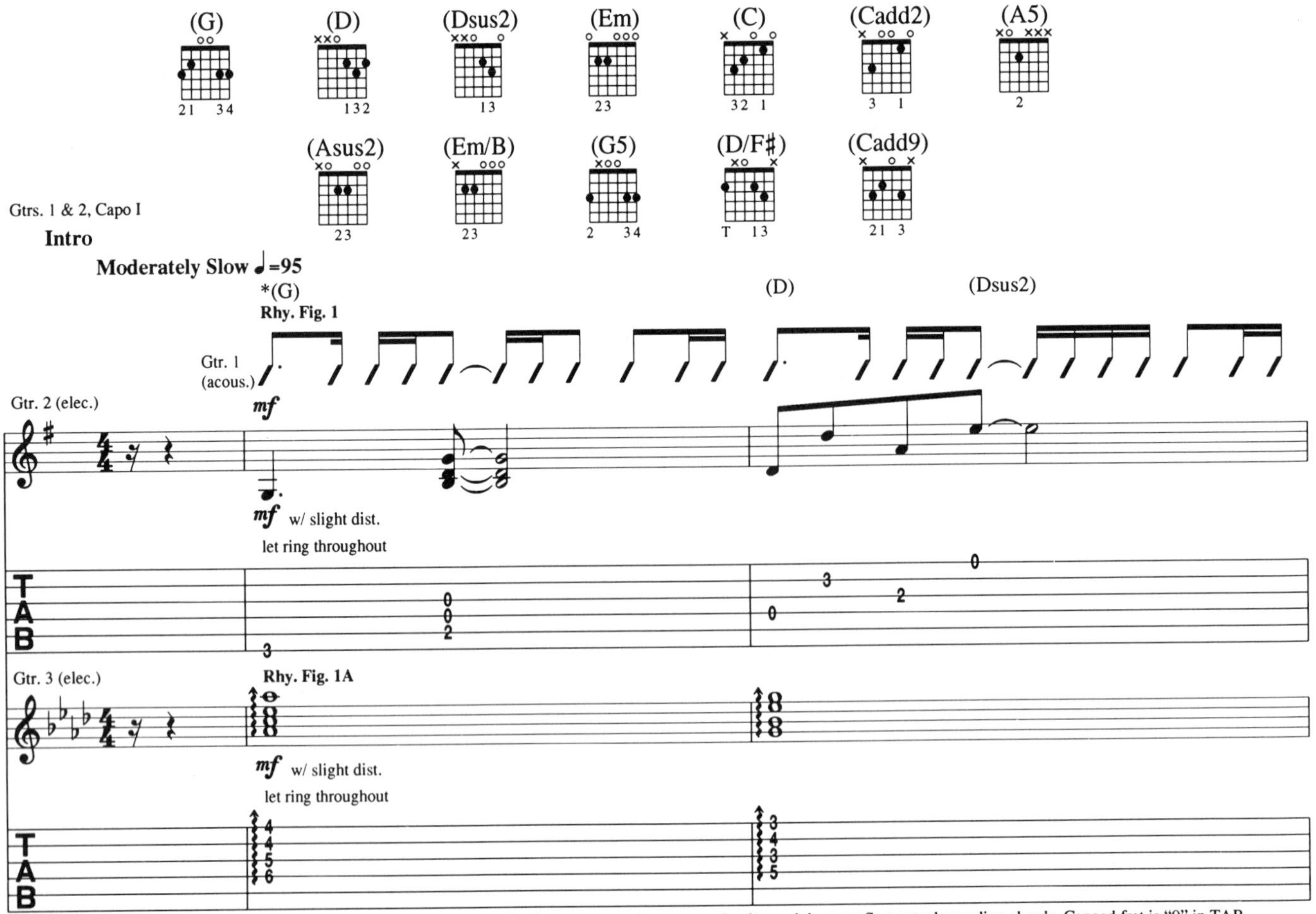

*Symbols in parentheses represent chord names respective to capoed guitar and do not reflect actual sounding chords. Capoed fret is "0" in TAB.

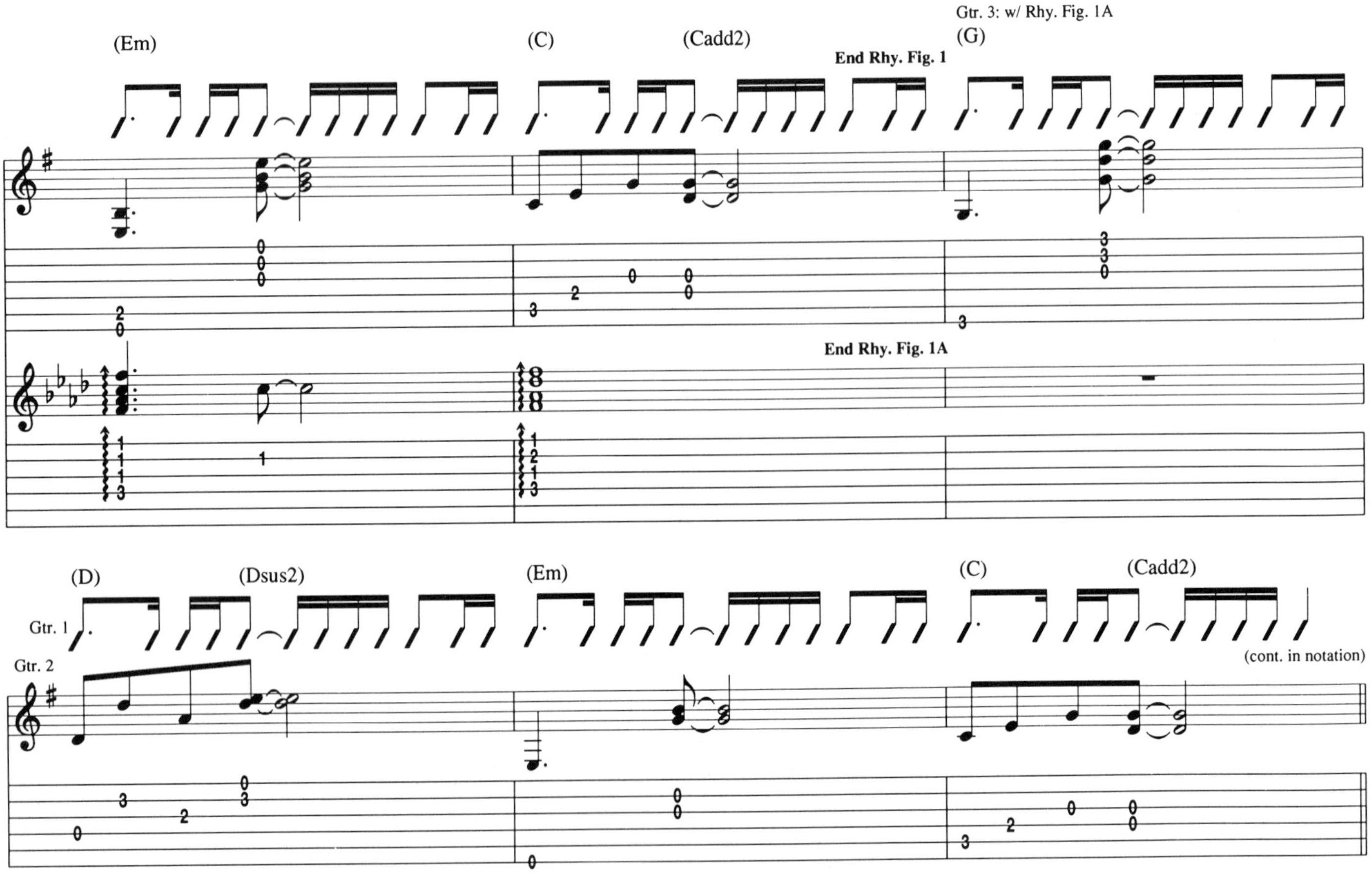

Verse
Fm
*(Em)
Db
(C)
Fm
(Em)
1. Well, Ko-dy sat _ down on __ the av - e-nue and tapped _ his feet _ to the
Gtr. 3
Rhy. Fig. 2A
Gtrs. 1 & 2
Rhy. Fig. 2
*Symbols in parentheses represent chord names respective to capoed guitars. Symbols above reflect actual sounding chord.
Db
(C)
Fm
(Em)
hum-min' of ___ the high - way. He watched _ the light __ shine down _ on the bro -

D♭
(C)
(G)
(D)
(Dsus2)
Gtr. 1
- ken glass _ and thought, _ "Well, I don't got _ no rea - sons yet."
Gtr. 3
End Rhy. Fig. 2A
Gtr. 2
End Rhy. Fig. 2
(Gtr. 1 cont. in slash)
Gtrs. 1, 2 & 3: w/ Rhy. Figs. 2 & 2A
Fm
(Em)
D♭
(C)
Fm
(Em)
And there it is ___ and there it was. Now, it ___ was clear _ to all _
D♭
(C)
Fm
(Em)
D♭
(C)
___ of us. ___ We kept _ this hat ___ of bro - ken dreams, _
(G)
Rhy. Fig. 3
(D)
(C)
(Cadd2)
End Rhy. Fig. 3
Gtr. 1
and we pulled _ them out _ when we need - ed them ______ a - round. _
Gtr. 3
Riff A
End Riff A
Gtr. 2
Rhy. Fig. 3A
End Rhy. Fig. 3A

𝄋 Chorus

Gtr. 1: w/ Rhy. Fig. 1, simile
Gtr. 2: w/ Rhy. Fig. 1, simile, 2nd time
Gtr. 4: w/ Fill 2, 2nd time

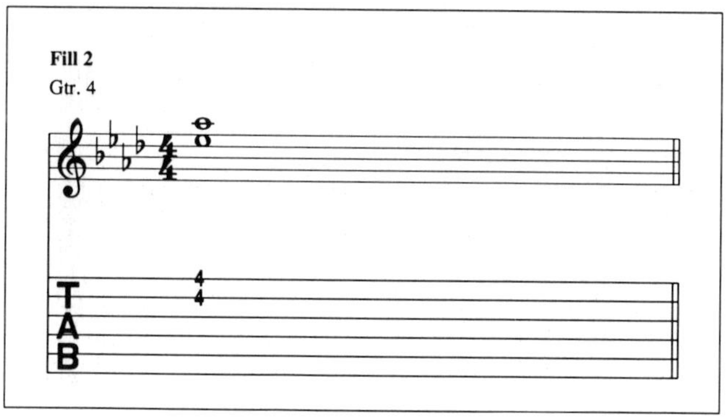

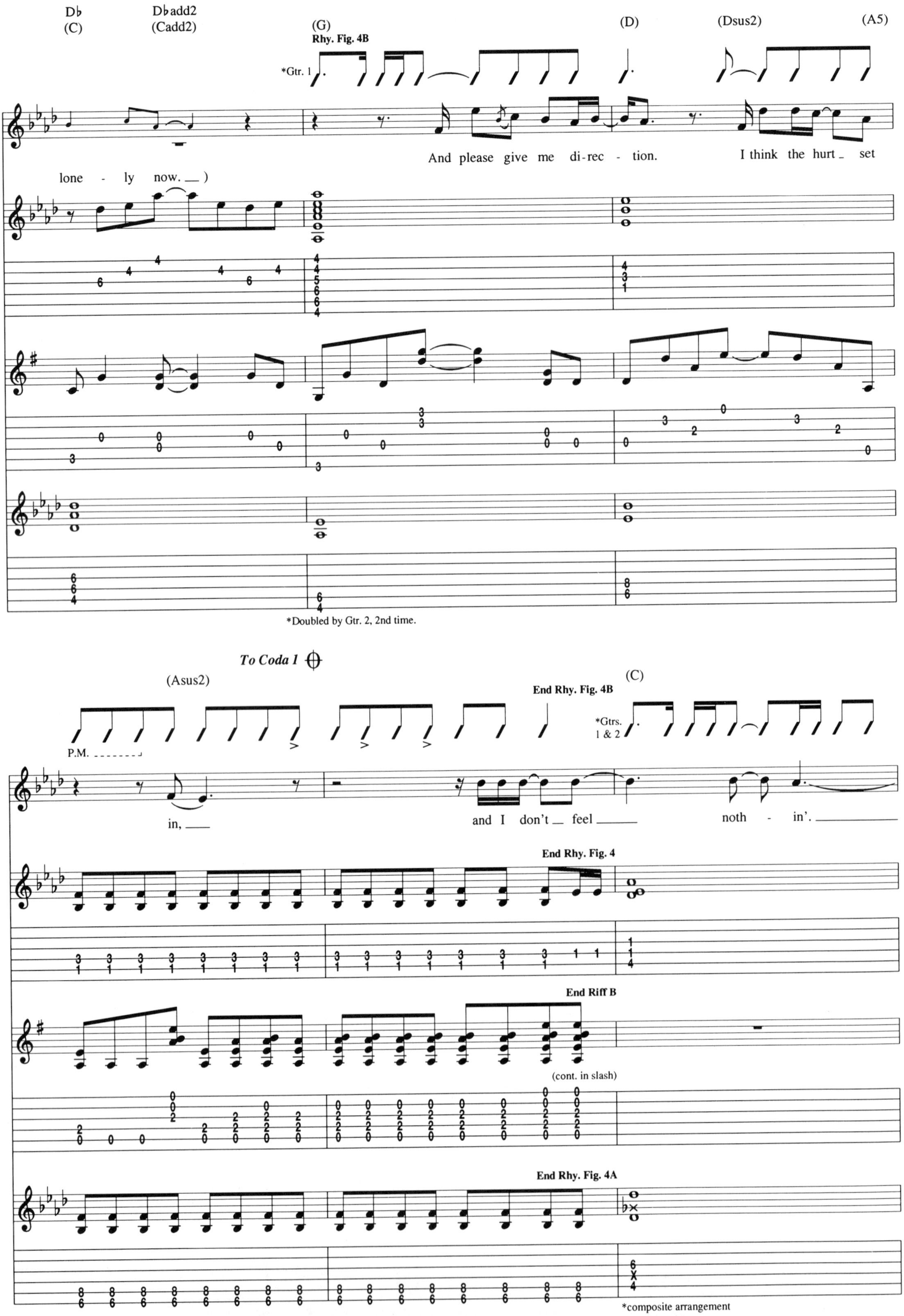
D♭ (C)
D♭add2 (Cadd2)
(G)
Rhy. Fig. 4B
*Gtr. 1
(D)
(Dsus2)
(A5)
lone - ly now.)
And please give me di-rec - tion.
I think the hurt set
*Doubled by Gtr. 2, 2nd time.
To Coda 1
(Asus2)
P.M.
End Rhy. Fig. 4B
(C)
*Gtrs. 1 & 2
in,
and I don't feel
noth - in'.
End Rhy. Fig. 4
End Riff B
(cont. in slash)
End Rhy. Fig. 4A
*composite arrangement

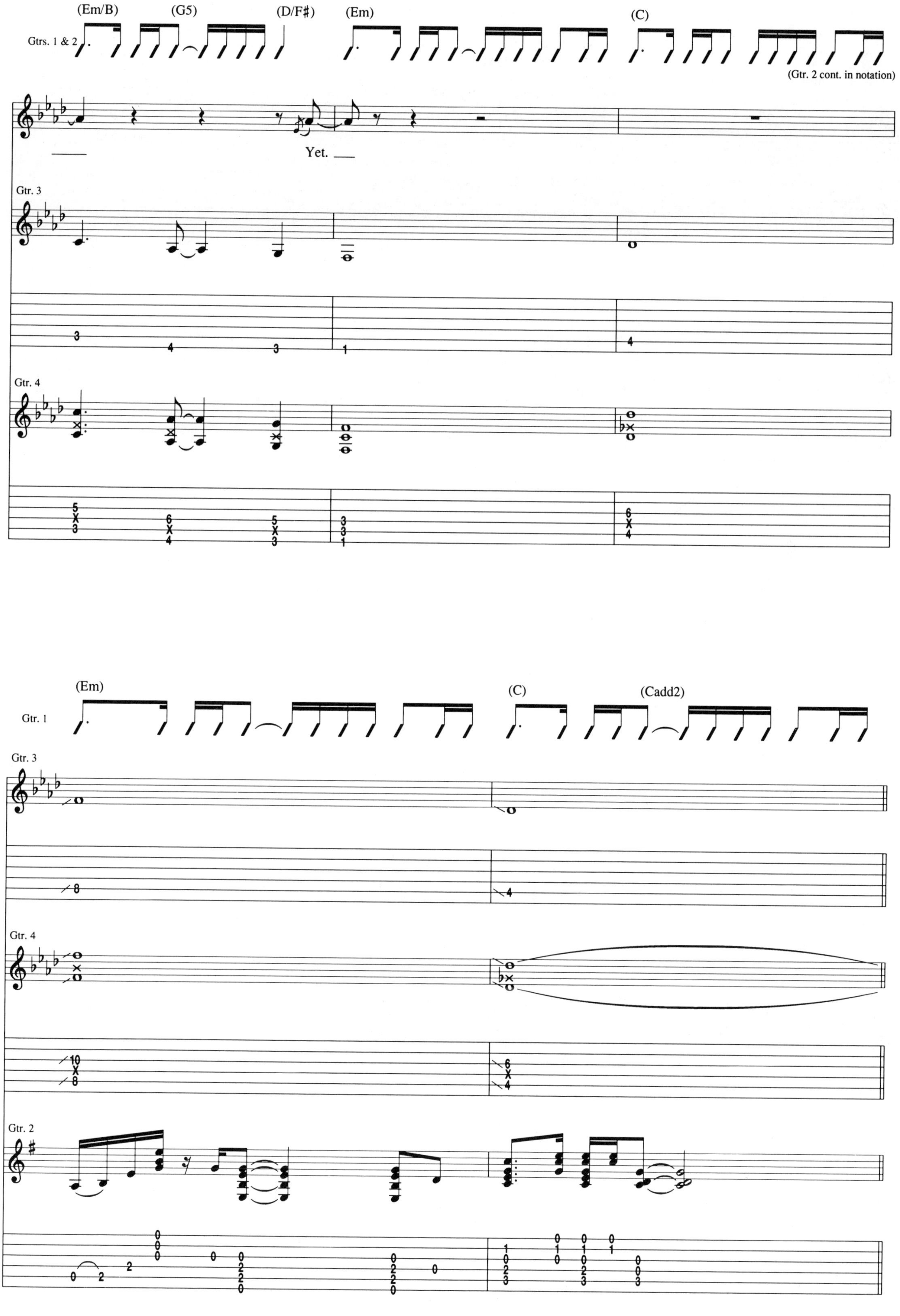
(Em/B)
(G5)
(D/F#)
(Em)
(C)
Gtrs. 1 & 2
(Gtr. 2 cont. in notation)
Yet.
Gtr. 3
Gtr. 4
(Em)
(C)
(Cadd2)
Gtr. 1
Gtr. 3
Gtr. 4
Gtr. 2

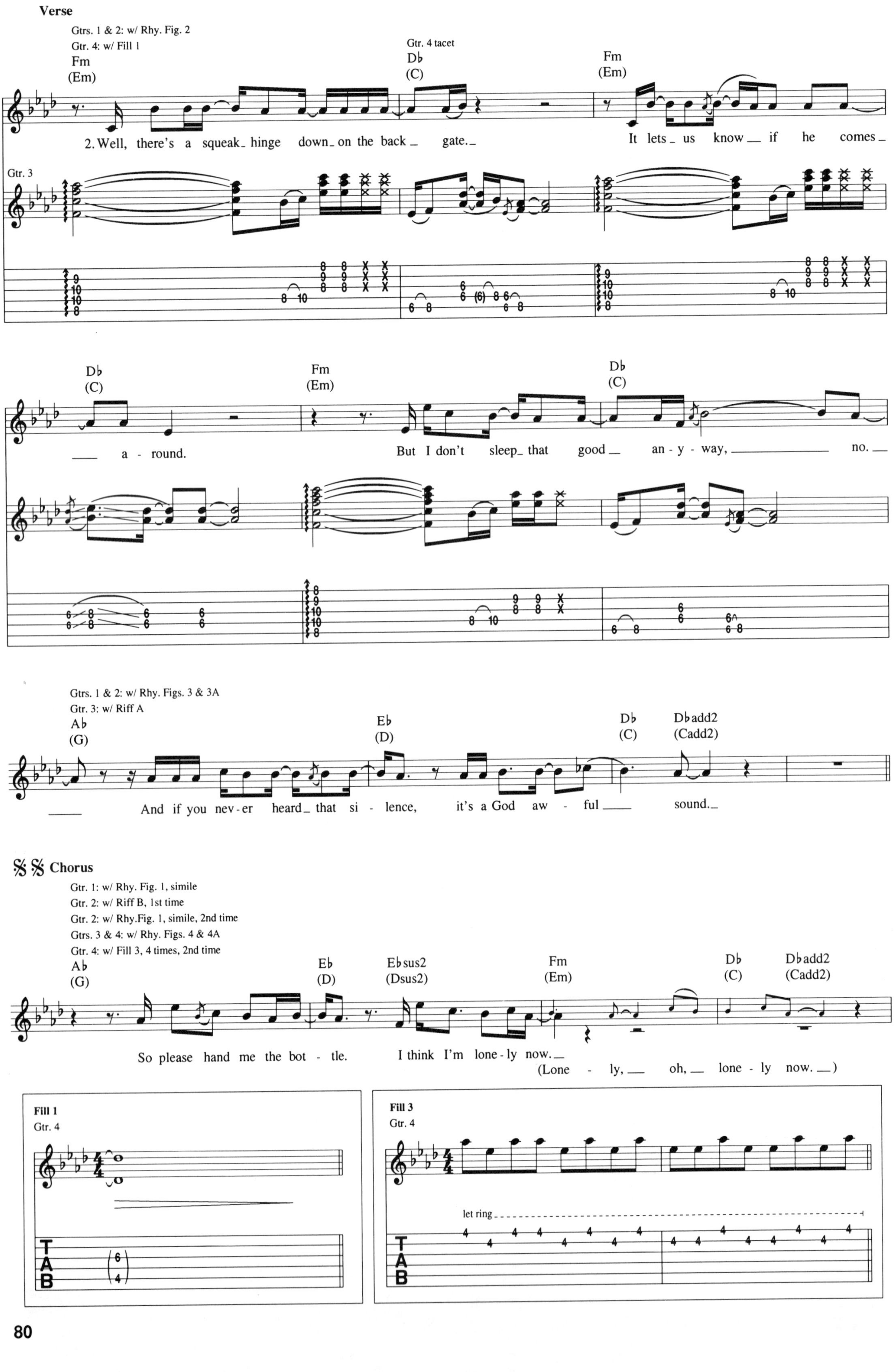
Verse
Gtrs. 1 & 2: w/ Rhy. Fig. 2
Gtr. 4: w/ Fill 1
Gtr. 4 tacet
Fm (Em)
Db (C)
Fm (Em)
2. Well, there's a squeak_ hinge down_ on the back_ gate._
It lets_ us know_ if he comes_
Gtr. 3
Db (C)
Fm (Em)
Db (C)
_ a - round.
But I don't sleep_ that good_ an - y - way, no._
Gtrs. 1 & 2: w/ Rhy. Figs. 3 & 3A
Gtr. 3: w/ Riff A
Ab (G)
Eb (D)
Db (C)
Dbadd2 (Cadd2)
_ And if you nev - er heard_ that si - lence, it's a God aw - ful_ sound._
Chorus
Gtr. 1: w/ Rhy. Fig. 1, simile
Gtr. 2: w/ Riff B, 1st time
Gtr. 2: w/ Rhy.Fig. 1, simile, 2nd time
Gtrs. 3 & 4: w/ Rhy. Figs. 4 & 4A
Gtr. 4: w/ Fill 3, 4 times, 2nd time
Ab (G)
Eb (D)
Ebsus2 (Dsus2)
Fm (Em)
Db (C)
Dbadd2 (Cadd2)
So please hand me the bot - tle. I think I'm lone - ly now._
(Lone - ly,_ oh,_ lone - ly now._)
Fill 1
Gtr. 4
Fill 3
Gtr. 4
let ring
T
A
B

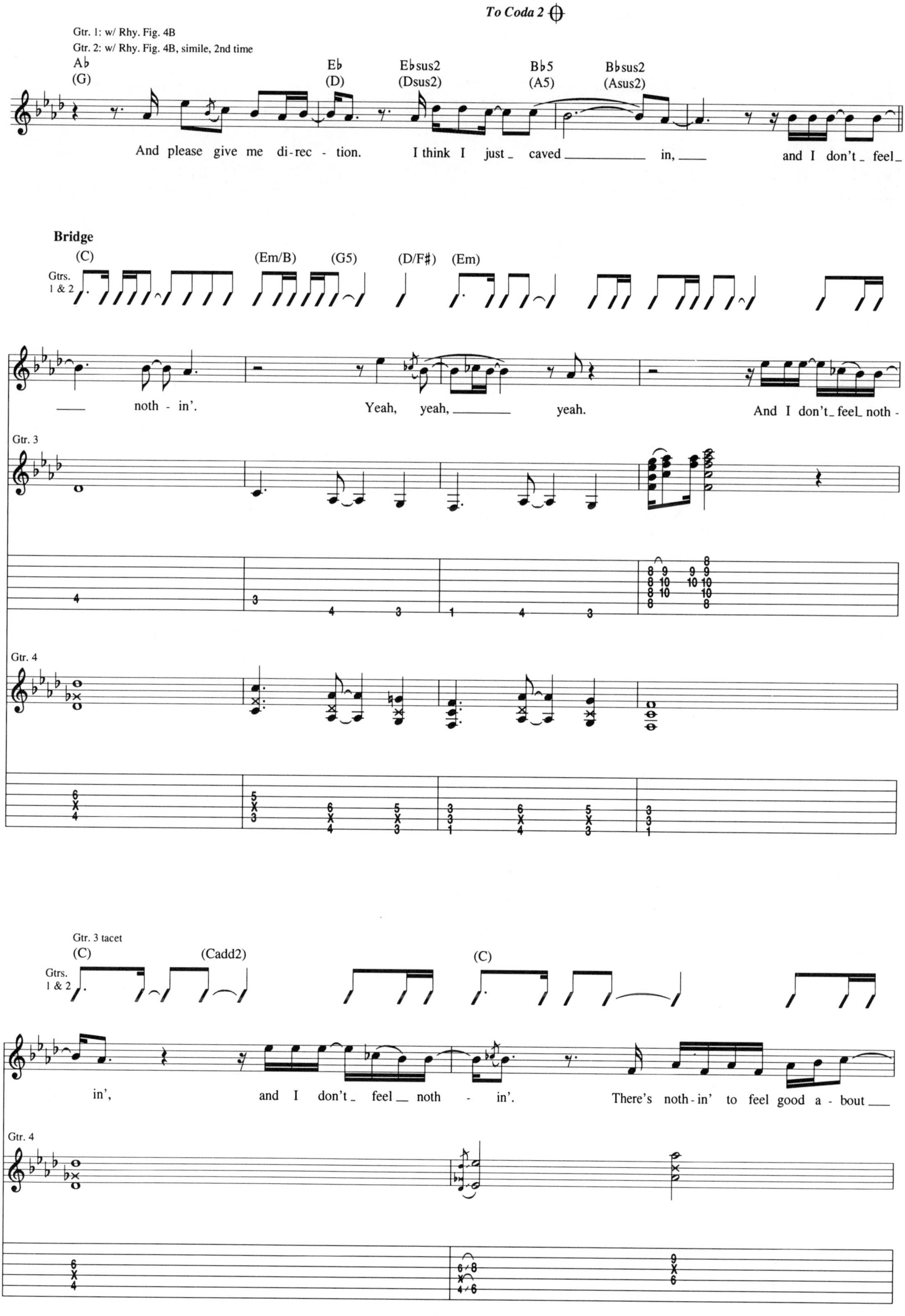
To Coda 2
Gtr. 1: w/ Rhy. Fig. 4B
Gtr. 2: w/ Rhy. Fig. 4B, simile, 2nd time
A♭ (G)
E♭ (D)
E♭sus2 (Dsus2)
B♭5 (A5)
B♭sus2 (Asus2)
And please give me di-rec - tion. I think I just_ caved ___ in, ___ and I don't_ feel_
Bridge
(C)
(Em/B)
(G5)
(D/F♯)
(Em)
Gtrs. 1 & 2
___ noth - in'. Yeah, yeah, ___ yeah. And I don't_ feel_ noth -
Gtr. 3
Gtr. 4
Gtr. 3 tacet
(C)
(Cadd2)
(C)
in', and I don't_ feel_ noth - in'. There's noth-in' to feel good a - bout ___

(Em)
(D)
here, yeah.
Verse
(Em)
Rhy. Fig. 5
(Cadd2)
End Rhy. Fig. 5
Gtrs. 1 & 2
3. And I don't much get down much to the av - e - nue.
Gtr. 4
Gtr. 3
Rhy. Fig. 5A
End Rhy. Fig. 5A
Gtrs. 1, 2 & 3: w/ Rhy. Figs. 5 & 5A, 2 times, simile
Fm
(Em)
D♭add2
(Cadd2)
Well, I could drive, but it takes so much to get there. Oh,
Gtr. 4

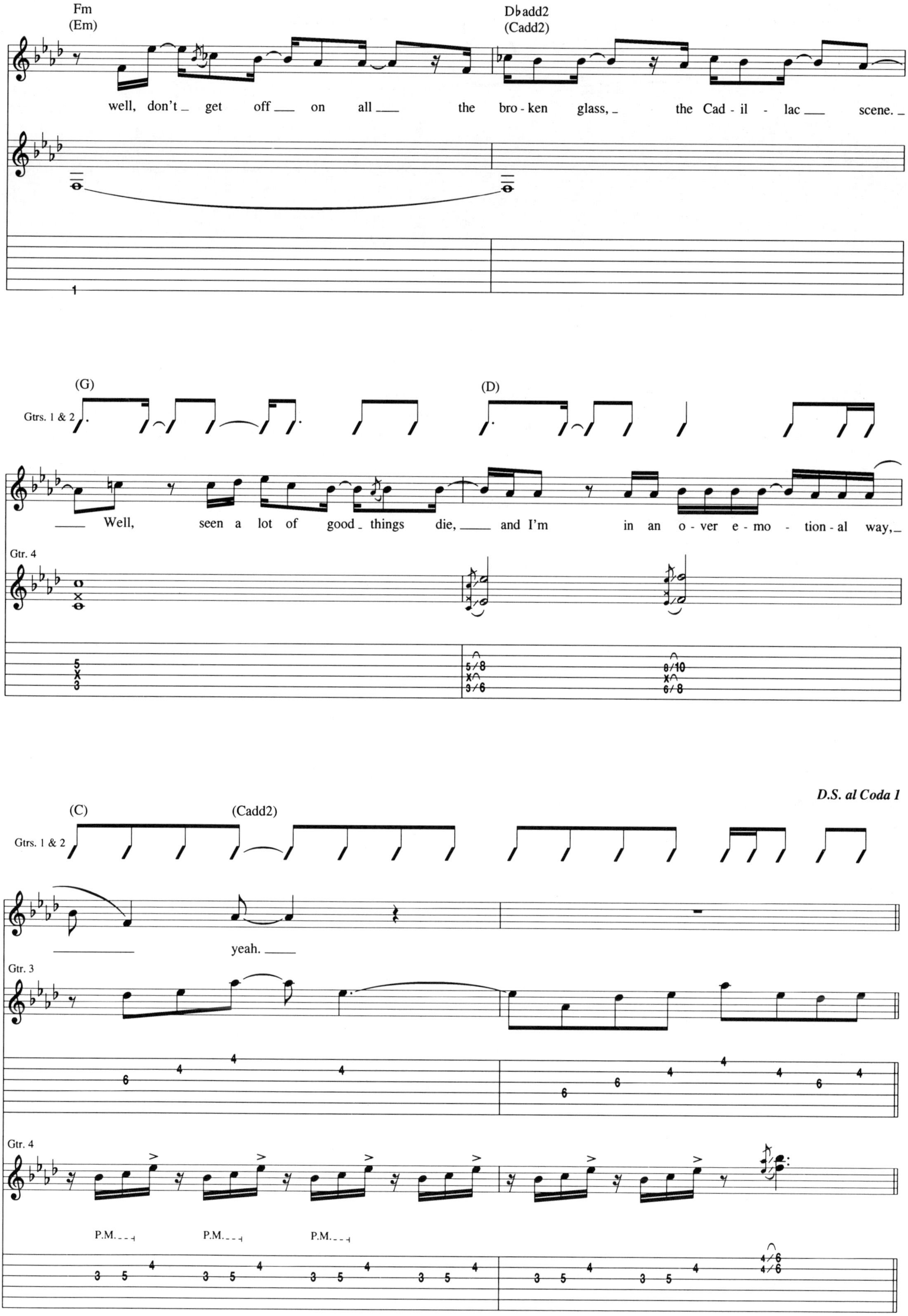
Fm
(Em)
Db add2
(Cadd2)
well, don't_ get off_ on all_ the bro-ken glass,_ the Cad-il-lac_ scene._
(G)
(D)
Gtrs. 1 & 2
_ Well, seen a lot of good_ things die,_ and I'm in an o-ver e-mo-tion-al way,_
Gtr. 4
D.S. al Coda 1
(C)
(Cadd2)
Gtrs. 1 & 2
yeah._
Gtr. 3
Gtr. 4
P.M.
P.M.
P.M.

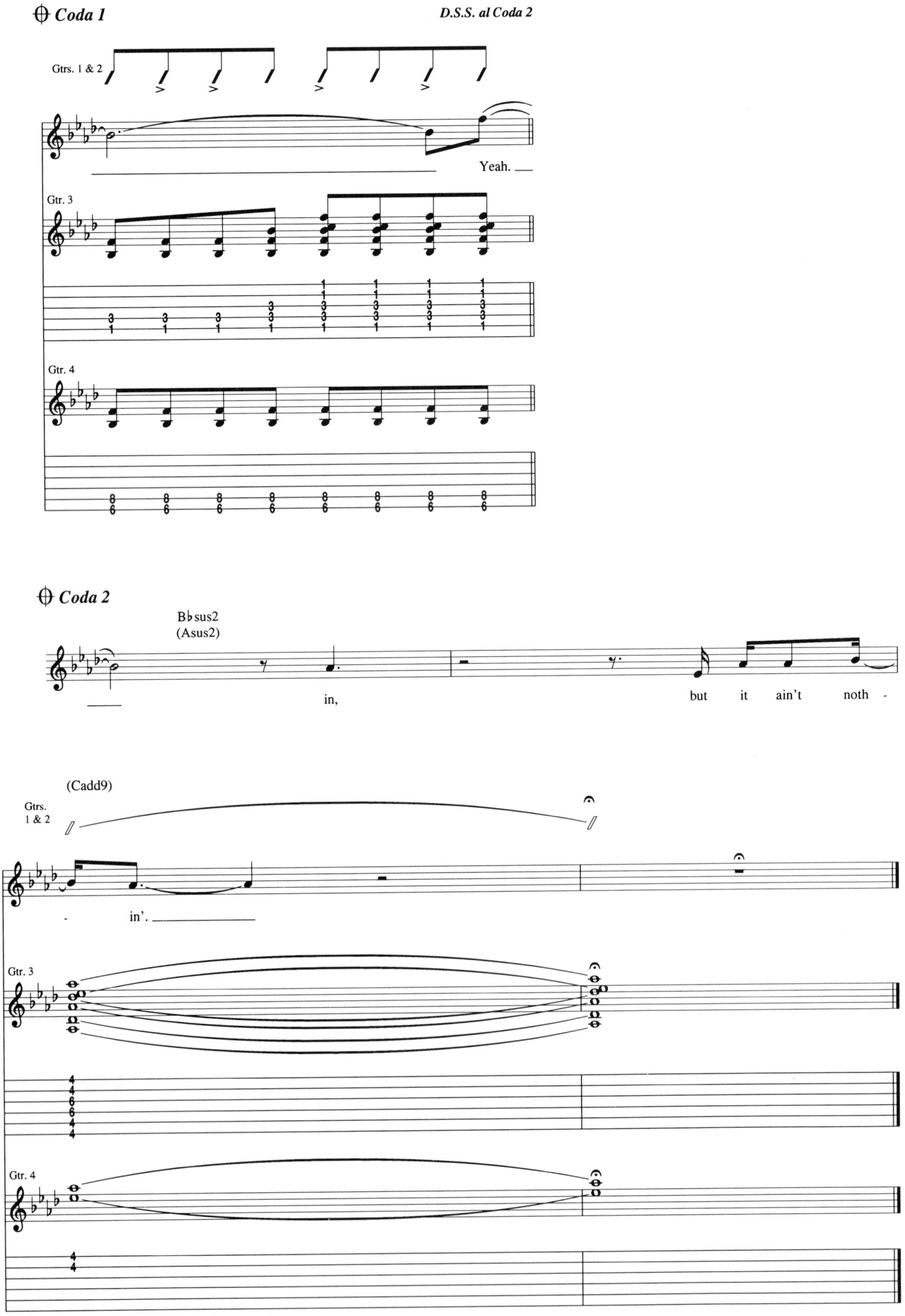
Coda 1
D.S.S. al Coda 2
Gtrs. 1 & 2
Yeah.
Gtr. 3
Gtr. 4
Coda 2
B♭sus2
(Asus2)
in,
but it ain't noth -
(Cadd9)
Gtrs. 1 & 2
- in'.
Gtr. 3
Gtr. 4

Busted

Written by Rob Thomas

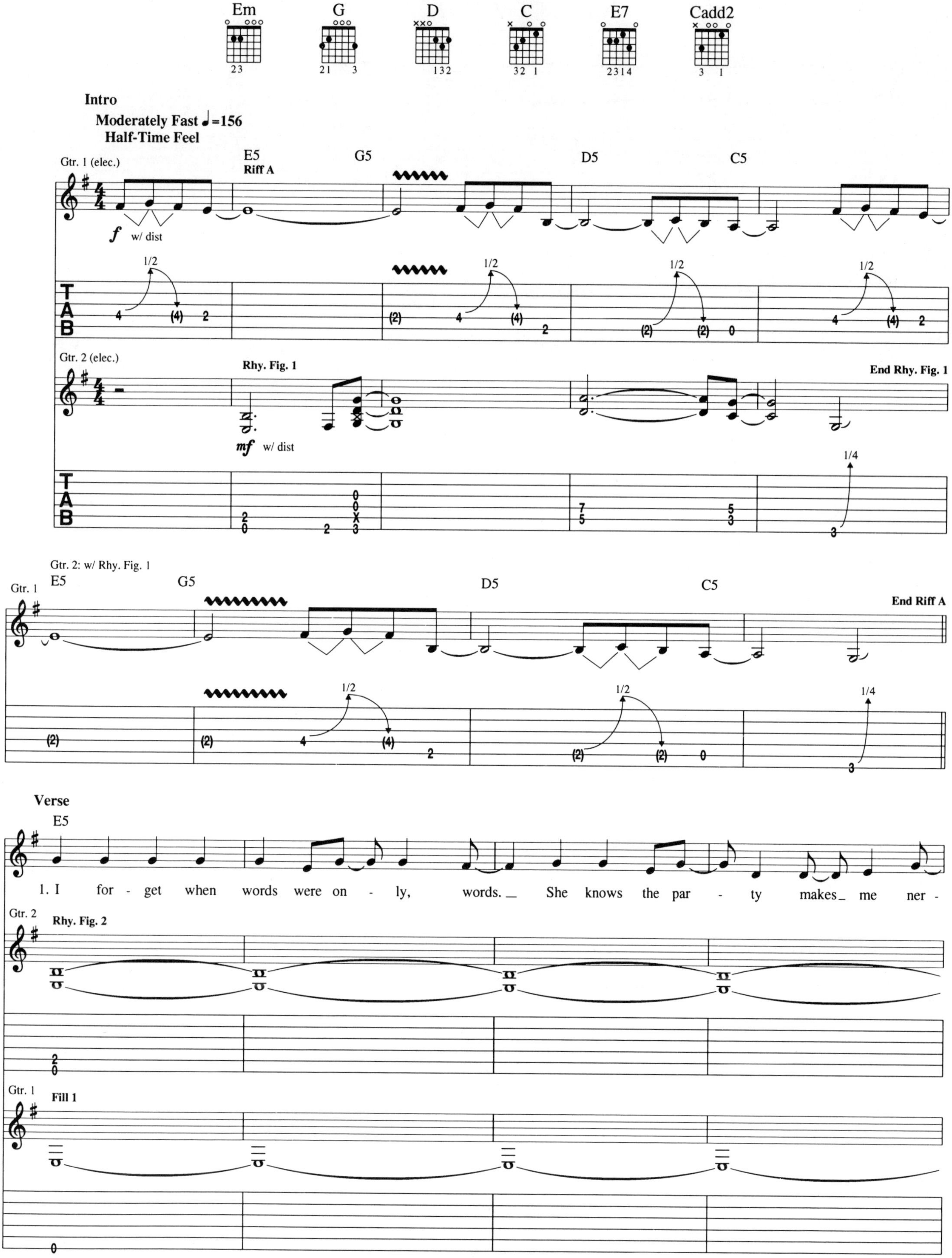

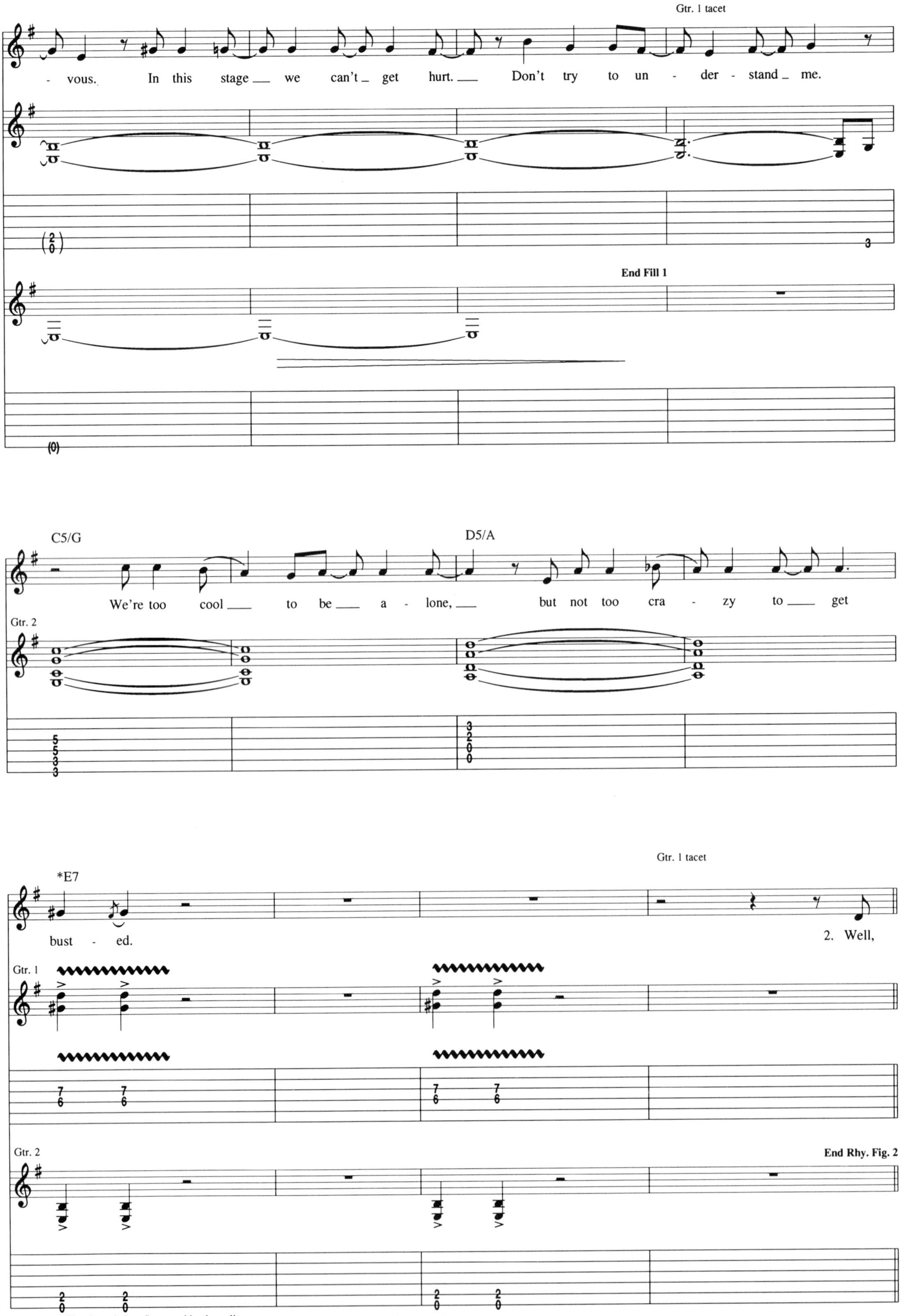
Gtr. 1 tacet
- vous. In this stage we can't get hurt. Don't try to un - der - stand me.
End Fill 1
C5/G
D5/A
We're too cool to be a - lone, but not too cra - zy to get
Gtr. 2
Gtr. 1 tacet
*E7
bust - ed.
2. Well,
Gtr. 1
Gtr. 2
End Rhy. Fig. 2

*Chord symbols reflect combined tonality.

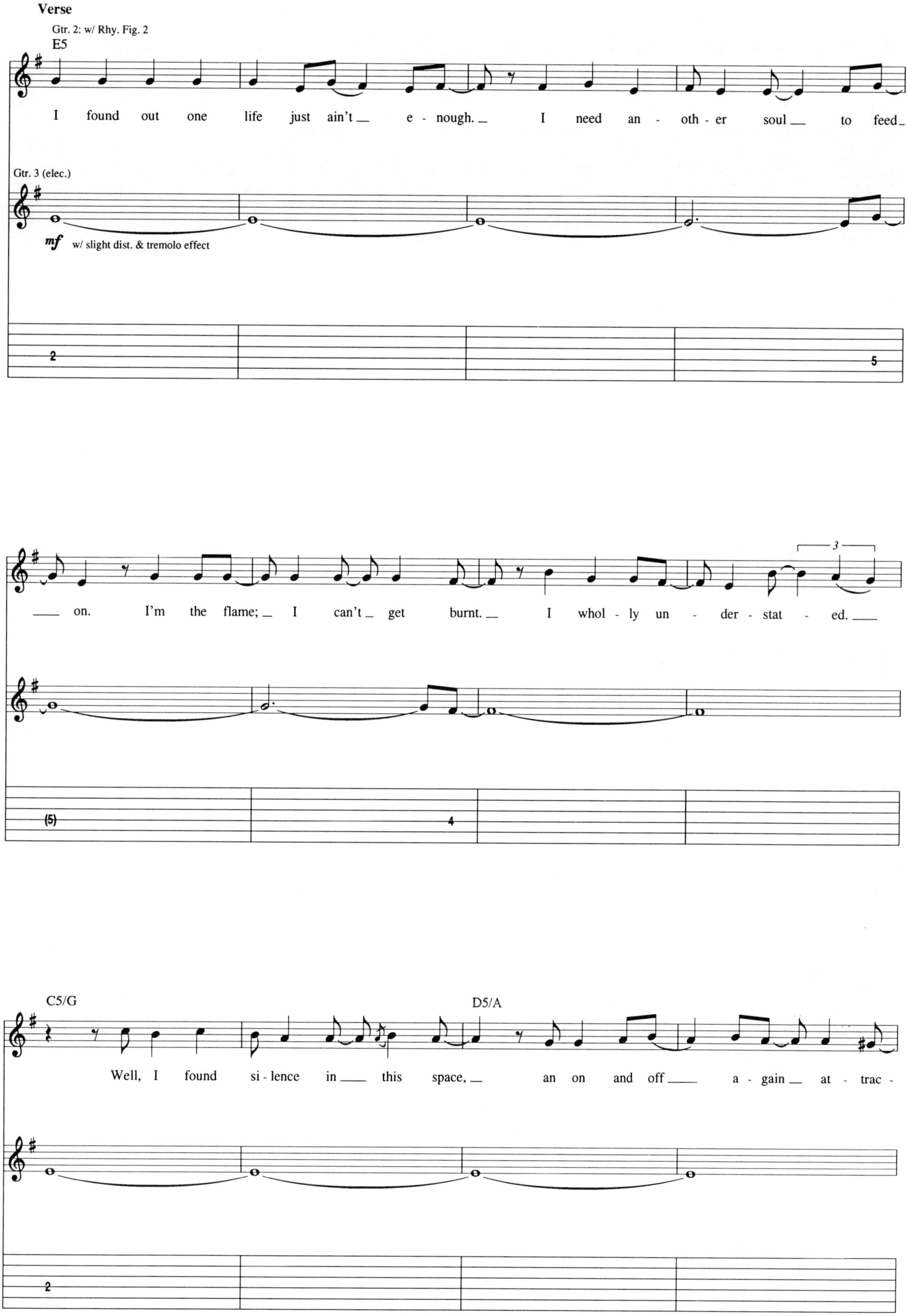
Verse
Gtr. 2: w/ Rhy. Fig. 2
E5
I found out one life just ain't e - nough. I need an - oth - er soul to feed
Gtr. 3 (elec.)
mf w/ slight dist. & tremolo effect
on. I'm the flame; I can't get burnt. I whol - ly un - der - stat - ed.
C5/G
D5/A
Well, I found si - lence in this space, an on and off a - gain at - trac -

Gtr. 3 tacet
E7
- tion.
Gtr. 1
End Half-Time Feel
C5/G
D5/A
Well, I need such a - maz - ing grace. Heav - en sweep me a - way. Ah, well,
Gtr. 3 Riff B
let ring throughout
Rhy. Fig. 3
Gtr. 1
End Rhy. Fig. 3
Gtr. 2 Rhy. Fig. 3A
End Rhy. Fig. 3A

Chorus
Em
Rhy. Fig. 4
G
D
C
End Rhy. Fig. 4
Gtr. 4 (acous.)
mf
love don't change, don't come a-round here. Don't wear my heart on your sleeve like a high school let -
Gtr. 3
End Riff B
Gtr. 1
Fill 2
End Fill 2
Gtr. 2
Riff C
End Riff C
Gtr. 2: w/ Riff C
Gtr. 4: w/ Rhy. Fig. 4
Gtr. 1 tacet
Em
G
D
ter. Don't strain, 'cause noth-in' ev - er comes from it, and the peo-ple we've be - come, well, they've
Gtr. 3

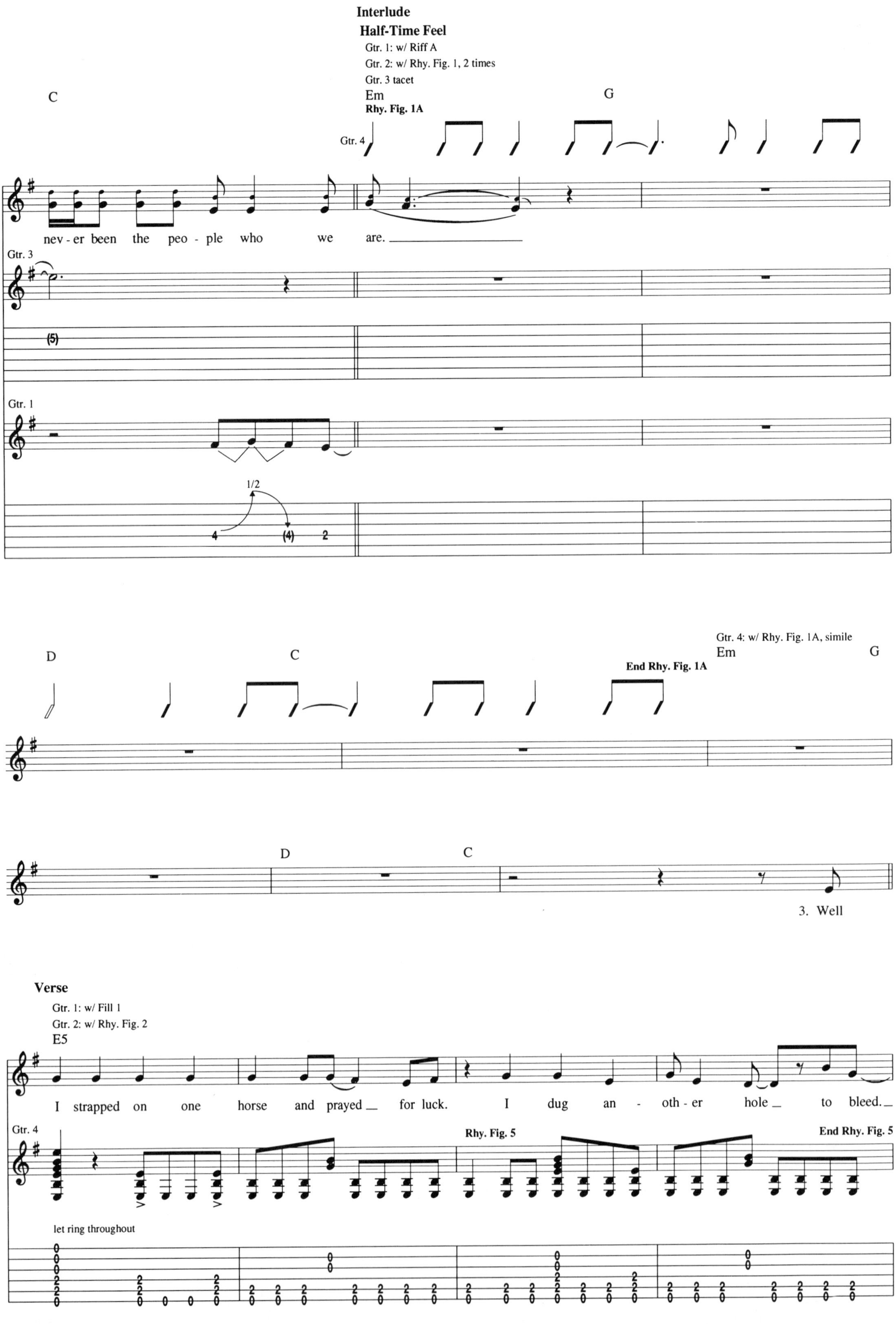
Interlude
Half-Time Feel
Gtr. 1: w/ Riff A
Gtr. 2: w/ Rhy. Fig. 1, 2 times
Gtr. 3 tacet
C
Em
G
Rhy. Fig. 1A
Gtr. 4
nev - er been the peo - ple who we are.
Gtr. 3
Gtr. 1
1/2
D
C
End Rhy. Fig. 1A
Gtr. 4: w/ Rhy. Fig. 1A, simile
Em
G
D
C
3. Well
Verse
Gtr. 1: w/ Fill 1
Gtr. 2: w/ Rhy. Fig. 2
E5
I strapped on one horse and prayed for luck. I dug an - oth - er hole to bleed.
Gtr. 4
Rhy. Fig. 5
End Rhy. Fig. 5
let ring throughout

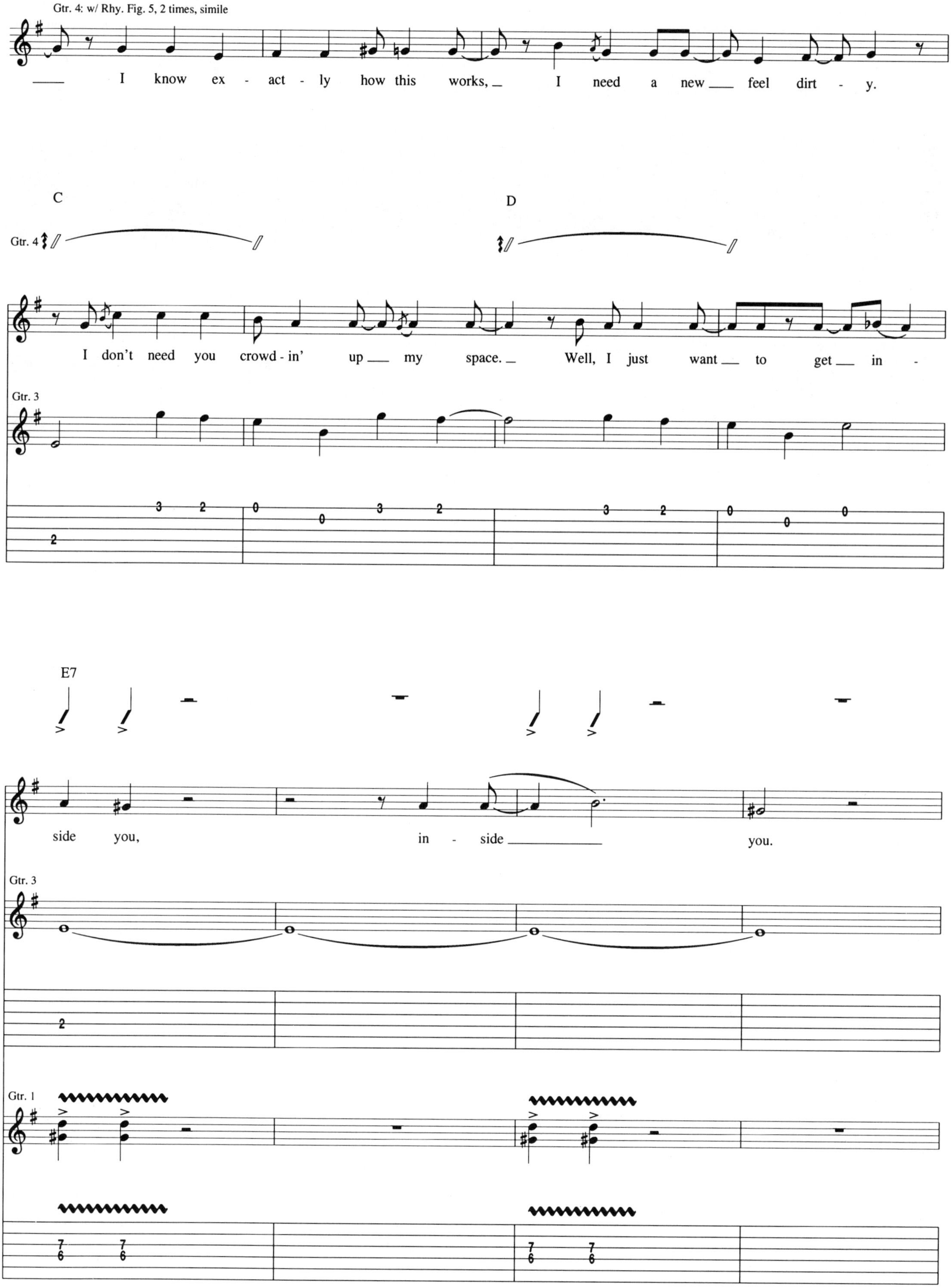
Gtr. 4: w/ Rhy. Fig. 5, 2 times, simile
I know ex - act - ly how this works, I need a new feel dirt - y.
C
D
Gtr. 4
I don't need you crowd - in' up my space. Well, I just want to get in -
Gtr. 3
E7
side you, in - side you.
Gtr. 3
Gtr. 1

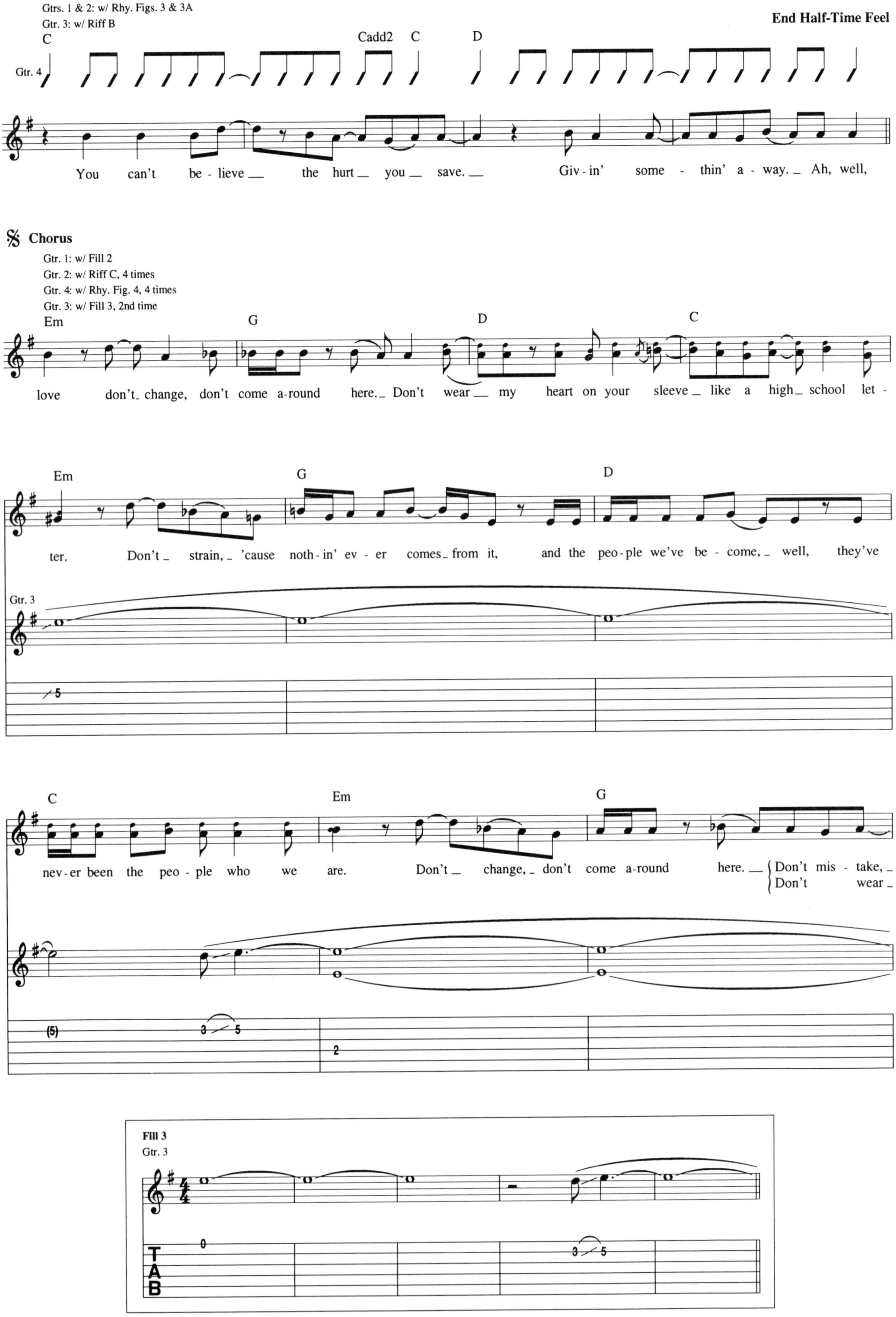

Gtrs. 1 & 2: w/ Rhy. Figs. 3 & 3A
Gtr. 3: w/ Riff B
End Half-Time Feel
C
Cadd2
C
D
Gtr. 4
You can't be - lieve ___ the hurt ___ you ___ save. ___ Giv - in' some - thin' a - way. ___ Ah, well,
Chorus
Gtr. 1: w/ Fill 2
Gtr. 2: w/ Riff C, 4 times
Gtr. 4: w/ Rhy. Fig. 4, 4 times
Gtr. 3: w/ Fill 3, 2nd time
Em
G
D
C
love don't change, don't come a-round here. ___ Don't wear ___ my heart on your sleeve ___ like a high ___ school let -
ter. Don't ___ strain, ___ 'cause noth - in' ev - er comes ___ from it, and the peo - ple we've be - come, ___ well, they've
Gtr. 3
nev - er been the peo - ple who we are. Don't ___ change, ___ don't come a-round here. ___ Don't mis - take, ___ / Don't wear ___
Fill 3
Gtr. 3
TAB

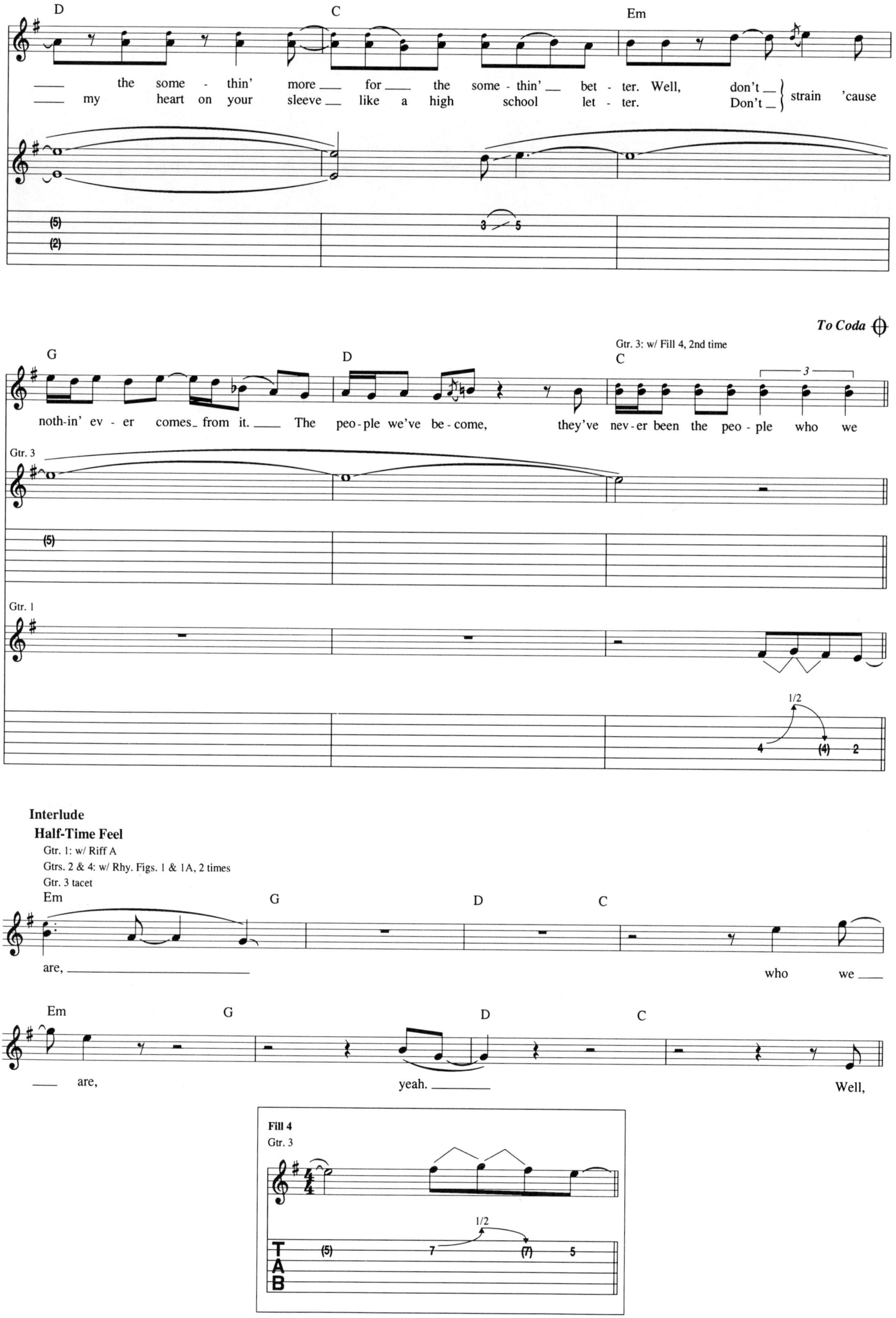
D
C
Em
the some - thin' more for the some - thin' bet - ter. Well, don't strain 'cause
my heart on your sleeve like a high school let - ter. Don't
To Coda
Gtr. 3: w/ Fill 4, 2nd time
G
D
C
noth-in' ev - er comes from it. The peo-ple we've be-come, they've nev-er been the peo-ple who we
Gtr. 3
Gtr. 1
1/2
Interlude
Half-Time Feel
Gtr. 1: w/ Riff A
Gtrs. 2 & 4: w/ Rhy. Figs. 1 & 1A, 2 times
Gtr. 3 tacet
Em
G
D
C
are, who we
are, yeah. Well,
Fill 4
Gtr. 3
1/2
T
A
B

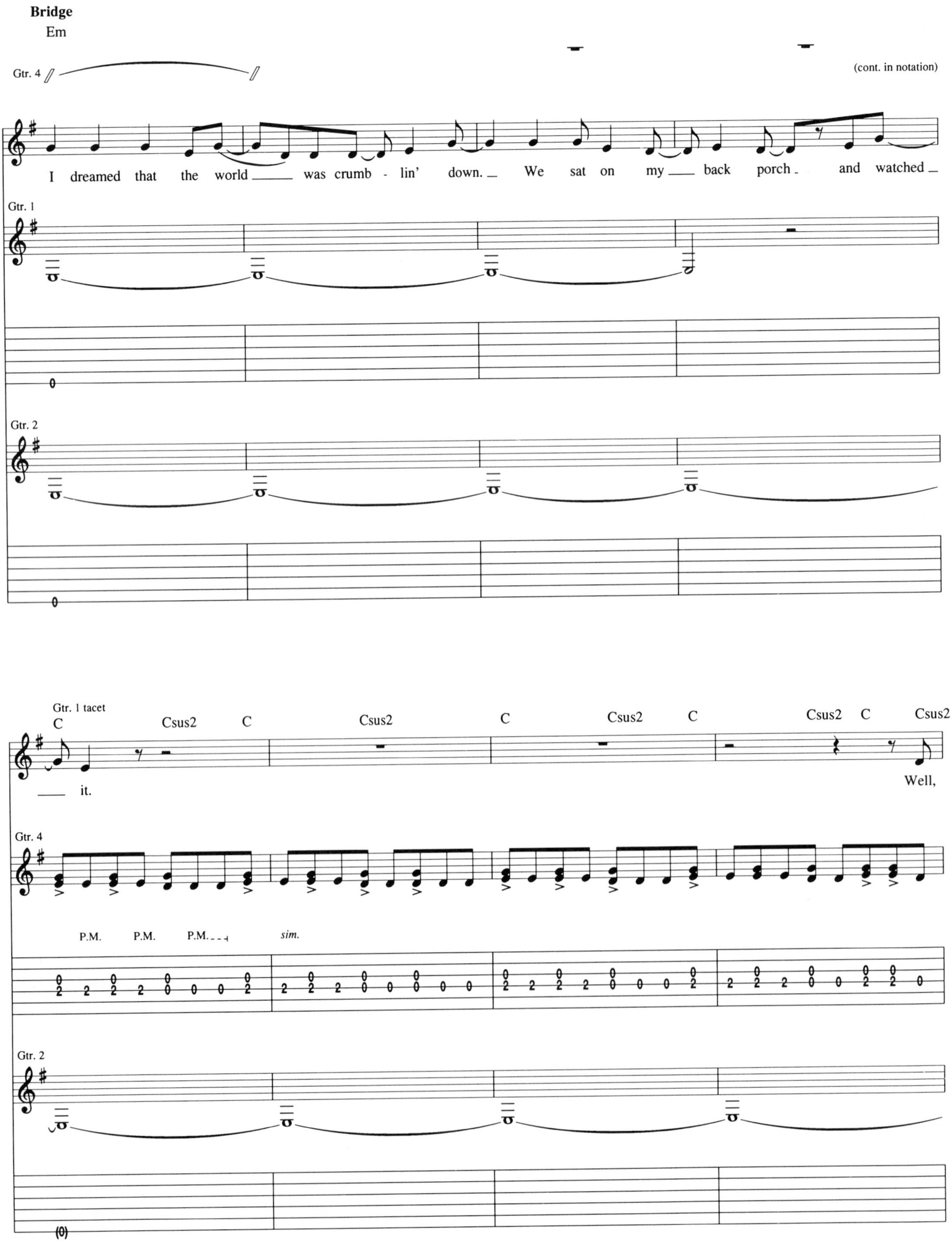
Bridge
Em
Gtr. 4
(cont. in notation)
I dreamed that the world was crumb - lin' down. We sat on my back porch and watched
Gtr. 1
Gtr. 2
Gtr. 1 tacet
C Csus2 C Csus2 C Csus2 C Csus2 C Csus2
it. Well,
Gtr. 4
P.M. P.M. P.M.
sim.
Gtr. 2

E5 E7 E5 Em E5 Em7 E5 E7 E5 Em7 E5
I dreamed that the build - in's all fell down. We sat on my back porch and we watched
fdbk.
C Csus2 C Csus2 C Csus2 C Csus2 C
it, yeah. Yeah, well,
(cont. in slash)

Em
G
Gtr. 4
I dreamed that the world was crumb - lin' down. We sat on my
Gtr. 1
Gtr. 2
divisi
C
back porch and watched it. In my head I heard the sound
D
Em
like fif - teen strang - ers danc - in'. But, oh, how I want you to

E
open
F#
2fr
G
know me. Well, oh, how I want you to know me. And,
D.S. al Coda
End Half-Time Feel
D
Gtr. 4
C
D
oh, how I wish I was some - bod - y else, ba - by. Oh, how I wish you could own, own me.
Gtr. 1
Gtr. 2

Coda
Outro
Gtr. 1: w/ Riff A
Gtrs. 2 & 4: w/ Rhy. Figs. 1 & 1A, 2 times
Em G D C
are,
(Ah,)
who we are,
who we are,
Gtr. 3
1/2
Em G D C
we are.
(Ah.)
1/4
Em
Gtr. 4
Gtr. 3
Gtr. 2
Gtr. 1

Shame

Written by Rob Thomas

Pre-Chorus
(G) (Em) (D) (Dsus2) (C) (G) (Em) (D)
Rhy. Fig. 2A
Gtr. 2
Fun - ny how it comes to pass, that all the good slips a - way. And there's no one a - round
Set your - self, sit - u - ate, like a fool try a - gain. There's no one a - round
Gtr. 1
Rhy. Fig. 2
(Dsus2) (C)
drums enter
(Em)
(C)
End Rhy. Fig. 2A
you can re - mem - ber be - ing good to you.
you can re - mem - ber be - ing good for you. So,
*Gtr. 1
End Rhy. Fig. 2
*Dbld. throughout by gtr. w/ ③, ④, ⑤ & ⑥ tuned up one octave.
Chorus
(G) (D) (Dsus2) (Am) (C) (Cadd2) (C)
Rhy. Fig. 3A
Rhy. Fig. 3
Shame, should - n't try you, could - n't step by you and o - pen up more
(G) (Em) (D) (Dsus2) (D) (Dsus2) (C) (Cadd2) (C) (Cadd2)
End Rhy. Fig. 3A
shame, shame, shame.
End Rhy. Fig. 3

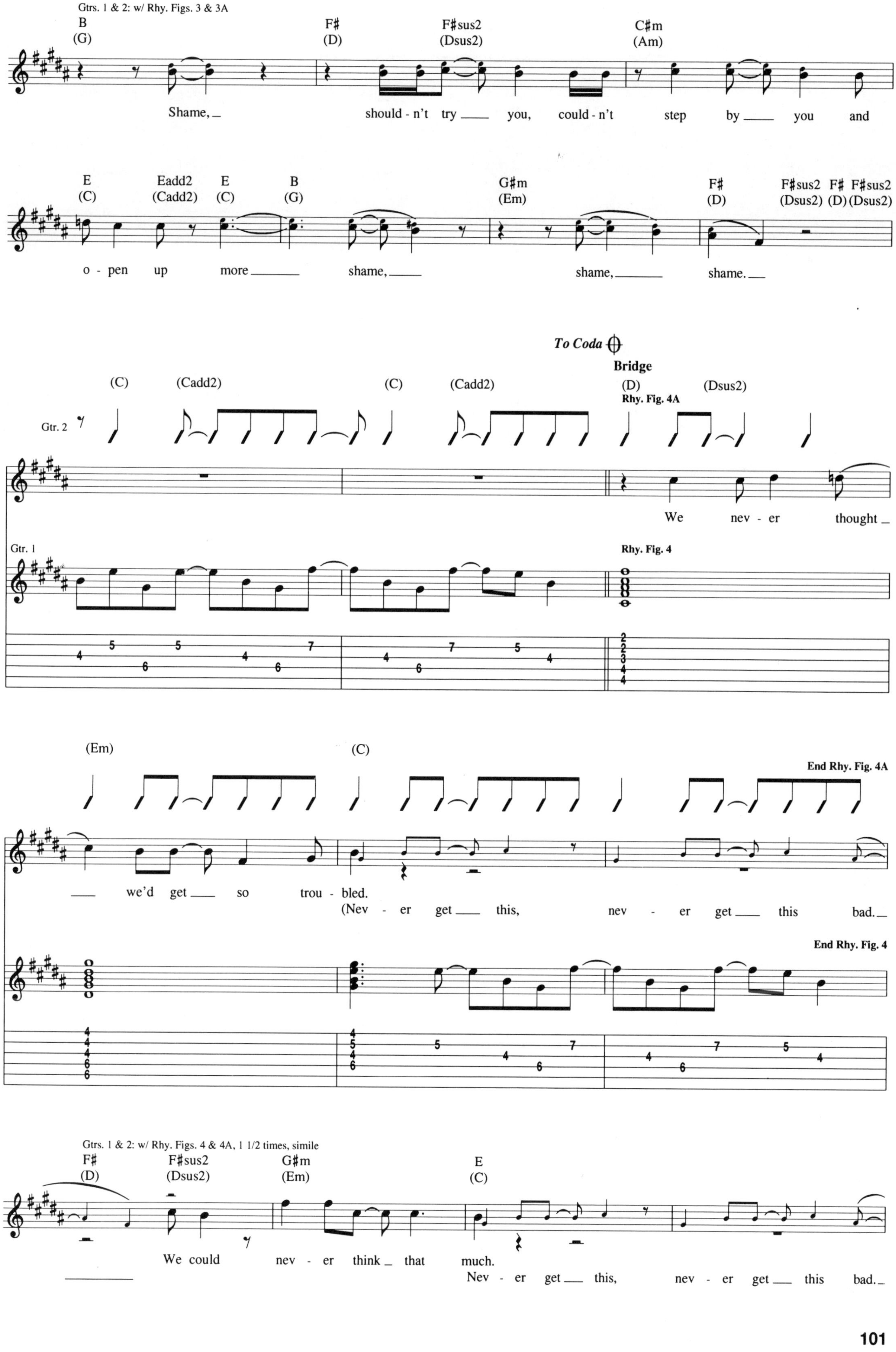
Gtrs. 1 & 2: w/ Rhy. Figs. 3 & 3A
B (G)
F♯ (D)
F♯sus2 (Dsus2)
C♯m (Am)
Shame, should - n't try you, could - n't step by you and
E (C)
Eadd2 (Cadd2)
E (C)
B (G)
G♯m (Em)
F♯ (D)
F♯sus2 (Dsus2)
F♯ (D)
F♯sus2 (Dsus2)
o - pen up more shame, shame, shame.
To Coda
Bridge
(C) (Cadd2) (C) (Cadd2) (D) (Dsus2)
Rhy. Fig. 4A
Gtr. 2
We nev - er thought
Gtr. 1
Rhy. Fig. 4
(Em) (C)
End Rhy. Fig. 4A
we'd get so trou - bled.
(Nev - er get this, nev - er get this bad.
End Rhy. Fig. 4
Gtrs. 1 & 2: w/ Rhy. Figs. 4 & 4A, 1 1/2 times, simile
F♯ (D)
F♯sus2 (Dsus2)
G♯m (Em)
E (C)
We could nev - er think that much.
Nev - er get this, nev - er get this bad.

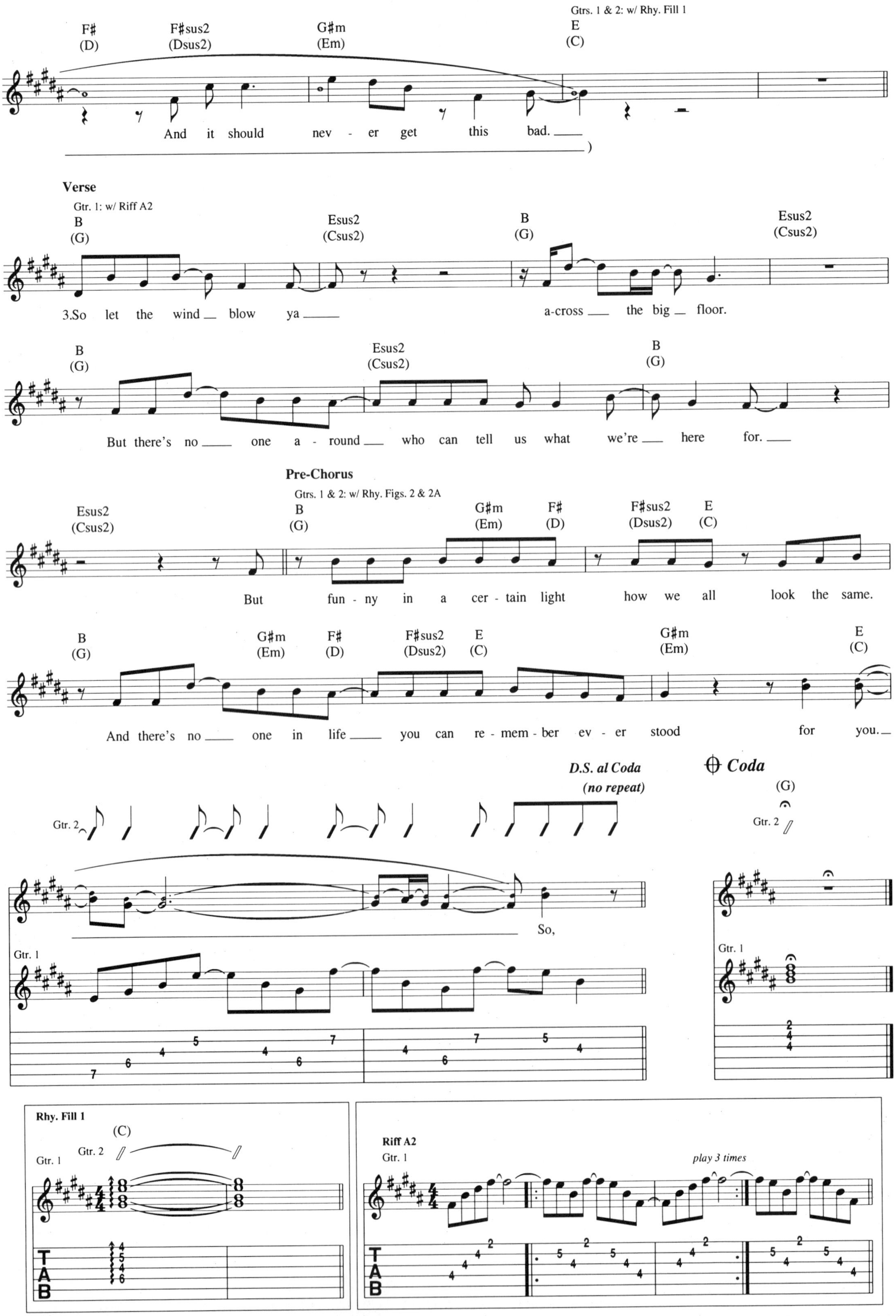
Gtrs. 1 & 2: w/ Rhy. Fill 1
F♯ (D) F♯sus2 (Dsus2) G♯m (Em) E (C)
And it should nev - er get this bad.
Verse
Gtr. 1: w/ Riff A2
B (G) Esus2 (Csus2) B (G) Esus2 (Csus2)
3.So let the wind blow ya a-cross the big floor.
B (G) Esus2 (Csus2) B (G)
But there's no one a - round who can tell us what we're here for.
Pre-Chorus
Gtrs. 1 & 2: w/ Rhy. Figs. 2 & 2A
Esus2 (Csus2) B (G) G♯m (Em) F♯ (D) F♯sus2 (Dsus2) E (C)
But fun - ny in a cer - tain light how we all look the same.
B (G) G♯m (Em) F♯ (D) F♯sus2 (Dsus2) E (C) G♯m (Em) E (C)
And there's no one in life you can re - mem - ber ev - er stood for you.
D.S. al Coda
(no repeat)
Coda
(G)
Gtr. 2
Gtr. 1
So,
Rhy. Fill 1
(C)
Gtr. 1
Gtr. 2
Riff A2
Gtr. 1
play 3 times

Hang

Written by Rob Thomas

G
Cmaj7
G
She burns all her notes.
And she knows __ she's been here too _ few years _
D5
Cmaj7
Gsus2
Gtr. 2 (acous.)
mf
(cont. in notation)
__ to feel _ this _ old. __
End Rhy. Fig. 1
Verse
Gtr. 1: w/ Rhy. Fig. 1, simile
*G
Cmaj7
2. He smokes his cig-a-rette.
He stays out-side __ 'til it's gone.
Rhy. Fig. 1A
Gtr. 2
let ring throughout
*Chord symbols reflect combined tonality.
Em7
D
Dsus2
D
If an-y-bod-y e-ver had a heart, __
well,

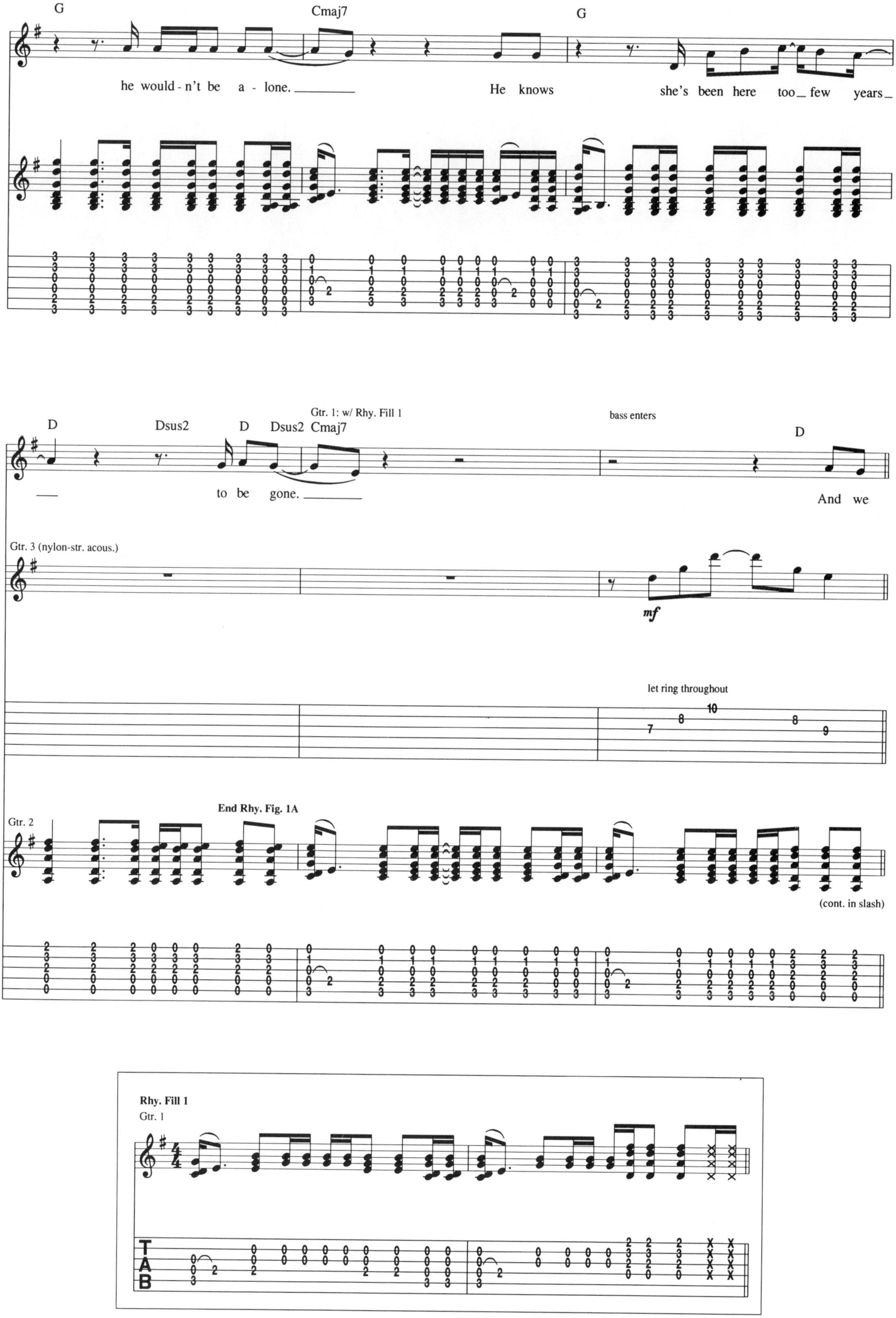
G
Cmaj7
G
he would-n't be a-lone.
He knows
she's been here too few years
D
Dsus2
D
Dsus2
Cmaj7
Gtr. 1: w/ Rhy. Fill 1
bass enters
D
to be gone.
And we
Gtr. 3 (nylon-str. acous.)
mf
let ring throughout
Gtr. 2
End Rhy. Fig. 1A
(cont. in slash)
Rhy. Fill 1
Gtr. 1
T
A
B

Chorus
G D/A Cadd2 C Cadd2 C G D/A
Rhy. Fig. 2
*Gtr. 2
al - ways say, it would be good to go a - way,
Riff A
Gtr. 3
*Dbld. by Gtr. 1, 2nd time.
To Coda
Cadd2 C Cadd2 C Em D Dsus2
End Rhy. Fig. 2
some - day. Yeah, but if there's noth - in' there to make things change, if it's the
(Ah.
End Riff A
C
Guitar Solo
Gtr. 2: w/ Rhy. Fig. 1A, 1st 4 meas., simile
G
same for you I'll just hang.
)
Gtr. 3
Gtr. 1
divisi
Gtr. 1 tacet
Gtr. 3
C

Verse

Gtr. 2: w/ Rhy. Fig. 1A, simile
G
C
3. The trou-ble, un - der - stand, is she got rea - sons he don't.
Em7
Fun-ny how I could-n't see at all
D Dsus2 D G
un - til she grabbed up her coat.
C G D Dsus2 D Dsus2
And she goes, she's been here too few years

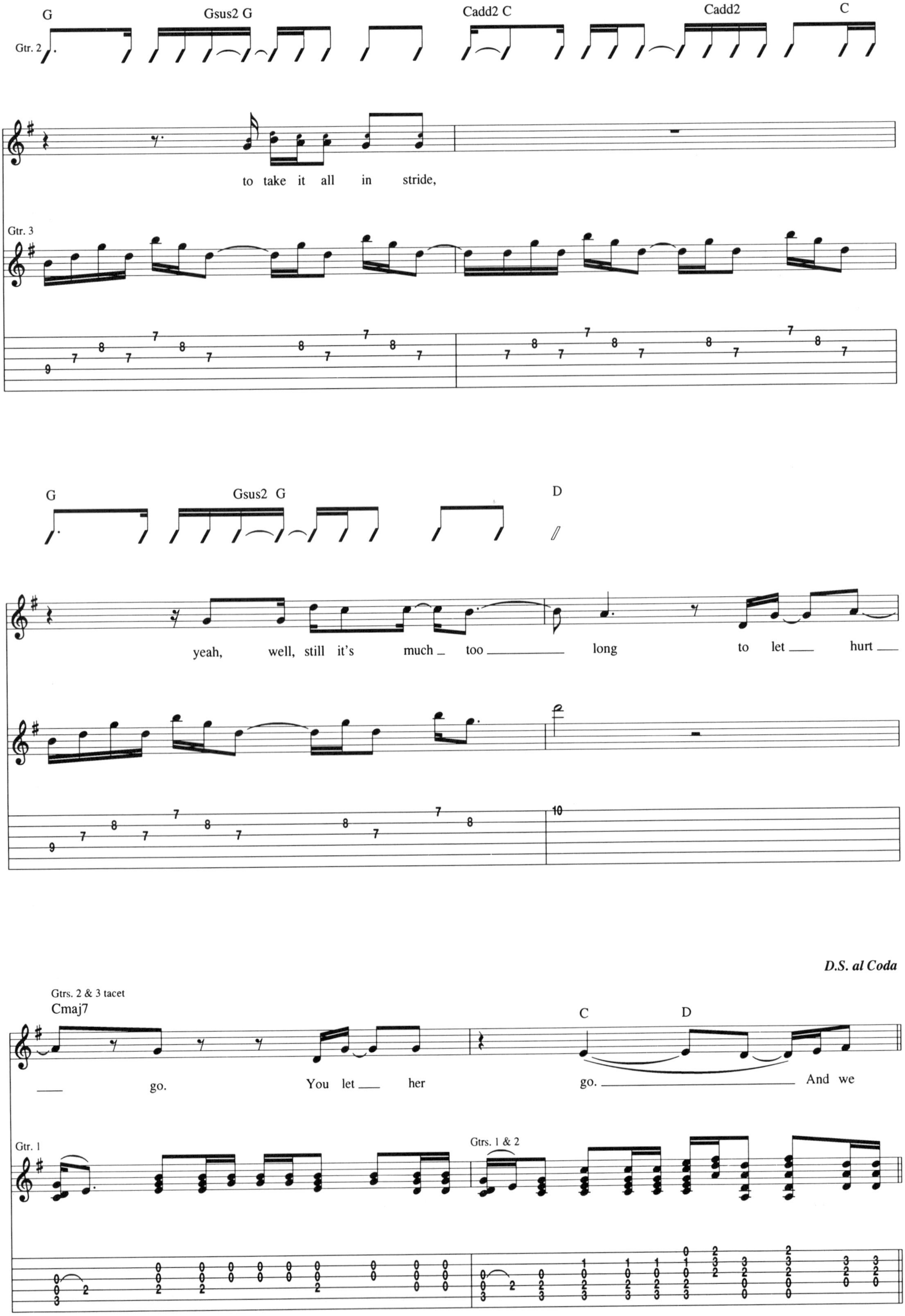
G
Gsus2 G
Cadd2 C
Cadd2
C
Gtr. 2
to take it all in stride,
Gtr. 3
G
Gsus2 G
D
yeah, well, still it's much _ too ___ long to let ___ hurt ___
D.S. al Coda
Gtrs. 2 & 3 tacet
Cmaj7
C
D
___ go. You let ___ her go. ___ And we
Gtr. 1
Gtrs. 1 & 2

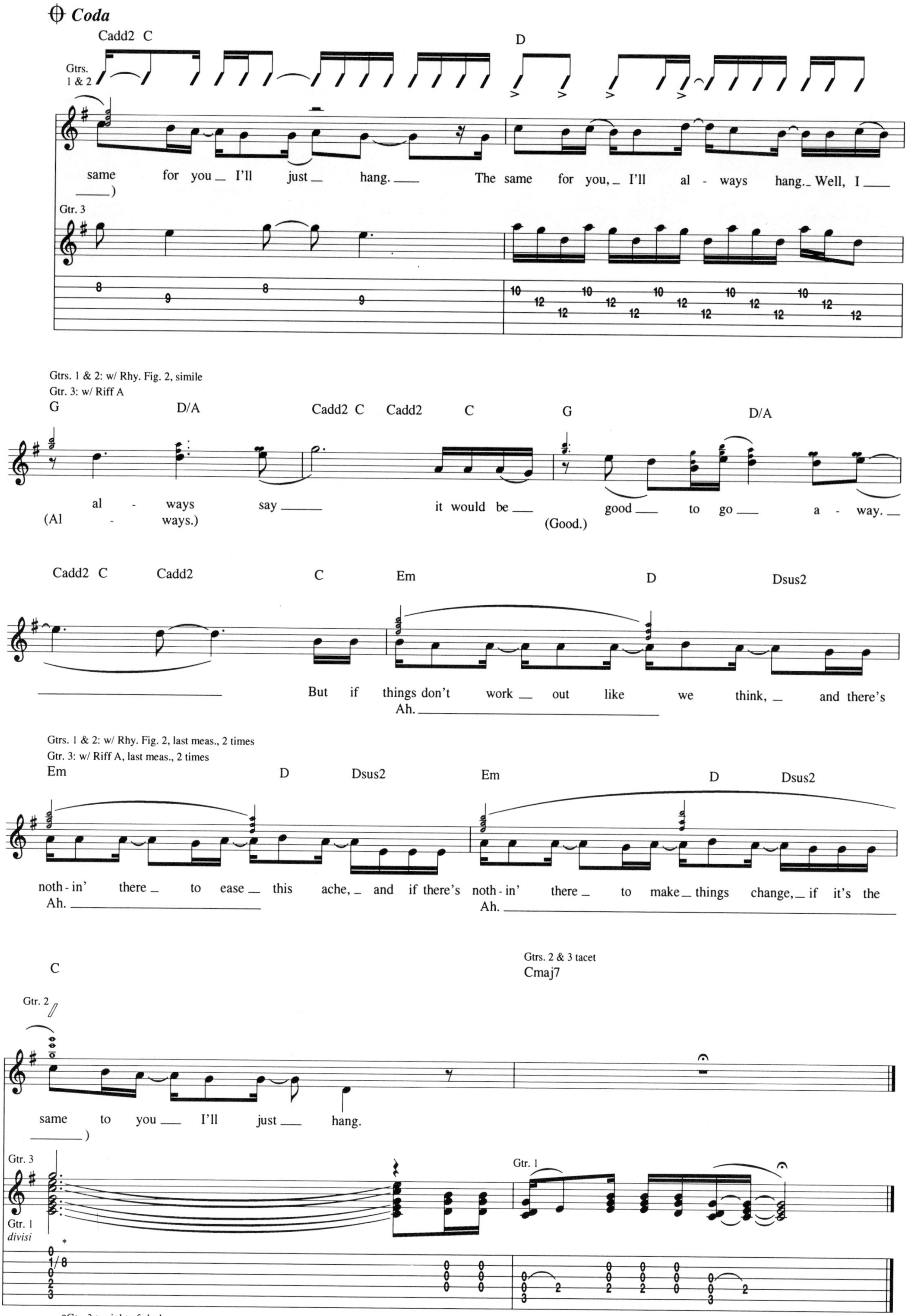

*Gtr. 3 to right of slash.

Guitar Notation Legend

Guitar Music can be notated three different ways: on a *musical staff*, in *tablature*, and in *rhythm slashes*.

RHYTHM SLASHES are written above the staff. Strum chords in the rhythm indicated. Use the chord diagrams found at the top of the first page of the transcription for the appropriate chord voicings. Round noteheads indicate single notes.

THE MUSICAL STAFF shows pitches and rhythms and is divided by bar lines into measures. Pitches are named after the first seven letters of the alphabet.

TABLATURE graphically represents the guitar fingerboard. Each horizontal line represents a a string, and each number represents a fret.

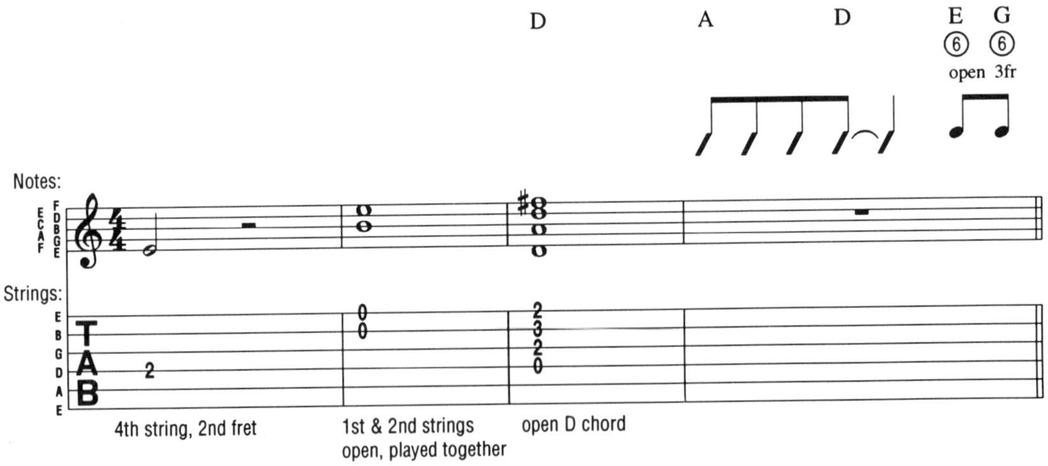

Definitions for Special Guitar Notation

HALF-STEP BEND: Strike the note and bend up 1/2 step.

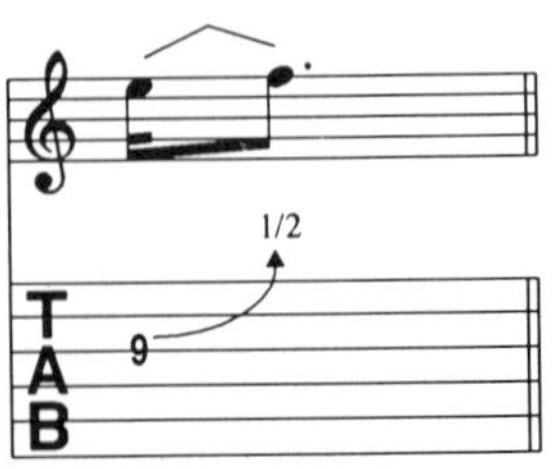

WHOLE-STEP BEND: Strike the note and bend up one step.

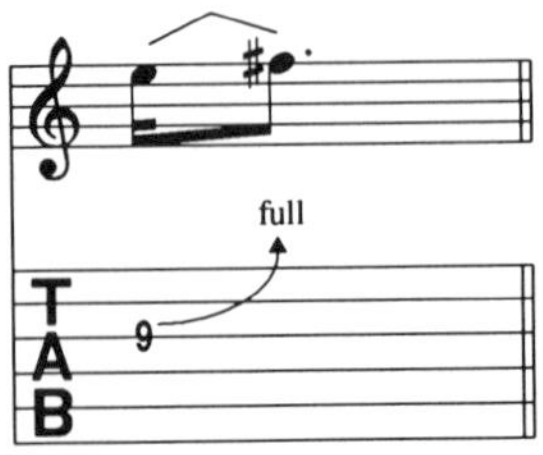

GRACE NOTE BEND: Strike the note and bend up as indicated. The first note does not take up any time.

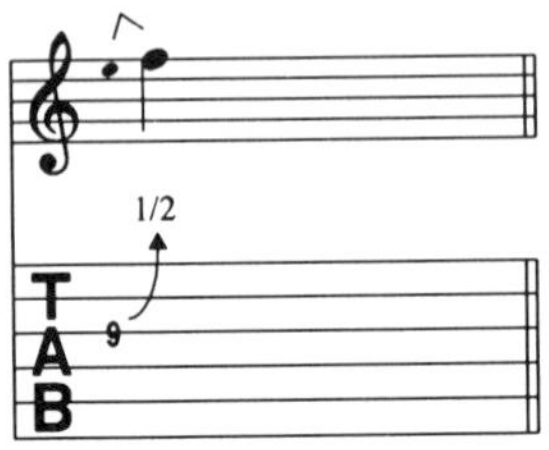

SLIGHT (MICROTONE) BEND: Strike the note and bend up 1/4 step.

BEND AND RELEASE: Strike the note and bend up as indicated, then release back to the original note. Only the first note is struck.

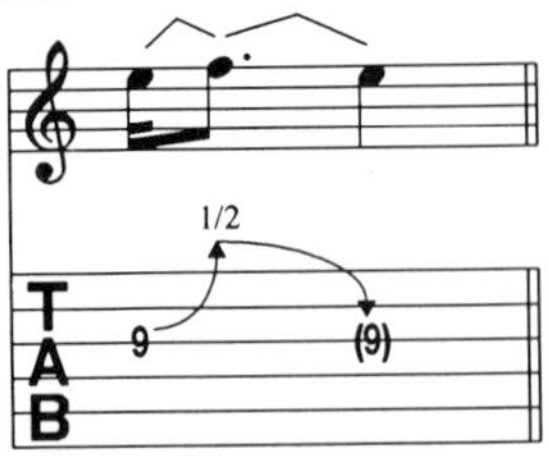

PRE-BEND: Bend the note as indicated, then strike it.

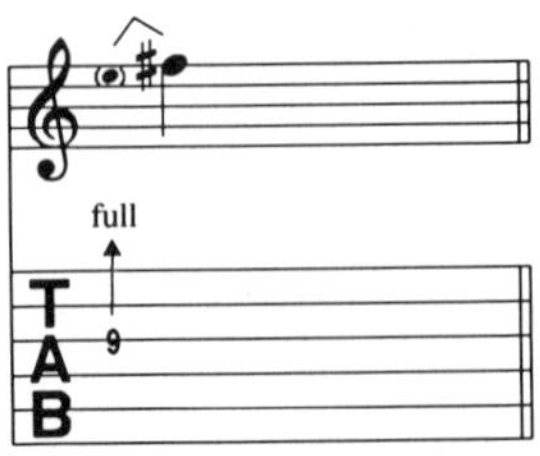

PRE-BEND AND RELEASE: Bend the note as indicated. Strike it and release the bend back to the original note.

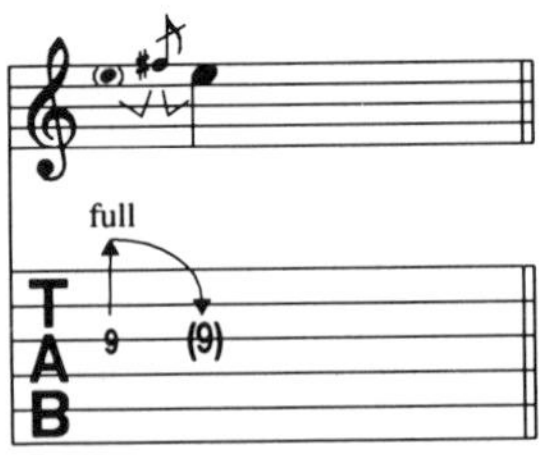

UNISON BEND: Strike the two notes simultaneously and bend the lower note up to the pitch of the higher.

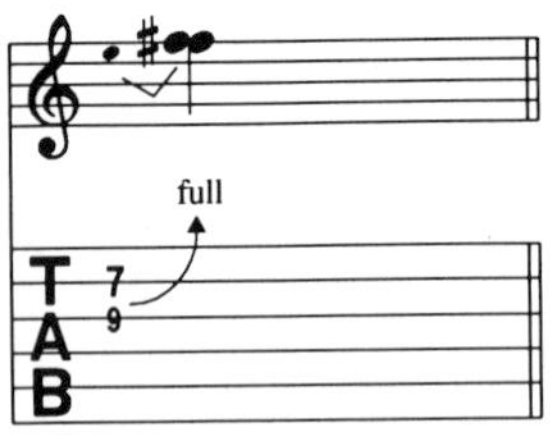

VIBRATO: The string is vibrated by rapidly bending and releasing the note with the fretting hand.

WIDE VIBRATO: The pitch is varied to a greater degree by vibrating with the fretting hand.

HAMMER-ON: Strike the first (lower) note with one finger, then sound the higher note (on the same string) with another finger by fretting it without picking.

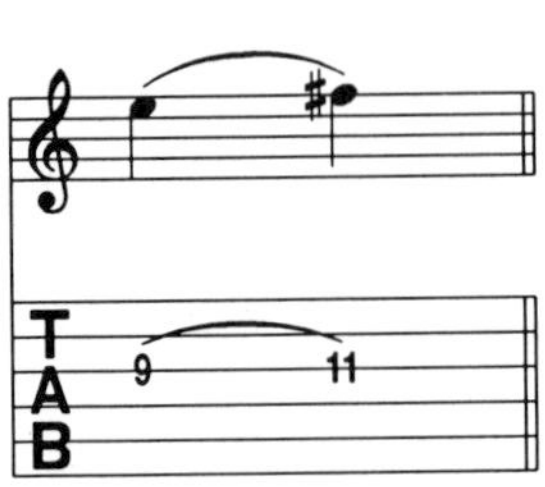

PULL-OFF: Place both fingers on the notes to be sounded. Strike the first note and without picking, pull the finger off to sound the second (lower) note.

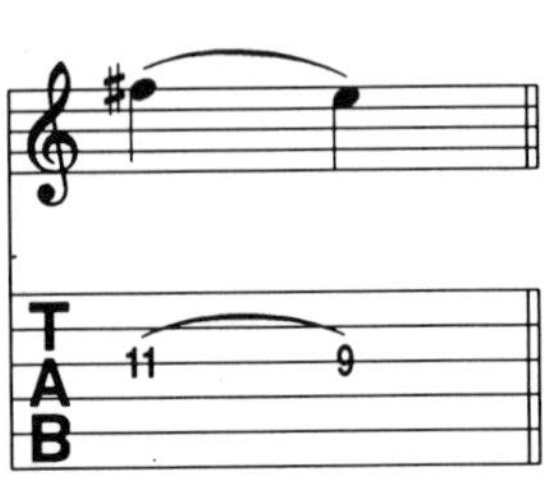

LEGATO SLIDE: Strike the first note and then slide the same fret-hand finger up or down to the second note. The second note is not struck.

SHIFT SLIDE: Same as legato slide, except the second note is struck.

TRILL: Very rapidly alternate between the notes indicated by continuously hammering on and pulling off.

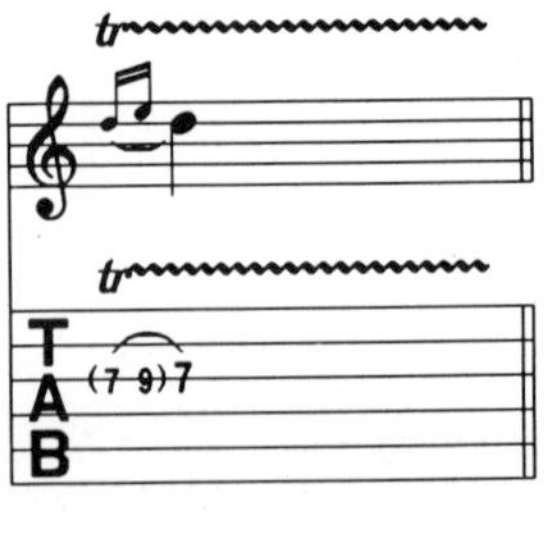

TAPPING: Hammer ("tap") the fret indicated with the pick-hand index or middle finger and pull off to the note fretted by the fret hand.

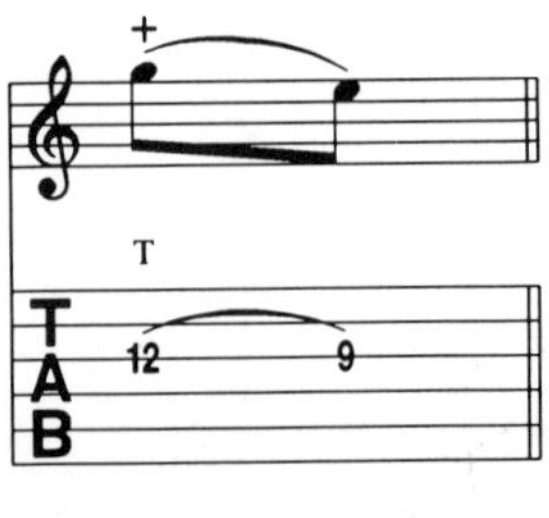

NATURAL HARMONIC: Strike the note while the fret-hand lightly touches the string directly over the fret indicated.

PINCH HARMONIC: The note is fretted normally and a harmonic is produced by adding the edge of the thumb or the tip of the index finger of the pick hand to the normal pick attack.

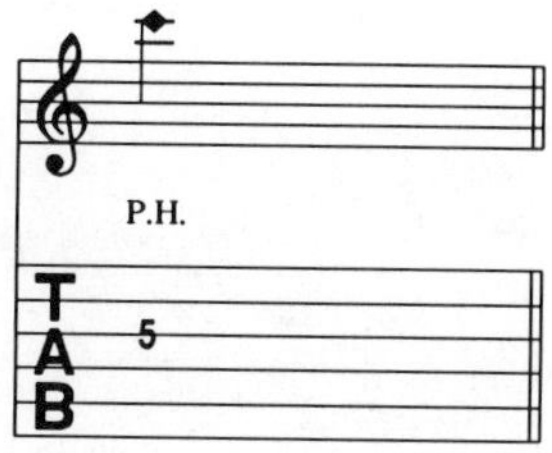

HARP HARMONIC: The note is fretted normally and a harmonic is produced by gently resting the pick hand's index finger directly above the indicated fret (in parentheses) while the pick hand's thumb or pick assists by plucking the appropriate string.

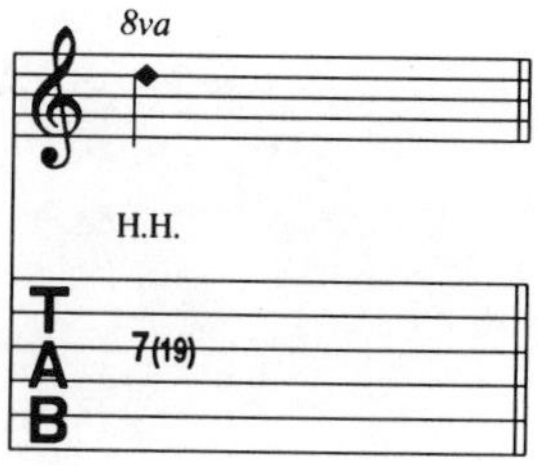

PICK SCRAPE: The edge of the pick is rubbed down (or up) the string, producing a scratchy sound.

MUFFLED STRINGS: A percussive sound is produced by laying the fret hand across the string(s) without depressing, and striking them with the pick hand.

PALM MUTING: The note is partially muted by the pick hand lightly touching the string(s) just before the bridge.

RAKE: Drag the pick across the strings indicated with a single motion.

TREMOLO PICKING: The note is picked as rapidly and continuously as possible.

ARPEGGIATE: Play the notes of the chord indicated by quickly rolling them from bottom to top.

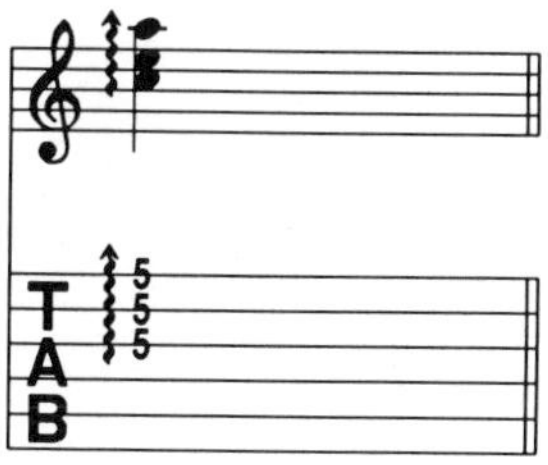

VIBRATO BAR DIVE AND RETURN: The pitch of the note or chord is dropped a specified number of steps (in rhythm) then returned to the original pitch.

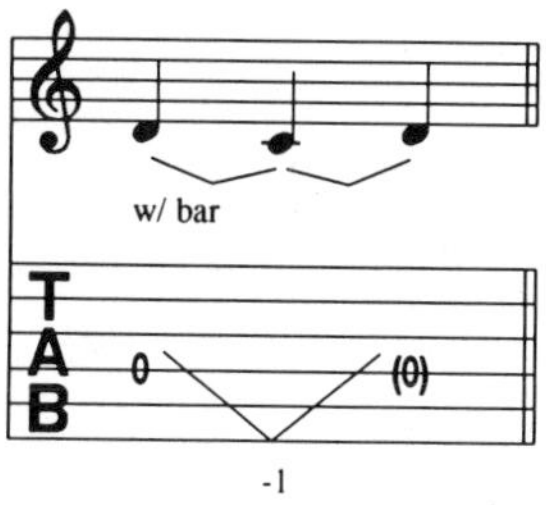

VIBRATO BAR SCOOP: Depress the bar just before striking the note, then quickly release the bar.

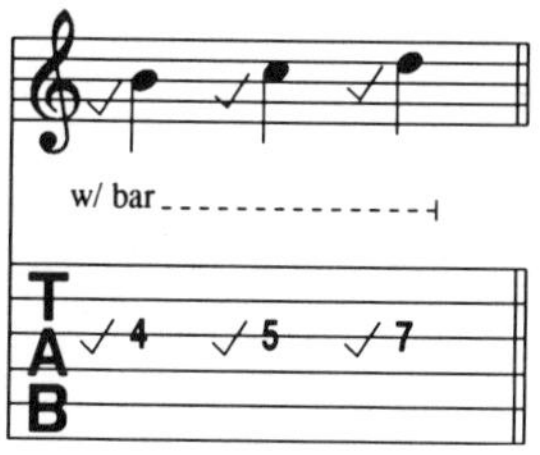

VIBRATO BAR DIP: Strike the note and then immediately drop a specified number of steps, then release back to the original pitch.

Additional Musical Definitions

 *(accent)* • Accentuate note (play it louder)

 *(accent)* • Accentuate note with great intensity

 *(staccato)* • Play the note short

⊓ • Downstroke

V • Upstroke

D.S. al Coda • Go back to the sign (𝄋), then play until the measure marked "***To Coda,***" then skip to the section labelled "***Coda.***"

D.S. al Fine • Go back to the beginning of the song and play until the measure marked "***Fine***" (end).

Rhy. Fig. • Label used to recall a recurring accompaniment pattern (usually chordal).

Riff • Label used to recall composed, melodic lines (usually single notes) which recur.

Fill • Label used to identify a brief melodic figure which is to be inserted into the arrangement.

Rhy. Fill • A chordal version of a Fill.

tacet • Instrument is silent (drops out).

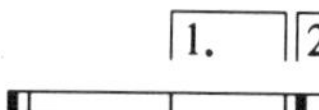 • Repeat measures between signs.

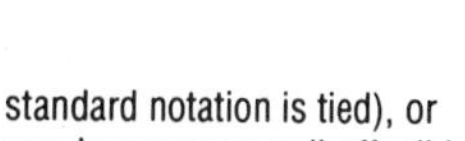

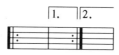

• When a repeated section has different endings, play the first ending only the first time and the second ending only the second time.

NOTE: Tablature numbers in parentheses mean:
1. The note is being sustained over a system (note in standard notation is tied), or
2. The note is sustained, but a new articulation (such as a hammer-on, pull-off, slide or vibrato begins, or
3. The note is a barely audible "ghost" note (note in standard notation is also in parentheses).

RECORDED VERSIONS

The Best Note-For-Note Transcriptions Available

RECORDED VERSIONS GUITAR

ALL BOOKS INCLUDE TABLATURE

00694909 Aerosmith – Get A Grip $19.95
00690199 Aerosmith – Nine Lives $19.95
00690146 Aerosmith – Toys in the Attic $19.95
00694865 Alice In Chains – Dirt $19.95
00660225 Alice In Chains – Facelift $19.95
00694925 Alice In Chains – Jar Of Flies/Sap $19.95
00694932 Allman Brothers Band – Volume 1 $24.95
00694933 Allman Brothers Band – Volume 2 $24.95
00694934 Allman Brothers Band – Volume 3 $24.95
00694877 Chet Atkins – Guitars For All Seasons $19.95
00694918 Randy Bachman Collection $22.95
00694880 Beatles – Abbey Road $19.95
00694891 Beatles – Revolver $19.95
00694863 Beatles – Sgt. Pepper's Lonely Hearts Club Band $19.95
00690174 Beck – Mellow Gold $17.95
00690175 Beck – Odelay $17.95
00694931 Belly – Star $19.95
00694884 The Best of George Benson $19.95
00692385 Chuck Berry $19.95
00692200 Black Sabbath – We Sold Our Soul For Rock 'N' Roll $19.95
00690115 Blind Melon – Soup $19.95
00690241 Bloodhound Gang – One Fierce Beer Coaster $19.95
00690028 Blue Oyster Cult – Cult Classics $19.95
00690219 Blur $19.95
00690173 Tracy Bonham – The Burdens Of Being Upright $17.95
00694935 Boston: Double Shot Of $22.95
00690237 Meredith Brooks – Blurring the Edges $19.95
00690043 Cheap Trick – Best Of $19.95
00690171 Chicago – Definitive Guitar Collection $22.95
00690010 Eric Clapton – From The Cradle $19.95
00660139 Eric Clapton – Journeyman $19.95
00694869 Eric Clapton – Live Acoustic $19.95
00694873 Eric Clapton – Timepieces $19.95
00694896 John Mayall/Eric Clapton – Bluesbreakers $19.95
00694940 Counting Crows – August & Everything After $19.95
00690197 Counting Crows – Recovering the Satellites $19.95
00690118 Cranberries – The Best of $19.95
00694941 Crash Test Dummies – God Shuffled His Feet $19.95
00694840 Cream – Disraeli Gears $19.95
00690007 Danzig 4 $19.95
00690184 DC Talk – Jesus Freak $19.95
00660186 Alex De Grassi Guitar Collection $19.95
00694831 Derek And The Dominos – Layla & Other Assorted Love Songs $19.95
00690187 Dire Straits – Brothers In Arms $19.95
00690191 Dire Straits – Money For Nothing $24.95
00690182 Dishwalla – Pet Your Friends $19.95
00660178 Willie Dixon – Master Blues Composer $24.95
00690089 Foo Fighters $19.95
00690042 Robben Ford Blues Collection $19.95
00694920 Free – Best Of $18.95
00690222 G3 Live – Satriani, Vai, Johnson $22.95
00694894 Frank Gambale – The Great Explorers $19.95
00694807 Danny Gatton – 88 Elmira St $19.95
00690127 Goo Goo Dolls – A Boy Named Goo $19.95
00690117 John Gorka Collection $19.95
00690114 Buddy Guy Collection Vol. A-J $19.95
00690193 Buddy Guy Collection Vol. L-Y $19.95
00694798 George Harrison Anthology $19.95
00690068 Return Of The Hellecasters $19.95
00692930 Jimi Hendrix – Are You Experienced? $19.95
00692931 Jimi Hendrix – Axis: Bold As Love $19.95
00660192 The Jimi Hendrix – Concerts $24.95
00692932 Jimi Hendrix – Electric Ladyland $24.95
00690218 Jimi Hendrix – First Rays of the New Rising Sun $24.95
00660099 Jimi Hendrix – Radio One $24.95
00690280 Jimi Hendrix – South Saturn Delta $19.95
00694919 Jimi Hendrix – Stone Free $19.95
00690038 Gary Hoey – Best Of $19.95
00660029 Buddy Holly $19.95
00660169 John Lee Hooker – A Blues Legend $19.95
00690054 Hootie & The Blowfish – Cracked Rear View $19.95
00690143 Hootie & The Blowfish – Fairweather Johnson $19.95
00694905 Howlin' Wolf $19.95
00690136 Indigo Girls – 1200 Curfews $22.95
00694938 Elmore James – Master Electric Slide Guitar $19.95
00690167 Skip James Blues Guitar Collection $16.95
00694833 Billy Joel For Guitar $19.95
00694912 Eric Johnson – Ah Via Musicom $19.95
00690169 Eric Johnson – Venus Isle $22.95
00694799 Robert Johnson – At The Crossroads $19.95
00693185 Judas Priest – Vintage Hits $19.95
00690073 B. B. King – 1950-1957 $24.95
00690098 B. B. King – 1958-1967 $24.95
00690099 B. B. King – 1962-1971 $24.95
00690134 Freddie King Collection $19.95
00694903 The Best Of Kiss $24.95
00690157 Kiss – Alive $19.95
00690163 Mark Knopfler/Chet Atkins – Neck and Neck $19.95
00690202 Live – Secret Samadhi $19.95
00690070 Live – Throwing Copper $19.95
00690018 Living Colour – Best Of $19.95
00694954 Lynyrd Skynyrd, New Best Of $19.95
00694845 Yngwie Malmsteen – Fire And Ice $19.95
00694956 Bob Marley – Legend $19.95
00690239 Matchbox 20 – Yourself or Someone Like You $19.95
00690020 Meat Loaf – Bat Out Of Hell I & II $22.95
00690244 Megadeath – Cryptic Writings $19.95
00690011 Megadeath – Youthanasia $19.95
00690236 Mighty Mighty Bosstones – Let's Face It $19.95
00690040 Steve Miller Band Greatest Hits $19.95
00690225 Moist – Creature $19.95
00694802 Gary Moore – Still Got The Blues $19.95
00690103 Alanis Morissette – Jagged Little Pill $19.95
00694958 Mountain, Best Of $19.95
00694895 Nirvana – Bleach $19.95
00694913 Nirvana – In Utero $19.95
00694883 Nirvana – Nevermind $19.95
00690026 Nirvana – Acoustic In New York $19.95
00120112 No Doubt – Tragic Kingdom $22.95
00690273 Oasis – Be Here Now $19.95
00690159 Oasis – Definitely Maybe $19.95
00690121 Oasis – (What's The Story) Morning Glory $19.95
00690204 Offspring, The – Ixnay on the Hombre $17.95
00690203 Offspring, The – Smash $17.95
00694830 Ozzy Osbourne – No More Tears $19.95
00694855 Pearl Jam – Ten $19.95
00690053 Liz Phair – Whip Smart $19.95
00690176 Phish – Billy Breathes $22.95
00690240 Phish – Hoist $19.95
00693800 Pink Floyd – Early Classics $19.95
00694967 Police – Message In A Box Boxed Set $70.00
00690125 Presidents of the United States of America $19.95
00690195 Presidents of the United States of America II $22.95
00694974 Queen – A Night At The Opera $19.95
00694910 Rage Against The Machine $19.95
00690145 Rage Against The Machine – Evil Empire $19.95
00690179 Rancid – And Out Come the Wolves $22.95
00690055 Red Hot Chili Peppers – Bloodsugarsexmagik
00690090 Red Hot Chili Peppers – One Hot Minute
00694892 Guitar Style Of Jerry Reed
00694937 Jimmy Reed – Master Bluesman
00694899 R.E.M. – Automatic For The People
00694898 R.E.M. – Out Of Time
00690014 Rolling Stones – Exile On Main Street
00690186 Rolling Stones – Rock & Roll Circus
00690135 Otis Rush Collection
00690133 Rusted Root – When I Woke
00690031 Santana's Greatest Hits
00694805 Scorpions – Crazy World
00690150 Son Seals – Bad Axe Blues
00690128 Seven Mary Three – American Standards
00690076 Sex Pistols – Never Mind The Bollocks
00120105 Kenny Wayne Shepherd – Ledbetter Heights
00690196 Silverchair – Freak Show
00690130 Silverchair – Frogstomp
00690041 Smithereens – Best Of
00694885 Spin Doctors – Pocket Full Of Kryptonite
00690124 Sponge – Rotting Pinata
00690161 Sponge – Wax Ecstatic
00120004 Steely Dan – Best Of
00694921 Steppenwolf, The Best Of
00694957 Rod Stewart – Acoustic Live
00690021 Sting – Fields Of Gold
00120081 Sublime
00690242 Suede – Coming Up
00694824 Best Of James Taylor
00694887 Thin Lizzy – The Best Of Thin Lizzy
00690238 Third Eye Blind
00690022 Richard Thompson Guitar
00690267 311
00690030 Toad The Wet Sprocket
00690228 Tonic – Lemon Parade
00694411 U2 – The Joshua Tree
00690039 Steve Vai – Alien Love Secrets
00690172 Steve Vai – Fire Garden
00660137 Steve Vai – Passion & Warfare
00690023 Jimmie Vaughan – Strange Pleasures
00660136 Stevie Ray Vaughan – In Step
00694835 Stevie Ray Vaughan – The Sky Is Crying
00690015 Stevie Ray Vaughan – Texas Flood
00694776 Vaughan Brothers – Family Style
00690217 Verve Pipe, The – Villains
00120026 Joe Walsh – Look What I Did...
00694789 Muddy Waters – Deep Blues
00690071 Weezer
00690286 Weezer – Pinkerton
00694970 Who, The – Definitive Collection A-E
00694971 Who, The – Definitive Collection F-Li
00694972 Who, The – Definitive Collection Lo-R
00694973 Who, The – Definitive Collection S-Y

Prices and availability subject to change without notice. Some products may not be available outside the U.S.A.

FOR MORE INFORMATION, SEE YOUR LOCAL MUSIC DEALER OR WRITE TO:

HAL•LEONARD CORPORATION

7777 W. BLUEMOUND RD. P.O.BOX 13819 MILWAUKEE, WI 5321

http://www.halleonard.com